THE EDUCATION OF AFRICAN-AMERICANS

THE EDUCATION OF AFRICAN-AMERICANS

EDITED BY

Charles V. Willie,
Antoine M. Garibaldi,
AND
Wornie L. Reed

Prepared under the auspices of the William Monroe Trotter Institute, University of Massachusetts at Boston

Auburn House
New York • Westport, Connecticut • London

Library of Congress Cataloging-in-Publication Data

The Education of African-Americans / edited by Charles V. Willie, Antoine M. Garibaldi and Wornie L. Reed.
p. cm.
Prepared under the auspices of the William Monroe Trotter Institute, University of Massachusetts at Boston.
Includes bibliographical references and index.
ISBN 0-86569-018-9 (alk. paper)
ISBN 0-86569-020-0 (pbk. : alk. paper)
1. Afro-Americans—Education. 2. Afro-Americans—Education—History. 3. Afro-Americans—Education (Higher) I. Willie, Charles Vert. II. Garibaldi, Antoine M. III. Reed, Wornie L. IV. William Monroe Trotter Institute
LC2717.E38 1991
370'.8996073–dc20 91-6356

British Library Cataloguing in Publication Data is available.

Library of Congress Catalog Card Number: 91-6356
ISBN 0-86569-018-9 (hardcover)
0-86569-020-0 (paperback)

First published in 1991

Auburn House, 88 Post Road West, Westport, CT 06881
An imprint of Greenwood Publishing Group, Inc.

Printed in the United States of America

∞™

The paper used in this book complies with the Permanent Paper Standard issued by the National Information Standards Organization (Z39.48–1984).

10 9 8 7 6 5 4 3 2 1

Copyright Acknowledgments

Contents

III
SCHOOL IMPROVEMENT

IV
POSTSECONDARY EDUCATION

V
SPECIAL ISSUES

Preface

In spring 1987 the William Monroe Trotter Institute for the Study of Black Culture at the University of Massachusetts at Boston initiated a national project, The Assessment of the Status of African-Americans. The project included study groups on six topics: employment, income, and occupations; political participation and administration of justice; social and cultural change and continuity; health status and medical care; family; and education. The study group on education included: Robert A. Dentler of the University of Massachusetts at Boston; Robert C. Johnson of St. Cloud State University; Meyer Weinberg of the University of Massachusetts at Amherst; and Charles V. Willie of Harvard and Antoine M. Garibaldi of Xavier University in Louisiana, who served as chair and vice-chair, respectively.

The project was developed to reflect upon the status of African-Americans since 1940 in each of the topical areas in anticipation of the results and analyses of the National Research Council's (NRC) Study Committee on the Status of Black Americans. The Trotter Institute and the more than 60 scholars who agreed to participate in the assessment project recognized that the NRC study would not only have significant implications for African-Americans but would also directly affect public policy. Thus, it was imperative that groups be formed prior to the release of the NRC study so that study group recommendations could stand on their own merits.

The education study group met in late May 1987 and drafted an agenda of significant educational issues ranging from early childhood education programs through postsecondary education public policy issues. Study group members chose topics within their areas of expertise and identified other notable researchers from across the country who have written extensively on these issues. As the list of contributors shows, the authors come from varied settings: secondary schools, private and public universities, historically black universities, and private organizations. They include white as well as black scholars representing a wide range of academic and experiential expertise in educational research.

In the solicitation for papers on the various issues, writers were asked to address three specific questions:

What do we know about this major issue?
What else do we need to know about this issue?
What should be done about this issue?

The authors were asked to pay particular attention not only to trends in the educational progression of African-Americans but also to analyze laws and policies that have had significant impacts on the educational preparation of African-Americans since 1940. Even more, they were requested to speculate on anticipated and unforeseen conditions that will affect the educational pursuits of African-Americans. Through these informal practices of forecasting, policy recommendations for federal, state, and local education agencies — as well as private foundations — could be offered.

Despite the pressures of limited time and limited financial support for this work, these scholars responded to our call and made significant contributions to this volume. Because of their generosity and commitment to the educational progress of African-Americans, it may not be necessary to repeat the last five decades of educational improvements with such slow and nondeliberate speed.

In addition to study group members and other contributors, we are indebted to a number of individuals for the production of this study. Special thanks are offered to: Duncan Nelson, manuscript editor; Linda Kluz and Suzanne Baker, production editors; Eva Hendricks; Gemima Remy; and Frances Stubbs, assistant director.

I

HISTORICAL PERSPECTIVES

Trends and developments in the education of African-Americans over the past 40 years are directly related to trends and developments in civil rights. At its inception in the 1940s, the modern civil rights movement had as one of its major goals improved education for blacks. Indeed, throughout the decades of struggle, the principal civil rights battles have involved education. In the first chapter of this volume, Meyer Weinberg describes the close relationship between civil rights efforts and educational improvements for African-Americans. He discusses the movement's primary legal strategy — to challenge the nation's dual, segregated system of education — yet also points out that the civil rights movement was by no means limited to the courts. As Weinberg states, educational change was also "written in the streets" through demonstrations, marches, and acts of civil disobedience. Looking to the present, Weinberg also discusses the unfinished agenda in urban education including underfunding, poor facilities and resources, and inequities among schools — with, of course, black students getting the short end.

In his chapter, Charles V. Willie discusses the private sector's response to the push by African-Americans to improve their educational situation. This response came largely from private foundations, one program of which — the Rockefeller Foundation's Equal Opportunity Program — Willie analyzes. This program's first effort in the 1960s was to respond to the "black revolt" by providing major white colleges and universities with funds to attract black students. Initially, predominantly black colleges and universities were considered outside the mainstream and were thus not funded. Willie uses the problematic aspects of the Rockefeller Foundation's efforts to illustrate the struggles between African-Americans and major societal institutions when both are ostensibly attempting to improve the educational outcome for black Americans. He concludes that there is no linear pattern of inevitable progress in the attainment of educational equity: for every two steps forward, he says, there is probably a step backward. Nevertheless, improvements were made during the 1960s, and if improvements are to continue they will be the result of the black community working in conjunction with establishment leaders.

1

The Civil Rights Movement and Educational Change

Meyer Weinberg

Since 1940 the single most important factor in the lives of African-Americans has been the rise of the civil rights movement. In the main, it was a movement of black people led by black people and has been deeply responsive to the historic goals and aspirations of blacks in America. When in 1963 a highly placed federal education official declared "Thank God for the civil rights movement," he was giving voice to the growing realization that the movement was becoming the principal engine for educational change in this country (Keppel, 1964). Marching blacks and their allies demanded a series of changes:

dissolution of structures of segregation and planned deprivation as a further guarantee of equal education;
employment of black personnel on all levels of schooling as an extension of traditional patterns of ethnic representativeness;
democratization of educational policy making by city authorities and school boards through black and other minority participation; and
eradication of institutional and personal racism from curriculum, instructional materials, student learning, employment and promotion practices, distribution of school funds, and other areas of schooling.

The kinds of changes demanded by the civil rights movement were not, of course, well received by many school personnel and researchers. For example, instead of acknowledging their share of the responsibility for poor student performance, numerous teachers and principals demanded that black parents first change their cultural practices. Researchers chimed in with diagnoses that found black children "culturally deprived." Black parents, who during the 1950s were regularly denounced in school circles for their alleged nonconcern with education, were in the 1960s repeatedly criticized for their "interference" in the form of picket lines and mass delegations. Furthermore, state departments of education as a whole hindered the new movement: throughout the South, state legislatures, state school officials, and court officers collaborated in frustrating parent and community efforts to improve black education. Occasional sparkling new buildings for black students proved to be empty educational shells (Moody, 1968); desegregation objectives were hobbled by crafty stratagems and endless delays.

Change was energized only by pressure from the civil rights movement. As Martin Luther King, Jr., said of the 1964 Civil Rights Act: "This legislation was written in the streets" (King, 1965). But while the result was a popular triumph, the administration of the law could not be carried out on those same streets. Evasion, both blatant and veiled, remained the norm. Thus, civil rights matters that should have been implemented readily and directly limped along and came to be portrayed as an educational excrescence, an interference with the purportedly "professional" personnel. Fair treatment of children was thereby negated as an education goal. Black children lost most from this regressive stance: they were not only denied the respect due every child, they remained academically ill served.

During the 1980s, the main currents of educational reform departed further than ever from the civil rights concerns of equity and equality. Entire documents on reform omit mention of desegregation and concern for equal treatment. Others ritually refer to the subjects three-quarters of the way through a document.

The readiest way to effect the narrow brand of achievement explicated in most of these reform proposals is by not ignoring equity concerns. If, by a year from now, black and other minority students were to match the academic achievement of white students, a tremendous growth in excellence would be recorded — one far beyond the vague and slender goals elucidated in the reports. By ignoring the obvious failures of the public schools for black and other minority children, the reform movement is excluding the most immediate — and pressing — avenue for improvement.

In large city public school systems, poor and minority children are regularly shortchanged in matters that are mediated through money: school facilities, teachers and other instructional personnel, curriculum, counseling, and more. On a per-student basis, less is spent on them than on others (Weinberg, 1983). In a sense, this pattern is simply an extension of pre–Civil War practice when, in 1860, proportionately 27 times more white children than black children attended school. Slaves, who numbered 4 million that year, were not permitted to become literate or to instruct their own children. It was not until the mid–twentieth century that school enrollment ratios of black and white children were similar. Even then, however, systematically inferior schools were the inevitable lot of black children. This was a matter of common, everyday knowledge. Only educational researchers seemed unaware of it.

In the early 1950s, when strategy for the critical school segregation cases was being set, lawyers challenged mandatory separateness rather than the deliberate inferiority of black schooling. The Supreme Court obliged and thus avoided ruling on the latter. It has still not done so. Systematically inferior schools for black and other poor and minority children have yet to be declared a violation of the Fourteenth Amendment.

Researchers in the field of educational finance have all but ignored intradistrict inequalities. As a result of various legal proceedings, however, detailed documentation of significant variations in per-pupil expenditures is on record. City school systems involved include New York; Los Angeles; Washington, D.C.; Chicago; and Hartford (Weinberg, 1983; Olds, 1982). Over 20 years ago, the Coleman Report erroneously concluded that school-by-school differences in academic achievement could not be explained by similar differences in tangible or purchasable factors. It stated that these latter differences were too insubstantial to make any significant difference. In fact, comparisons among schools of actual per-student expenditures were not included in the report (1966).

Superintendents and school boards have avoided exploration of actual expenditures by race among schools. Because of the obvious political implications of any findings, the basic financial data are guarded as holy objects unfitted for plebeian scrutiny. Thus, governmental inquiries into intradistrict inequalities are almost unknown. (Interdistrict inequalities lack such obvious political implications and thus study of these transactions is more open to systematic investigation. The only losers can be other districts in the state or the state treasury itself.) And while about a decade ago Congress enacted a law requiring a formal study of, among other things, intradistrict inequalities, the law was never carried out.

The persistence of intradistrict inequalities when black students continue to receive the lesser share of programs and resources reminds us of the unfinished civil rights movement in education. In view of the above problems, an adequate study to address intradistrict inequalities requires:

a truly nationwide study defining the extent of such inequality;
a definitive statement of the educational costs of such inequality;
a plan to remedy the consequences of such inequality;
a congressional enactment declaring intradistrict inequalities a violation of the Fourteenth Amendment's guarantee of equal protection (the amendment itself provides for congressional explication); and
a research program ascertaining whether intradistrict inequalities supplant or supplement more commonly cited factors in educational disadvantages.

REFERENCES

Coleman, J. S. (1966). *Equality of educational opportunity.* Washington, DC: U.S. Department of Health, Education, and Welfare.

Keppel, F. (1964, April-May). Thank God for the civil rights movement. *Integrated Education, 2*, pp. 9–12

King, M. L., Jr. (1965, March 15). Let justice roll down. *Nation*, pp. 269–70.

Moody, A. (1968). *Coming of age in Mississippi.* New York: Dial Press.

Olds, W. (1982). *Intra-district school finance study in a large New England city.* Unpublished doctoral dissertation. University of Massachusetts, Amherst.

Weinberg, M. (1983). *The search for quality integrated education: Policy and research on minority students in school and college.* Westport, CT: Greenwood Press.

2

The Social and Historical Context: A Case Study of Philanthropic Assistance

Charles V. Willie

The contributions of established institutions to the education of blacks and other minorities are frequently functions of challenge and response. Left with their own inclinations to do good according to their assessment of situations, dominant people of power seldom "do the right thing." This case history of one foundation's attempt to respond to the civil rights revolution demonstrates the value of subdominant people of power establishing the agenda for educational reform to which dominants should respond. When dominants attempt to set the agenda for educational reform, they usually proceed in a trial-and-error fashion, resulting in much wasted motion.

The General Education Board, established by John D. Rockefeller, Sr., in 1902, spent between $62 and $63 million for the purpose of advancing elementary, secondary, and higher education among blacks (Rockefeller Foundation, n.d., p. 3). Despite these and numerous other Rockefeller-initiated contributions, it was not until 1963 that a broad-scale program in equal opportunity was launched by the Rockefeller Foundation. The foundation's Equal Opportunity Program was formulated because it was, on one hand, an extension of what the foundation had done in the past, but, on the other hand, it was a response to a set of new circumstances in society. An assessment of the leadership development component of that program is the focus of this report.

A NEW SET OF CIRCUMSTANCES

The new set of circumstances confronting the nation following World War II was the decision by racial minorities to cease cooperating in their own oppression. This decision was dramatized by Rosa Parks, a black woman who on December 1, 1955, in Montgomery, Alabama refused to give up her seat near the front of the bus in the section reserved by custom for whites. Because of her refusal to move, she was removed from the bus by police. That action was the beginning of what writer Anthony Lewis characterized as the "Negro revolt." In his book, *Portrait of a Decade,* Lewis observed that "something more was at stake . . . than bus segregation." He described "the stubborn sacrifice and determination" that blacks manifested in their boycott of segregated buses after the Parks incident as a signal of the "end to the subservient, satisfied mood [among blacks] that whites always thought they had seen" (Lewis, 1965, pp. 60–62). Neither the nation nor the foundation could respond to blacks as they had in the past — on the terms of the white majority. Instead, new patterns of race relations would be negotiated. In effect, new occasions would teach new duties for individuals and institutions. The new duty the Rockefeller Foundation accepted in 1963 was designing and implementing the Equal Opportunity Program.

The proximity of the founding date of the new Rockefeller program and that of the March on Washington is not a coincidence. Institutional action and individual expression of discontent often work together to produce peaceful change (Lewis, 1965, p. 71). Blacks and others who opposed racial segregation in the early 1960s had perfected the technique of "nonviolent direct action" and had used it in many communities. This approach was demonstrated by Martin Luther King, Jr., the main speaker at the August 28, 1963, March on Washington rally. King called nonviolent resistance not only a technique but a way of life. That summer more than a quarter of a million people gathered at the Lincoln Memorial and made the March on Washington one of the largest nonviolent direct action efforts of the century. The participants demonstrated for a "full and speedy program of civil rights." According to the *New York Times,* the crowd was "good natured" but "dead serious" (200,000 March, 1963, p. 1). King said, "Nothing could be more tragic than for men to live in these revolutionary times and fail to achieve the new attitudes and the new mental outlooks that the new situation demands." He described racism as "the hound of hell which dogs the tracks of our civilization" and suggested that new attitudes about race relations in the United States were essential (King, 1968, pp. 170, 173).

Despite King's characterization of white racism as hell, one may note in the analysis that follows that the initial projects funded in the Equal Opportunity Program were designed to change blacks, not whites. That is, the projects were for the purpose of helping blacks overcome what whites described as a sense of inferiority, but they did nothing about whites, some of whom suffered from a sense of superiority.

RESPONSE TO THE MARCH ON WASHINGTON

The Rockefeller Foundation responded to the ferment of the 1960s that culminated in the 1963 March on Washington by seeking suggestions and advice from "a large array of experienced and informed people, both black and white." For example, meetings were held with the leadership of the Southern Regional Council as one way of signaling that the foundation was considering "program transition from the advancement of basic knowledge to efforts to find solutions to selected problems of major importance" (Rockefeller Foundation, n.d., pp. 6–8).

There was strong sentiment within the foundation "to publicly align itself with efforts to eliminate discrimination against the Negro." The issue was how to be effective. By the end of 1963, the foundation had taken a small step toward actualizing the sentiment that existed among some of its staff, officers, and trustees. It appropriated $2.5 million for the United Negro College Fund's special centennial campaign and initiated a new area of program concentration called Toward Equal Opportunity for All (Rockefeller Foundation, n.d., p. 8).

During the first years of the new program, "the foundation gave primary attention to finding ways to improve higher educational opportunities for disadvantaged minorities." The goal was to qualify talented minorities for full participation in the mainstream of American life. The foundation believed that "the soundest way to accomplish this seemed to be to help open the doors of good universities to minority group candidates" (Rockefeller Foundation, 1968, p. 116).

With this goal in mind, a series of grants were made to help predominantly white, selective colleges and universities recruit students from minority groups. In September 1964, the first recruits enrolled in such universities as Duke, Emory, Tulane, and Vanderbilt. Institutions such as Antioch, Carleton, Grinnell, Oberlin, Occidental, Reed, and Swarthmore, which were characterized by the foundation as "strong liberal arts colleges," received grants in 1964 and 1965 to recruit more minority students. By 1966 and 1967 this program had extended to Bowdoin, Brooklyn College of the City University of New York, Claremont, Cornell, and the University of California at Los Angeles. Annual expansion of the program was possible because knowledge had been gained from three foundation-sponsored pilot programs for identifying "promising minority students." These pilot programs were undertaken at

Princeton, Dartmouth, and Oberlin as early as 1963 (Rockefeller Foundation, 1968, p. 116).

An analysis of the grant-making practice of the foundation during the first three years of the new Equal Opportunity Program revealed its understanding of the issue. To the foundation, "equal opportunity" translated as "equal educational opportunity." The foundation gave itself the task of increasing "the flow of Negro students to the better colleges and universities" as a way of implementing equal educational opportunity (Rockefeller Foundation, 1964, p. 60). The foundation was struggling to read the signs of the time: the 1955 bus boycott in Montgomery, the numerous demonstrations in the late 1950s and early 1960s, and the March on Washington in 1963. It wanted to make an appropriate response, but the response was largely conditioned by what the foundation had done in the past and by what liberal members of the white majority thought was appropriate.

BLACK INSTITUTIONS OF HIGHER EDUCATION

At the outset of the Rockefeller Equal Opportunity Program, the foundation gave black colleges \$2.5 million; subsequent grants totaling \$8.3 million were given over the five-year period from 1963 to 1968 to strengthen these schools (Rockefeller Foundation, 1968, p. 124). At that time none of the predominantly black schools was identified by the foundation as a "strong liberal arts college," and none was granted funds to attract "talented" and "promising" minority students to its campus. The expressed goal of the program was to increase the flow of blacks and other minorities into "strong liberal arts colleges." Although probably not intended, phrases like "strong colleges," "good colleges," "prestigious colleges," and "selective colleges" turned out to be synonyms for "predominantly white colleges" in the grant-making activity of the foundation in implementing its new Equal Opportunity Program.

Clearly, the Rockefeller Foundation did not consider predominantly black colleges to be in the mainstream. It is strange that these institutions, in light of their contribution to the current events of that period, were thought to be a sideshow rather than part of the main event in higher education. After all, it was the "Negro revolt" or "racial revolution" that stimulated the foundation to establish the new program in the first place. Black author John A. Williams described the central role of black students in black colleges in the civil rights movement this way: "The activities seem to be in the command of youth; it was the time of the sit-ins. . . . The sit-ins commenced on February 1, 1960. The place was

North Carolina A. and T. College in Greensboro. The students were directly influenced by the Montgomery bus boycott with its nonviolent philosophy; its effectiveness persuaded the black youth that they, too, could successfully employ it" (1970, p. 37). North Carolina Agricultural and Technical State University was predominantly black.

Williams said that the basic aim of the sit-ins was "to spur [the nation] into action to abolish the system that insured the life of degradation for the majority of its nonwhite citizens." Following the sit-ins came the freedom rides to desegregate interstate buses and bus stations. Freedom riders were beaten and humiliated. Nevertheless, as Williams reported, during the first half of the 1960s students from Fisk University and other black schools climbed aboard new buses everyday to continue the movement (1970, pp. 48–49).

Although predominantly black colleges had strengthened their students to exhibit such courage in the face of danger, the foundation looked upon these schools as places for poor blacks who could not afford to attend college away from home or for blacks who were unable to "qualify for admission to selective colleges." The attitude of the foundation was that it was desirable for blacks to attend a "better college" if they could, which meant — in the opinion of the foundation — a predominantly white selective college. This attitude was reflected in the *President's Five-Year Review* in 1968 by this indecisive statement: "How long the productivity of aiding these [predominantly black] institutions will outweigh the promise of competing opportunities is difficult to predict" (Rockefeller Foundation, 1968, p. 124).

In providing their students with the courage and commitment to resist racial oppression, the predominantly black colleges were without peer. The problem was that the foundation and most of the other predominantly white institutions in America tended to discount protest and resistance — even nonviolent resistance — as being of any value in the civil rights movement. They preferred to emphasize increased opportunities.

Providing a better chance by facilitating admission to institutions of higher education that were previously more or less closed to racial minorities was one way of increasing opportunities. This approach, of course, was under the control and direction of the white majority, while protest and resistance to discrimination was under the direction and control of racial minorities. The foundation's Equal Opportunity Program did not support advocacy and resistance efforts during its first three years. It was interested in racial cooperation and integration, not racial confrontation and demonstration. The wisdom of Frederick Douglass in noting that one cannot have rain without thunder and lightning was not heeded.

The signals that the foundation gave to racial minority communities during the early years of the new program were confusing. On one hand, it gave a clear signal that it wanted to help disadvantaged racial minorities. On the other hand, by focusing largely on talented black students who could qualify or be qualified for admission to predominately white, selective schools, it telegraphed a strong message that black colleges were second best and not worthy of participating in a program of integration. For instance, the foundation could have awarded grants to black colleges to recruit white students as a contribution to integration and equal opportunity, but it did not.

The goal of the foundation's program was not seriously challenged by racial minorities when it began because there was hope at the time that minorities would be invited to join the mainstream and exercise all of the rights and privileges attached thereto. Blacks and other racial minorities had a dream, and they were sure that America and its institutions, including the Rockefeller Foundation, would help them fulfill that dream. They believed that their dream was the American dream. The year in which the foundation launched the Equal Opportunity Program, Louis Harris found in a nationwide survey that nearly two-thirds of African-Americans believed that the attitudes of whites would be better in about five years (Brink & Harris, 1964). By 1968, however, the dream had not been fulfilled. Brutality and violence had not waned; the gap between blacks and whites was widening in some areas; and in that year, King, the esteemed nonviolent leader of African-Americans, was murdered.

TRAGIC EVENTS

Even before King's death, the momentum of the March on Washington was slowed by other tragic events. John F. Kennedy, the youngest president this nation ever had, who was known to be favorable to guaranteeing the civil rights of minorities, was murdered on November 22, 1963. To some it appeared that the nation was coming apart at the seams. There were other killings in 1964 and 1965 and more violence in subsequent years up to 1968. Black communities in several cities erupted in rioting.

By 1966 white hostility to desegregation was so severe that James Meredith, the first black student admitted to the University of Mississippi, could not complete his Freedom March to demonstrate that it was safe for blacks to walk the highways of that state. He was wounded by a shot in the back only a day after he began his march (King, 1968, p. 23).

A public statement of the mistrust of whites by blacks in America was one outcome of the Meredith Freedom March in Mississippi. King had related the story of the beginning of the black-imposed separatist movement and the diminution of nonviolence as a direct action technique. After Meredith was wounded, the Congress of Racial Equality (CORE), the Student Nonviolent Coordinating Committee (SNCC), and the Southern Christian Leadership Conference (SCLC) joined together to finish the Freedom March "in order to demonstrate to the nation and the world that Negroes would never again be intimidated by the terror of extremist white violence" (King, 1968, p. 24). As the marchers continued down the meandering highway in the sweltering heat, the sentiments of blacks seemed to change, observed King. During the afternoon they sang "We Shall Overcome," but many would not sing the stanza about "black and white together." King said that Stokeley Carmichael of SNCC wanted to de-emphasize the participation of whites in the call for people to join the march. (As late as 1964 SNCC was an interracial association.) One black, whose attitude reflected that of others, said, "I'm not for that nonviolent stuff anymore."

Although King pleaded for the leaders "to see the morality of making the march interracial," he found that he was fighting an uphill battle. Another representative remarked: "This should be an all-black march. We don't need any more white phonies and liberals invading our movement." Reflecting upon these happenings later, King said, "I should have known that in an atmosphere where false promises are daily realities, where deferred dreams are nightly facts, where acts of unpunished violence toward Negroes are a way of life, nonviolence would eventually be seriously questioned" (King, 1968, pp. 24–28).

During the first half of the 1960s, leaders such as Malcolm X and others had urged blacks "to use self-defense and even retaliation against acts of violence by whites" (Zinn, 1964, p. 222). By and large, however, these calls had gone unheeded because of the victories of the nonviolent technique and the momentum of the civil rights movement generated by the successful March on Washington. Such successes had created a sense of optimism for the future. By 1968, though, the mood had changed. In a book published that year, the year in which he was killed, King said, "The Negro has been wrong to toy with the optimistic thought that the breakdown of white resistance could be accomplished at a small cost" (King, 1968, p. 20). As the costs soared, blacks despaired and became bitter.

BLACKS IN WHITE INSTITUTIONS

There was trouble in the academy too. By 1966, Archie Epps, a Louisiana-born black who at that time was assistant dean of Harvard, described the multiple expectations that people had of him at that school. According to Epps, "one [expectation] is that I will, or should, lose my Negroness and just become a gentleman, or that I should gratefully accept this opportunity that Harvard has bestowed on me" (Brink & Harris, 1966, p. 118).

The testimony of a black student at a predominantly white college in upstate New York revealed the stress of integration for the minority when nothing is done to deal with the majority's sense of superiority. This student said:

> People weren't that militant when I came here in 1967. I think it was still the hope of many black people to get into the American mainstream. . . . They put me in a hall with 500 girls, all white except me. . . . Being isolated, I began to get into the system of having mainly white friends as my good friends. . . . Little incidents started happening. My white friends would make some mistakes in what they'd say and do. They would hurt my feelings. But I would take into account that they were really my friends and sometimes they do make errors. . . . We used to always study together for exams in one course. The content for one exam was about prejudice and poverty. They didn't call me in when they were studying. When I found out they had already studied and did not include me, I asked why and was told that one of the girls said Negroes were inferior and the other girls said they thought it wouldn't be right to include me in the study session after that type of attitude had been aired. Then Martin Luther King died and a lot of places began to be burned and a lot of those liberals — when the fire got nearer to their doorsteps — a lot of attitudes started coming out. Around this time, the Union of Black Collegians got to be more active. I began to make a break there and began to look at myself and this so-called friendship. Ever since then, I've been developing more intense attitudes about myself and people. . . . Someone once said I had to go to a white school to find out I was black. And that is exactly what happened to me (Willie & McCord, 1972, pp. 4-5).

This is the testimony of a black person who wanted to trust whites, who was optimistic that blacks and whites could do things together and be friends. In 1967, she pursued the goal of integration in higher education. In the end, she was disappointed. Some of her liberal white friends were untrustworthy. The Rockefeller Foundation did not consider this variable in its program of one-way integration that brought blacks into white institutions for the good that would accrue to blacks. The foundation had no plan for overcoming the prejudice of whites.

So the experience of integration that the Rockefeller Foundation launched so boldly for the purpose of bringing blacks into the mainstream at "good colleges and universities" was in some instances bringing blacks into a briar patch rather than a rose garden. The integrated setting sometimes turned out to be an ivy-covered jungle full of predators rather than the promised land.

ESTRANGEMENT BETWEEN BLACKS AND WHITES

Probably no other event caused black educators to mistrust white liberals more than a *Harvard Educational Review* article, "The American Negro College" by Christopher Jencks and David Riesman, published in the winter 1967 issue. Despite their liberal credentials and their knowledge of the negative effects of stereotyping, these white educators lumped all black colleges together and labeled them an "academic disaster area" (Jencks & Riesman, 1967, p. 26). Stephen Wright, Benjamin Mays, Hugh Gloster, and Albert Dent wrote forceful rejoinders and strongly defended black colleges (1967, pp. 451–68). They were clearly hurt by such an inappropriate characterization of the schools they had served, and they said so. Wright even questioned the intentions of the Harvard social scientists. He suggested that they had not tried to be "honest and fair." Although a few black educators spoke out against Jencks and Riesman, most suffered silently.

This analysis indicates that, by 1967, estrangement between blacks and whites in higher education was real, despite the new efforts to achieve integration. A study of black students at white colleges concluded that "with more interaction between the races on campus as the number of black students increases, the level of trust between blacks and whites appears to decrease. This may be due to an unmasking effect, which the increased interaction has produced" (Willie & McCord, 1972, p. 103). Apparently, the Equal Opportunity Program of the foundation had not considered how to deal with this unanticipated consequence of its grant-making activity.

Anthony Lewis (1965) described the roots of the veiled separatist movement among blacks that became public after Meredith was shot in his Freedom March in Mississippi in 1966. According to Lewis, "The promise of that happy day in Washington [August 28, 1963] could not be kept." The violence had a deadening effect on the drive for integration, and blacks became increasingly distrustful of whites. When the summer riots erupted in 1964, "the estrangement of the whites and Negroes of the

North worsened." There was also increasing talk among blacks about self-determination and self-defense, while, according to Lewis, there was increased talk about whether "extremists would capture the support of the northern Negro community." The one constructive element in all of this, said Lewis, was "the removal of illusion." He believed it was healthier that blacks and whites were "frankly talking about each other's faults" (Lewis, 1965, pp. 219, 220, 223, 228).

Meanwhile, John Munro, formerly a dean at Harvard, demonstrated by his actions that there was educational work worth doing at schools that were not predominantly white or described as selective. Rather than devoting all of his efforts toward recruiting minority students for Harvard in accordance with the guidelines of the Rockefeller Foundation or other philanthropic organizations, Munro left Harvard in 1967, at the age of 54, to teach at the predominantly black Miles College in Birmingham, Alabama. After ten years of teaching at a more or less open-admission school, Monro said, "Practically all our freshmen are invisible to the selective colleges." He said there was no reason why some of the Miles students should not be admitted to any school they wished to attend because "the truth is — and all of us on the open door campuses know this from experience — that a serious percentage of our 'invisible' students are well above average in intellectual ability" (Munro, 1978, p. 235).

CHANGE IN GRANT-MAKING PRACTICE

These rapid changes in events had a significant impact upon the Rockefeller Foundation and its Equal Opportunity Program. If they did not bring about a change in policy, they certainly brought about a change in practice. At the beginning of the program, schools such as Princeton, Dartmouth, and Oberlin were identified as excellent settings for minority students. These were predominantly white schools. By the close of 1964, Morehouse and Spelman, two predominantly black colleges in Atlanta, had been added to the list. They were given a grant to "jointly undertake an experiment with about sixty exceptionally talented but underprivileged boys and girls from the tenth grade." These students were brought to the college campuses each summer for three years to receive eight weeks of intensive instruction in reading, composition, mathematics, and chemistry (Rockefeller Foundation, 1964, p. 66). In 1965, Knoxville College, a predominantly black institution, was funded to provide a summer program "for students from predominantly Negro high schools in small towns and rural areas of the South." The Knoxville program offered "counseling and training in study skills, with special emphasis on obtaining high scores in national qualifying examinations for college admission and scholarship aid" (Rockefeller Foundation, 1965, p. 66). Grants also went to the predominantly black Tuskegee Institute and Hampton Institute for "remedial and enrichment work" in prefreshman summer courses. Students who were handicapped in their language and mathematics skills were exposed to prefreshman and postfreshman summer courses to broaden their horizons and strengthen their skills. These grants were made to provide supplemental studies for under-prepared college students.

The small grants given to predominantly black schools were in no way comparable to the larger sums that had been granted to the predominantly white, selective colleges and universities to recruit minority students. Yet, they indicated that the foundation was becoming sensitive to the growing feeling in the black community that there was a conspiracy in the nation to discount the value of black institutions in the drive toward integration.

Although in 1964 and 1965 the Rockefeller Foundation looked with favor upon a few black colleges as capable of identifying promising and talented black students and routing them into higher education, the basic orientation of the foundation and white educators in general was that black institutions of higher education were inferior. Thus, the American Council on Education, in cooperation with Educational Services Incorporated, was asked by the Rockefeller Foundation to arrange a series of summer institutes at predominantly white universities in the United States for teachers from predominantly black colleges. In 1964, there was a summer institute in mathematics at the University of North Carolina. In 1965, there was one in English at Indiana University, one in economics at Wayne State University, and one in business administration at New York University. The foundation sponsored these institutes because of its belief that "the key figure in the educational picture is the teacher." The summer institute was a setting in which black college professors could "keep up with the latest developments in their fields" (Rockefeller Foundation, 1965, p. 68).

These projects and the foundation grants that supported them indicated that the sharply focused Equal Opportunity Program of 1963 to increase the flow of potentially gifted black students into first-rank colleges and universities had gone slightly out of focus. Apparently, the initial goal was too narrow. A grant to the Friends Neighborhood Guild in Philadelphia in 1965 was an example of the enlarged concept of the program. This group had a good record "of constructive and imaginative community work." The foundation hoped that through a counseling program, high school students in slum communities would be "encouraged to finish high school and [that] students of potentially superior ability [could be] guided toward college" (Rockefeller Foundation, 1965, p. 74). Even though grants such as this one indicated that the foundation was beginning to recognize that the "trickle down" approach — that is, placing talented black youth at "selected institutions with a leadership position in America" — was not sufficient to break down the barriers retarding integration in higher education (Rockefeller Foundation, 1968, p. 116), it followed a traditional course of action. It turned to liberal white organizations and funded them to help poor blacks. Invariably, the white groups identified solutions that, from their own perspectives, would be beneficial for blacks and other racial minorities. They then proceeded to act upon their own definition of the situation without checking to determine if they and those who were to receive the help had similar perceptions of the problem and prescriptions for the solution.

This practice changed SNCC from an integrated to a separatist organization between 1964 and 1966. King said Stokeley Carmichael's resistance to including whites in the Meredith Freedom March "had its psychological roots in the experience of SNCC in Mississippi during the summer of 1964, when a large number of northern white students had come down to help." According to King, "What the SNCC workers saw was the most articulate, powerful and self-assured young white people coming to work with the poorest of the Negro people — and simply overwhelming them. That summer Stokeley and others in SNCC had probably unconsciously concluded that this was no good for Negroes, for it simply increased their sense of their own inadequacies" (King, 1968, p. 28).

During the years 1964 to 1966 the Rockefeller Foundation was only beginning to understand the negative impact whites could have on the civil rights movement. Yet, evidence of change was on the docket. For instance, more grants were made to black institutions as part of the Equal Opportunity Program, and the Atlanta University Center, Fisk University, and Lincoln University were added to the list of grant recipients. The foundation admitted in its 1966 annual report that "in addition to helping more Negroes qualify for top-ranking colleges, attention must be given to strengthening the predominantly Negro institutions." That attention came in the form of grants to black institutions for the purpose of "improving education in the colleges which train the public school teachers" (Rockefeller Foundation, 1966, p. 107). In the same year, the foundation also identified the Woodrow Wilson

Teaching Internship Program, which it had supported for three years, as an important part of its Equal Opportunity Program. The foundation's annual report described that program this way: "Woodrow Wilson fellows were placed in teaching positions for one year . . . at Negro colleges requesting them. They [were] freed from part of their teaching schedule to supervise special projects, promote intellectual interests and activities, and help students of exceptional ability prepare for admission to graduate and professional schools" (Rockefeller Foundation, 1966, p. 110).

Beyond enlarging the focus of the Equal Opportunity Program to accommodate projects at black colleges, the foundation developed a concern not only for what it had designated as the mainstream, but also for activities within the black community. This change in grant making was a response to the mood of minorities who in 1966 were beginning to question whether racial integration should be the primary goal of the freedom movement.

COMMUNITY ORGANIZATION

In line with this new interest in predominantly black institutions, the Rockefeller Foundation made a three-year grant to the National Urban League (NUL) in 1967 to expand its Leadership Development Program to ten cities. The NAACP Legal Defense Fund was also awarded a grant to establish a community service division to aid minorities through counseling and other assistance in employment and welfare. These grants were designed, more or less, to help the inhabitants of the ghetto's working-class and poor blacks. The foundation stated its intent this way: "Whereas the intent of the original Program had been to draw on upper- and middle-class Negroes, the effort now aimed increasingly at development of neighborhood leaders and local civic leaders." Organizations like the NUL and NAACP were funded, however, because they gave promise of linking ghetto dwellers with society at large. For example, it was explained that the NUL project would contribute to a "more effective transition of the Negro into the world outside the ghetto" (Rockefeller Foundation, 1968, p. 26). Thus, although the foundation was beginning to snatch a quick look at minority ghettos, its main focus was still on the larger society and how to bring minorities into it.

The foundation accepted the fact that its sharply focused program on increasing the number of able, talented, and promising minorities in selective institutions of higher education was becoming somewhat blurred. By entertaining proposals for grants to community organizations, the foundation, through its grant-making action, expressed doubt about the efficacy of the narrow approach it had originally taken. In light of this change, the second round of three-year grants to Antioch, Grinnell, Oberlin, and Reed colleges to support their minority recruitment programs was identified as terminal. The foundation decided in 1966 and 1967 that the time had come to phase out primary emphasis on experimental projects in higher educational opportunities for minorities (Rockefeller Foundation, 1968, p. 26).

INSTITUTIONAL CHANGE AND INDIVIDUAL ENHANCEMENT

As it began to look at the full range of racial minority populations, the foundation began to realize that enhancing the opportunities of only those individuals it had determined to be talented and able was not enough. In fact, it stated in the *President's Review and Annual Report* of 1966: "The Foundation's long-range objective was to accelerate institutional changes in America's educational system that would result in the training of Negro leaders and facilitate their entry into the mainstream of American life" (pp. 146–51).

The foundation had settled upon the goal of aiding young black individuals by providing them new educational opportunities, yet it had not sought to change the institutions in which they matriculated. In fact, little attention was given to the white higher education system into which black students were brought. A small grant of $11,000 was made to a black sociology professor at Oberlin College in 1967 to study the adjustment problems of minority group students at Oberlin and similar colleges, but nothing else was done.

Although the foundation was becoming more directly involved with the problems of the urban ghetto and was beginning to award grants that had to do with advocacy and community organization, it did not abandon its long-standing interest in education. Indeed, one could classify the foundation's involvement with education as a love affair of the past that would not be denied, that would not let go. In 1968 the trustees directed the foundation to place primary emphasis on the "improvement of elementary and secondary schools in major urban areas, with specific attention to schools serving the social, educational, and related needs of the students, parents, and others in the neighborhood." The trustees also called for the "development and training of responsible and competent leadership in minority groups, particularly in urban ghettos," and a "study of the nature and causes of the development and perpetuation of urban ghettos, and of the means required for their elimination as areas of involuntary residence" (Rockefeller Foundation, 1968, pp. 126–27). Thus, although education was still included in the new emphasis, it did not hold the spotlight alone. Not only was higher education de-emphasized in favor of grade school and high school, but social change as a goal of foundation grant-making activity was highlighted as a major concern. By the close of 1968, the foundation was more interested in institutional change than in producing changes within individuals alone. Without a doubt, the Rockefeller Foundation made a radical shift in its policy with reference to projects that would receive priority for funding in the Equal Opportunity Program.

A DECISIVE YEAR: 1968

It is appropriate to classify 1968 as a decisive year in contemporary U.S. history. The changes that occurred in our national life during that year were profound. King's murder on April 4 ended the age of optimism in race relations in this nation. Two months later, in June, Senator Robert Kennedy was killed. Prior to King's and Kennedy's deaths, on March 2, the President's Commission on Civil Disorders was reported to the nation. The commission's findings were grim: "White racism is essentially responsible for the explosive mixture which has been accumulating in our cities since World War II." Racism and riots, it added, would split the nation into "two societies, one black, one white — separate and unequal — unless massive and costly remedies are begun at once" (Associated Press, 1968, p. 64).

The predictions of the commission were played out in the aftermath of King's death. The Associated Press described what happened as "a paroxysm of arson and looting in more than 100 cities and towns across the nation." This was the tally: "two score deaths, 21,000 arrests; damage mounted to uncounted millions of dollars. More than 30,000 National Guardsmen and 20,000 regular troops were called to duty to quell the violence." The Associated Press made this observation: "The people were jolted into new awareness of the urgency of the race problem" (1968, p. 70). Truly this was a crisis — a turning point in the nation's history, a challenge to its survival.

Fortunately, the President's Commission on Civil Disorders had already pointed the way toward racial reconciliation in the form of over 160 recommendations. Two that apparently were meaningful to the Rockefeller Foundation were the call for increased efforts to eliminate de facto segregation in the nation's schools and the need for improved training programs in coping with, and communicating, the Negro's plight. The resolution of the trustees of the Rockefeller Foundation that gave new direction to the Equal Opportunity Program grew out of the social context of the happenings in 1968.

Having decided upon a new emphasis for its Equal Opportunity Program, the Rockefeller Foundation found itself in the embarrassing position of not having an officer on the staff of the Social Science Division, where the program was housed, who had professional knowledge of public schools or personal and professional experience with ghetto communities. Yet, a report on foundation activities during the 1960s described the difficulty in implementing the new directives of the Equal Opportunity Program with the in-house staff. The report indicated that the process of selecting appropriate projects from the "avalanche of requests for help . . . was a far more difficult and uncertain task than many might suppose." It explained that one of the most important reasons for the difficulty was that there were no "real experts, in the sense of specialists who are skilled in achieving the indicated results" (Rockefeller Foundation, n.d., pp. 66–67).

DIVERSIFYING THE PROFESSIONAL STAFF

The foundation bit the bullet and deliberately decided to diversify its professional staff, which was racially imbalanced. Thus, at the beginning of 1969, a search for an appropriate staff member was launched. The search was successful. Before the end of that year, the foundation had appointed a black professional who had been a public school teacher and who had served as principal of an inner-city school. Moreover, he had had administrative experience at the national level as assistant for Urban Education to the U.S. Commissioner of Education. Within two years, this officer had recruited another minority group staff member who had been an intern in two big city school systems, assistant principal in an urban high school, and administrative assistant to a superintendent of schools (Rockefeller Foundation, n.d., p. 72). Together these staff members fashioned a leadership development program that attempted to fulfill the dual goals of the Equal Opportunity Program. Their initiatives brought the blurred Equal Opportunity Program back into focus.

The Equal Opportunity Program that existed before the minority staff was recruited to help implement it was concerned with bringing minorities into the mainstream of American life as well as changing educational institutions. The program attempted to bring blacks into the mainstream with the projects it supported at the selective colleges and universities. In the end, it discovered that this was an elitist program that catered to the affluent sector of the black population and had little identifiable impact on institutions. The program then attempted to influence institutions with the projects it sponsored in community organization but was uncertain about which projects to support. For example, the report on the first decade of the Equal Opportunity Program stated that "the Foundation has made occasional grants to support organizations directly engaged in the struggle against anti-Negro prejudice and discrimination in the United States. These have always been exceptional grants, outside the designated areas of program effort. And grants for support of litigation were explicitly avoided" (Rockefeller Foundation, n.d., pp. 104–5).

THE NEW THRUST

The two new staff members worked with others to fashion a new thrust that, under the directives of 1969, would fulfill both goals of the Equal Opportunity Program — bringing minorities into the mainstream and changing institutions. They emphasized leadership development and created, first of all, the Superintendents' Training Program, which facilitated direct learning through internships with outstanding superintendents in major school systems. After the internship year, the participants usually accepted important administrative posts in the decision-making hierarchy of public school systems. In such positions, these administrators were able to aid ghetto schools through their impact upon the total system and its priorities. This leadership development approach recognized that ghetto schools, in spite of whatever deficits might exist within them, were products of the policies of the total educational system. The Superintendents' Training Program taught minorities how to implement change in the total educational system rather than restrict them to leadership positions in the ghetto. Before long, the Superintendents' Training Program became the centerpiece of the foundation's Equal Opportunity Program. Other leadership development efforts for institutions other than education were modeled after it.

The emphasis on education as a means of increasing opportunities for minorities was an old interest of the Rockefeller Foundation that received new stimulation by the Supreme Court decision in *Brown v. Board of Education* (1954, 1955). Concerning the *Brown* decision, Richard Kluger said, "probably no case ever to come before the nation's highest tribunal affected more directly the minds, hearts, and daily lives of so many Americans. . . . The decision marked the turning point in America's willingness to face the consequences of centuries of racial discrimination" (Kluger, 1975, p. x). The nation, including its foundations, did not know how to handle this new situation. Experimentation was the order of the day. Old institutions were trying new approaches. Thus, the Rockefeller Foundation administered some of its own leadership development programs to determine the most efficacious approach to ending the age of officially sanctioned discrimination. It was a new situation in which the foundation had to learn by doing.

REFERENCES

Associated Press. (1968). *The world in 1968.* New York: Author.

Brink, W., & Harris, L. (1964). *The Negro revolution in America.* New York: Simon & Schuster.

Brink, W., & Harris, L. (1966). *Black and white.* New York: Simon & Schuster.

Brown v. Board of Education, 347 U.S. 483 (1954); 349 U.S. 294 (1955).

Jencks, C., & Riesman, D. (1967). The American Negro college. *Harvard Educational Review, 37,* 3–60.

King, M. L., Jr. (1968). *Where do we go from here.* Boston: Beacon Press.

Kluger, R. (1975). *Simple justice.* New York: Vintage Books.

Lewis, A. (1965). *Portrait of a decade.* New York: Bantam Books.

Monro, J. (1978). Teaching and learning English. In C. V. Willie & R. R. Edmonds (Eds.), *Black colleges in America.* New York: Teachers College Press.

Rockefeller Foundation. (1964, 1965, 1966). *President's review and annual report.* New York: Author.

Rockefeller Foundation. (1968). *President's five-year review and annual report.* New York: Author.

Rockefeller Foundation. (n.d.). *Toward equal opportunity for all: A summary report of the foundation's efforts in this program, 1963–1974.* New York: Author.

200,000 march for civil rights in orderly Washington rally: President sees gains for Negro. (1963, August 29). *New York Times,* p. 1.

Williams, J. A. (1970). *The king God didn't save.* New York: Coward-McCann.

Willie, C. V., & McCord, A. S. (1972). *Black students at white colleges.* New York: Praeger.

Wright, S. J., Mays, B. E., Gloster, H. M., & Dent, A. W. (1967). The American Negro college: Four responses and a reply. *Harvard Educational Review, 37,* 451–68.

Zinn, H. (1964). *SNCC, the new abolitionists.* Boston: Beacon Press.

II

ELEMENTARY AND SECONDARY EDUCATION AND DESEGREGATION

One of the primary concerns in elementary and secondary education since World War II has been school desegregation. This focus has been central because education is traditionally seen as the primary means of social mobility for African-Americans and because it is through desegregation that blacks can have access to the same facilities and instruction as whites.

It is commonly acknowledged that in 1944 Gunnar Myrdal and his associates were prescient about a number of events that were to unfold in black-white relations in the United States following the war. What they did not foresee, however, was the occurrence and impact of the U.S. Supreme Court's decision in *Brown v. Topeka* in 1954. In the first chapter in this section on desegregation, Robert A. Dentler examines how the United States arrived at this case — and the resulting decision — in the mid-1950s, and then how the country got to *Brown* III in 1987.

Dentler reports that the *Brown* decision had an impact on the learning opportunities of black students in only one ten-year span — 1966 to 1976. He argues that during the preceding decade virtually no school desegregation plans had explicit educational components and that most efforts were instead concerned with the elimination of racial injustices in school district policies and practices. According to Dentler, while desegregation plans did contain important educational components during the decade 1966 to 1976, such progress came to a standstill during the 1980s.

Charles V. Willie also examines school desegregation in his chapter in this section of the volume. Citing two benefits of desegregation — a decline in the school dropout rate for black students and an increase in the high school graduation rate for all students — Willie states his belief that desegregation is the most important enhancement to education in the United States in recent years.

One alternative to desegregation discussed by Willie is the "effective schools" movement, a growing effort to transform black neighborhood schools by emphasizing strong leadership, an orderly environment, a climate of high expectations, and continuous monitoring of student progress. Willie argues that, although this movement appears to be successful, it has not had enough saturation to displace desegregation as the best option for improving the educational experience of black students. In the end, Willie makes an argument for "controlled choice" — a school desegregation model plan that permits parents to choose a school on a districtwide basis.

Finally, Willie also discusses the nature and process of school desegregation and how African-Americans have reacted to it. While he points out that more blacks favor desegregation than oppose it, he suggests that those blacks who oppose the process do so because blacks have borne the brunt of efforts to desegregate (i.e., busing). These blacks, as well as others, he says, may be looking for systemic reform rather than cosmetic changes.

3

School Desegregation since Gunnar Myrdal's *American Dilemma*

Robert A. Dentler

In the matter of education, Gunnar Myrdal and his associates demonstrated an informed and enduringly sound perspective on the policy of schooling in the social history of black America and in the emergence of African-Americans from the caste system of the post-Reconstruction era. Myrdal noted that learning was given nearly transcendent importance in the black community ever since the slave system had denied blacks opportunities to achieve literacy (1944). Prior to World War II, schooling was next to godliness: it enabled one to read the Bible and offered the best means for improving one's social status. In fact, the marks of learning were etched more sharply into the black class structure than the white structure. A college education was, before the war, a guarantee of topmost community standing. Myrdal's grasp of the de jure system of school segregation in the South was firm as well, although he erred a bit in assuming that northern educational opportunities for blacks were far more equitable than later events revealed them to be.

Myrdal and associates were also prophetic in depicting the dynamic and accelerating relation between black educational attainment and social protest. They foresaw not only how race relations would be different in postwar America but how change would be fostered and intensified by what was learned in school. While they could not foresee the baby boom of the 1950s or the impact of that boom on public educational services, their comprehension of the magnitude of the northward migration of black households from 1941 through 1944 was accurate. This understanding provided them with a sense of how this redistribution would affect educational opportunity, but it did not allow them to anticipate the scope of social and economic change in America in the postwar era or the role of desegregation in that change.

In 1944, public school desegregation was not a rallying cry among African-Americans, their interest groups, or the civil rights leadership in general. Indeed, school segregation and desegregation were not deemed important enough topics to be listed in Myrdal's index, and his chapter "The Negro School" contains only four paragraphs on desegregation. He wrote:

> There is a further controversy as to whether Negro education ought to be segregated or not. In the North the official opinion among whites is that segregation is not compatible with equality, but, as we have seen, much segregation is actually in effect as a consequence of residential segregation and of gerrymandering districts and granting permits to transfer. In the South direct segregation in schools is a necessary means of keeping up the tremendous financial discrimination against Negro schools. . . . Negroes are divided on the issues of segregated schools (p. 901).

This brief treatment ends with a long, now-famous quotation from W. E. B. Du Bois about the unimportance of school segregation, taken from an article he published in 1935 (Myrdal, p. 902). With the NAACP focused on efforts to open graduate and professional schools to black students and to raise black teacher salaries in the South, Myrdal's attribution of low salience to desegregation was not only understandable, it was an accurate estimate of trends between 1935 and 1944.

Nonetheless, one cannot get from *An American Dilemma* a valid profile of the state of public education in those times. There are good citations from the painstaking research of Doxey Wilkerson about shortages and racial inequalities in the allocation of resources, and there is an observation about the need for postwar federal financing of school construction, yet the nearly incredible dilapidation of public systems and the corresponding extremes in deprivation for black students get very brief review.

One question explored in this paper, then, is how this country arrived at *Brown v. Board of Education* I and II in 1954 and 1955 — a step not really foreseen by Myrdal's otherwise often prophetic work — and how it then arrived at *Brown* III in 1987 — the case that represented the completion of the cycle of school racial desegregation and left us pointed in the direction of a return to segregation. The same question invites consideration of the related question of how desegregation and what Gunnar Myrdal called the issue of the Negro school have become one and the same.

HISTORICAL TRENDS

In her history of American education from 1945 to 1980, Diane Ravitch (1983) narrates the deprived state of public schooling, particularly for rural blacks and whites. She quotes Florence Christmas, a black teacher from Copiah County, Mississippi, who told a Senate Education and Labor Committee hearing in 1945 that she and three other teachers taught 190 children all subjects in grades five through eight and received $60 a month for six months. According to Christmas, the other teachers were each paid less than $50 a month. Of 6,000 black teachers in Mississippi, 5,000 received less than $600 a year and held factory jobs during the off-months in order to live. In Copiah County in the same year the average salary for white teachers was $889.53 compared to an annual average for black teachers of $332.58; and of the 126 black teachers employed by the district, 122 had no college degree. Pay and qualifications were better in the other Deep South states, but not by much (p. 4).

Robert A. Dentler (1987) found that the demographic explosion of the baby boom, beginning in 1946, intersected with the depleted and substandard condition of public school systems throughout the nation. New school facilities had not been built, with some exceptions, from 1930 to 1945. About 2,400 new schools were built in 1946, and the annual number rose to 4,700 by 1950, reaching 8,200 a year by 1955. Nevertheless, the U.S. Office of Education forecast a nationwide shortage of nearly half a million classrooms by 1960.

District organization was also a mess. There were more than 101,000 school districts in 1946, whereas today there are about 15,000. Obsolete equipment, dilapidated firetrap buildings, small and underfunded districts, badly underpaid teachers with a third of all teachers teaching out of field, triple lunch shifts due to overcrowding, and a kind of curricular and programmatic bankruptcy steeped in intellectual confusion about what was needed in the postwar era summed up the state of public education between 1946 and 1960.

Black households were located precisely where they could experience the most negative brunt of these deprivations: in remote rural counties and villages throughout the South and in certain northern cities where industrial dislocations, suburbanization, and military demobilization had left legions of the unemployed in their wake. The degradation of vast sectors of Detroit, Cleveland, Gary, Chicago, St. Louis, and East St. Louis, for example, began as the war machines wound down.

To the uninformed, school desegregation efforts did not appear to be intimately related to these educational trends, and in some respects they were not. The more comprehensive and pervasive doctrine of racial separation was crumbling in a variety of policy domains under the impact of forces unleashed by the war. Employment practices, housing covenants, and some aspects of public accommodations were sectors in which the legal foundations of racial segregation and discrimination began to be shattered after 1946. This shattering was brought about through the new strength experienced by black interest groups and civil rights organizations as a result of shared wartime interests. These groups, together with organized labor, mounted a successful march on Washington in 1950. In addition, President Harry Truman's dwindling public support pushed him in 1947 to try to cultivate black support by cautious extensions of civil rights principles through federal executive orders. During this same time, Truman's solicitor general's office began to innovate legally against discrimination as well (Elman, 1987).

Success in several graduate and professional education cases in the late 1940s generated new interest within the NAACP Legal and Education Defense Fund in contesting racial segregation in public elementary education. In fact, there was an unmistakable and steady evolution in case law that made a more direct assault on the *Plessy v. Ferguson* (1896) doctrine feasible (Kluger, 1976). However, it is vital to understand that the substance of the cases that came to comprise *Brown v. Board of Education* in 1954 grew out of deeply authentic attempts by black parents to cope with the deprivations of public schooling for their children in those postwar years.

There were five different cases at the base of the Supreme Court's 1954 *Brown* decision (Newman et al., 1978, p. 80). In one, from Clarendon County, South Carolina, black sharecroppers led by their school teacher petitioned the school board for bus transportation to their children's school. A second grew out of the efforts of poor parents to protest overcrowding in all-black schools in the District of Columbia. A third emerged from Prince Edward County, Virginia, where high school students took political action into their own hands after their parents failed in a protest. In a fourth case in Topeka, Kansas, black parents sought to reverse policies under which their children traveled to black schools far from home while passing white schools closer to home. The fifth case came out of Wilmington, Delaware, where the inequalities between gravely substandard black schools and superior white schools was a corollary to times when all public schools in that state were of poor quality.

The leading defense fund attorney, Thurgood Marshall, was certainly concerned with revitalizing the Fourteenth Amendment to the Constitution through *Brown*. His overarching goal was litigative victories that would uncouple the power of the state from all policies that used race as a criterion for action or for neglect, but his tactical aim in education was to force the advent of quality in public instruction and educational services by the device of redistributive justice. If white parents in the 21 states where public education was segregated under law had to send their offspring to the black shacks on the edges of town and across the county rivers because students could no longer be assigned to buildings by race, Marshall reasoned that the shacks would disappear quickly and be replaced by decent facilities and qualified staff capable of delivering effective programs. Racial separation had meant, since the time of the Emancipation Proclamation, that most black public schools were physically, programmatically, and operationally inferior to most white schools. There were exceptions, to be sure, but Marshall aimed at the widest target.

Three distinctive features of the *Brown* decision profoundly affected its implementation and the societal consequences it would have for black America. In the customary import of Supreme Court cases on national social policy, the first of these features had an extraordinarily positive impact. In 1954 the Warren Court ruled that racially segregated public schools were by definition unconstitutional because they were an affront to black students, and because that affront could forever damage children's hearts as well as minds. In this decision (which became known as *Brown* I) the Court's repudiation of the idea of separate but equal was moral, psychological, and social scientific. It was more than a legal decision, and it would radiate across every domain in which racial segregation and discrimination were practiced in the United States, far beyond public schooling in its consequences (Newby, 1967).

The second important feature of *Brown* was the clause "with all deliberate speed," which was written into the Court's 1955 *Brown* decision, commonly known as *Brown* II. As one of the architects of this clause has noted:

> [W]e were the first to suggest . . . that if the Court should hold that racial segregation in public schools is unconstitutional, it should give district courts a reasonable time to work out the details and timing of implementation of the decision. In other words, "with all deliberate speed."
>
> The reason I'm so proud of that proposal is that it offered the Court a way out of its dilemma, a way to end racial segregation without inviting massive

> disobedience, [and] a way to decide the constitutional issue unanimously without tearing the Court apart (Elman, 1987, p. 827).

If "all deliberate speed" slowed the remedial process to something less than a snail's pace over the years, a third feature of *Brown* often brought it to a halt. This was the decision in *Brown* II that left the implementation of desegregation to local school authorities, subject to the supervision of federal district judges. In other words, the fox was made responsible for repairing the chicken coop and binding the wounds of the hens under supervision from courts known for their lack of administrative capabilities.

In spite of these limitations, the hue and cry from segregationists, defenders of institutional racism, and opportunistic politicians of the North as well as the South has never dimmed in more than three decades, so bold and far-reaching was *Brown* as a blow to segregation (Hawley et al., 1981). As Ravitch remarks in her history of that era, "Never before had the Supreme Court reached so deeply into the lives, laws, and mores of so many people; nearly half the states of the nation were living according to laws that the Court had ruled unconstitutional. Approximately 40% of the public school pupils in the nation were enrolled in segregated systems" (1983, p. 127).

THE OVERALL REMEDIAL RECORD

One reason race never declines in significance in American society is that domestic policy commitments to further the decline, even when they become the law of the land, travel through spiraling circles of cultural disenchantment. The policy of separate but equal, for example, had some viability for diminishing the onerous features of a racial caste system, but only if the equality principle had been pursued, not to mention fulfilled — which it never was during the six decades that the *Plessy* (1896) decision prevailed. So, too, had what Myrdal called the American credo — the constitutional and moral philosophy of anticategorical coequality central to the national culture — always remained a vision rather than a field of action.

The same has also been true with school desegregation. What desegregation meant to social policy under federal law came to be defined swiftly in the aftermath of *Brown* I and II. A public school district has been racially desegregated when its governance is unitary rather than dual — that is, when policy and policy implementation take place within inclusive rather than racially fragmented and barriered domains; when students, staff, and resources are distributed according to universal criteria that produce equality of treatment and uniformity of access to programs; and when the historic ravages of discrimination have been countervailed by affirmative efforts of many kinds.

The policy principles include equal treatment, equality of opportunity, and active elimination of the vestiges of past wrongs based on race. These meanings evolved in the case law and in legislation and executive orders across the three branches of federal government from about 1938 to 1955. As political resistance to the import of *Brown* mobilized, however, the meanings grew confused through constant challenge and local defiance.

The first steps toward genuine compliance with *Brown* were taken by some of the big city school systems in border states. Early pioneers included Baltimore, the District of Columbia, Wilmington, and Louisville. Border states as a whole followed next, with affirmative steps being taken in Kentucky, Tennessee, and Maryland before 1960. Some northern and western states, such as New York and California, followed by 1962.

The Deep South began to mobilize resistance as soon as *Brown* I was announced. When Little Rock's board of education moved to enroll nine black students in its Central High School in 1957, Arkansas governor Orville Faubus's defiance was restrained at last by nothing less than the arrival of armed federal troops in armored vehicles.

For all of the clarification of law and educational policy that took place between *Brown* I in 1954 and Little Rock in 1960, when the Supreme Court ruled state school closing laws unconstitutional in *Cooper v. Aaron* (1958), school desegregation did not move forward by much year by year. No more than 2 percent of black students were enrolled in biracial public schools in eight of the states of the Deep South by 1962, and in three of those states — Alabama, Mississippi, and South Carolina — total school segregation still prevailed.

The period of peak action toward large-scale and substantial school desegregation ran from 1966, when the Department of Justice and the U.S. Office of Education within the Department of Health, Education, and Welfare (HEW) became executive agency initiators, regulators, and enforcers of progress toward compliance with *Brown* and the 1964 Civil Rights Act, to 1976, when all but a few of the court cases in big northern city districts had been resolved. In turn, the peak year within this decade was probably 1972, because by that time nearly all Deep South districts had moved toward compliance with one or another among widely varied versions of a federal court order to desegregate.

An HEW statistical report prepared in 1974 (Orfield, 1978, p. 56, footnote 48) estimated that roughly 3.2 million of the nation's 9.8 million minority students were enrolled in unsegregated public schools. The level of continuing segregation was highest among black students: four in every ten of them were enrolled in racially identifiable and isolated schools. Gone were the thousands of schools that had been 100 percent black before *Brown*. But, of course, the great preponderance of such schools — both throughout the Deep South and in the nation's largest cities, North and South — had simply become schools that were 90 percent black or white.

Compliance with constitutional law thus never reached the half-way mark. If the rate of progress since 1974 was to hold for the future, moreover, compliance in excess of 50 percent would never be achieved since housing segregation has continued to intensify annually, complicating the historic ease with which cross-race schooling could have been accomplished in the period 1960 to 1970. In addition, most social scientists agree that the rate of change toward desegregative compliance, if measured not in student composition of enrollments but in sources of political and educational resistance or avoidance, has slowed since 1981. Even during the 1970s, federal executives under the Nixon and Ford administrations opposed school desegregation vigorously, and the House of Representatives labored to limit the extent to which judicial policy was advanced. Court decisions, however, continued very consistently to sustain *Brown* (at least until *Milliken v. Bradley* in 1974), and federal agency initiatives were substantial in the early 1970s.

With the advent of the Reagan administration, however, a quarter of a century of slow, often disenchanting, and uneven movement toward compliance with *Brown* drew to a close. The Department of Justice's Civil Rights Division was pared down to a sliver of its former self. Its advocacy for desegregation remedies narrowed correspondingly to an occasional drumbeat for magnet school development. The Office for Civil Rights within the Department of Education, as well as other arms of that cabinet agency, withdrew from most school desegregation efforts at regulation, problem solving, and local-level intervention. The U.S. Commission on Civil Rights, long a bastion of policy support for school desegregation, turned against its own record and became an advocate for inaction. Federal district and appellate judicial appointments, hundreds of which took place between 1981 and 1987, were made with an eye to limiting investments in any aspect of school desegregation. There were, in other words, just a few brief years — a decade at most (1966 to 1976)

— during which the far-reaching policy of *Brown* had a direct impact on the learning opportunities of black students.

In 1987, 33 years after *Brown* I had been decided by the Supreme Court, it was reopened as a law case in Topeka, Kansas. District court judge Richard Rogers had agreed in 1979 to rehear the case in order to test the allegation that vestiges of a racially dual school system still existed in Topeka. By the time Rogers had reheard the case, the political climate had changed dramatically. Dozens of urban districts were petitioning for the withdrawal of court jurisdiction. The idea of racial imbalance had declined tremendously in policy significance since 1979. Rogers, in declaring the Topeka Board of Education racially unitary in April 1987, acknowledged that "racial balance does not exist in the district's schools," but concluded that this was not a result of school board policy or "covert intentional segregation" (*Brown v. Board of Education,* 1987). *Brown* III thus added one more nail to what many saw as the coffin of court-ordered school desegregation.

DESEGREGATION POLICY DISPUTES

Great, dramatic policy decisions such as *Brown* are seldom based on much awareness, let alone exhaustive advance impact analysis, of what will evolve in and around the locus of change. Thurgood Marshall and Robert Carter knew from more than a decade of civil litigation that they would accomplish something of profound importance for black Americans if they won their case, yet we have evidence to show that even these best informed and most seasoned warriors for racial equity had limited insight into what would come in the aftermath of *Brown.*

For instance, it took roughly 15 years to develop the full range of tools needed to accomplish school desegregation. Initially districts such as Louisville reassigned students by attendance zones in ways that broke up the old one-race arrangements and then invited parents to apply for the schools they preferred. But the choosing was not controlled; it was not what is now called "majority to minority transfer." It entailed free and open changes back and forth with the result that all schools were mixed racially but some of the mixes were very skewed.

So, too, in the early years thousands of black educators were put out of work or transferred to positions they did not want or were not qualified to perform because desegregation in many districts consisted of shutting down black schools and merging their students into previously all-white schools. Ideas about equitable methods for recruiting, assigning, and retaining black educators did not take effective form until the early 1970s. Vocational education, special education for exceptional and handicapped students, and bilingual and other programs for lingual minorities all required technically distinctive remedial plans and action. It took more than a decade for such programs to be invented, tested, and installed. Transportation, student safety and security provisions, compensatory and development programs, and race relations within schools were other realms in which special tools had to be developed.

Desegregation research, planning, innovation, and field testing also did not move forward very rapidly. State education agencies were, with few exceptions, committed to avoiding this policy issue (Dentler, 1984). Universities and colleges had few knowledgeable experts to contribute, and no schools introduced programs of training and assistance until late in the 1960s. Under the Elementary and Secondary Education Act of 1965, federally funded research and development centers and regional laboratories took up a bit of the slack. For example, a center at Johns Hopkins University began to pioneer in desegregation research and evaluation, and the Center for Urban Education in New York City became a laboratory for school desegregation. Desegregation assistance centers, some of which have been maintained for over 20 years at their respective universities and agencies, were funded in 1967.

Generally, however, technical needs in desegregation were great while the availability of technical help was not. But, since this was a period of substantial innovation and applied research in professional education generally, desegregation planners began to beg, borrow, and adapt ideas and approaches from adjacent fields as the span of their own practice widened.

In the first decade after *Brown,* desegregation plans were crude and essentially noneducational in content. De jure separation ended, some schools were paired with one another or attendance zones altered, and biracial staffs were merged and retrenched. Instructional programs were usually left untouched. There were sometimes brief race relations trainings carried out for teachers and sometimes for student leaders, but this domain developed as slowly as others.

Social scientists began to evaluate desegregation plans as they were implemented. Most of the early years of evaluation research are summarized in a kind of metareview by Nancy St. John (1975). Seminal as the first 15 years were in stimulating better policy planning, the research was, when revisited, very naive. With few exceptions, researchers assumed that an appropriate test of the effectiveness of school desegregation was whether student achievement increased. They also often hypothesized that achievement gains should be associated with significant improvements in the racial balances of enrollments, as if this feature of the desegregation plans was a positivistic determinant of academic learning. Coleman's landmark survey of school segregation and desegregation (1966) took this line of reasoning a step further. It concluded that schooling itself was not a determinant of verbal achievement among white students but that family background was the main determinant of academic learning.

Overall, social scientists who attempted to evaluate the emerging desegregation plans tended to lack an awareness that nearly all school desegregation plans from 1955 through 1965 had no explicit educational components. Most desegregation efforts concerned the elimination of racial injustices in school district policies and practices — a goal that, at least initially, was not perceived as extending to the need for reform in teaching and learning activities and cocurricular practices. Some school practitioners were enthusiastic about racial integration and concentrated on social learning and improving human relations within schools. These practitioners also concentrated on correlative matters, such as multicultural curricular approaches and black studies. Social scientific evaluators, however, emphasized traditional achievement "outcomes" and began to find over and over again that desegregation did not improve those outcomes uniformly or substantially for minority students.

For a time it seemed that the swifter and more certain desegregative tools developed in the 1960s, the more intense was the contrast between desegregation as a goal and school learning as an aim of black parents. Teachers and administrators reinforced this contrast in their fear that the politics of desegregation would detract from school resources and programs of instruction.

As white resistance to the black revolution intensified, moreover, disillusion about cultural assimilation and racial integration became more intense. By 1968 black power and community control themes came to be pitted against the earlier call for desegregation (Rogers, 1968; Willie, 1978). The ideal of desegregation began to go out of fashion in young adult circles, as the racial protest movement shifted from the hands of middle-aged black ministers to those of the college students from the sit-ins.

In Atlanta, ten years of contentious confusion around school desegregation was resolved essentially through a compromise that emphasized increased black leadership control over public schooling in exchange for a de-emphasis on student and staff redistribution (Willie, 1984). Desegregation thus no longer represented all that was positively good and valuable to black establishment leaders, attorneys, and educators.

Derrick A. Bell, Jr. (1980), a scholar of constitutional law, and Ronald Edmonds (1978), a leading professional school administrator and professor, labored together and apart to reinterpret *Brown* and its implications for public education during the early 1970s. Bell had been a trial attorney with the NAACP Legal Defense Fund before joining the Harvard law faculty. He argued with considerable authority that the implementation of *Brown* I and II should emphasize the delivery of quality educational services to minority students. If necessary, Bell wrote and debated frequently, interracial exposure, and certainly racial balance, could well be sacrificed in preference for improved teaching and learning opportunities. Some experts who reviewed Bell's point of view believed it contained the theme of racial separatism as an acceptable and enduring feature of American society. Some even thought that what Bell sought was for blacks to be separate but more than equal. The *Milliken v. Bradley* II Supreme Court decision seemed to come out of this perspective. Where metropolitan desegregation was desirable but legally infeasible, said the Court, and where states had historically contributed to segregation and discrimination, city school systems could seek to enhance their permanently one-race or all-black public schools at state expense. St. Louis, among a few other large urban districts, adopted this approach. Edmonds (1979) also pioneered in developing the concept and operating specifics for the "effective school." He particularized the Bell strategy by elaborating what would be needed if one were to design and maintain effective schools for learners, especially black learners, who had historically been most deprived of opportunities.

It thus took educators, desegregation planners, attorneys, and judges 15 to 20 years since *Brown* to master the challenge of how to plan and implement school desegregation methods that work. In the first half of this period, plans were usually devoid of educational components. In the second half, those components began to be devised and installed. The best plans went beyond these, however, to include features for administrative decentralization, citizen participation, independent monitoring and evaluation, and even capitalization reforms for funding districts and upgrading their facilities and equipment.

Decision makers also learned that even the desegregation plan that has everything may work badly if it is badly implemented. For instance, Cleveland's court orders, coming late in 1978 (almost the final stage in the policy evolution of desegregation), seemed like one such plan. It was comprehensive, sophisticated, and reflected the best that had been learned over the years in other systems. In these ways, the Cleveland plan was exemplary. It has not worked, however, because the Cleveland board has become an agency characterized by wrangling ill will and racial division, while its central office bureaucracy has not divested itself of hegemony over either money or operating power in order to distribute it downward through the schools (Dentler & Flowers, 1987). It should be noted too that these devolutions are probably correlates of the economic fact that Cleveland, like many other industrial giants in the Midwest, suffered severe business setbacks for more than a decade.

WORKABLE REMEDIES

By 1974, the Supreme Court decisions amounted in aggregate to prescriptions for future state and local remedial plans to right the wrongs of racial segregation. For example, the Court had made it clear that an acceptable plan was one that "worked and worked now" (*United States v. Montgomery County,* 1969) to eliminate racial dualism in public school systems and the vestiges of discrimination carried over from such systems. The workability of a plan was to be assessed in terms of feasibility of implementation, not public clamor. Thus, what the Court called practicalities — very long distances for transportation or geographical barriers such as mountains and rivers without bridges — could be taken into account and result in exceptions. Public opposition, whether overt white fears or threats of white flight, was discounted as immaterial. Remedies were also to be systemic rather than aimed at a few schools within a district. They were to affect the treatment of all racial and ethnic groups, not place the burdens of change on black families alone. Later on, the Court began to emphasize the more conservative principle that the scope of each historical wrong should be the yardstick by which each remedial component should be measured.

In other words, as the decades of litigative experience unfolded between 1954 and 1974, judges, attorneys, and their educational experts began to evolve, always with guidance from circuit courts of appeal and from the Supreme Court, guidelines for planning, adopting, and then scheduling the implementation of a desegregation remedy. Open enrollment plans and student transfers that were not controlled for cross-race effects, for example, were eliminated as allowable options after they had been adopted in dozens of districts in the South. One-way busing provisions became suspect along with other plans in which the full burden of remediation fell on the shoulders of black parents and children (although on occasion such plans were adopted as late as the 1970s, as in Indianapolis) (Dentler et al., 1983). Plans that affected one set of schools but ignored others were also increasingly rejected over the years, although plans of this kind were occasionally approved as late as 1975. Houston's desegregation plan, for example, has gone essentially unmodified in recent years, even though it leaves more than 100 elementary schools racially isolated and more than 90 percent black. Standards evolved, then, but were often ignored because regional and local variability continued to be enormous.

By far the most controversial feature of the school desegregation plans that evolved between 1965 and 1975 was two-way cross-busing in support of racially balanced enrollments in all or most of the schools within a district. As white fears about having their children assigned to schools located in residentially black neighborhoods were intensified by political leaders who played upon those fears, veto groups composed of white parents sprang up in many cities and suburbs, especially in the urban North and West. These groups devised a rhetoric for opposing desegregation. The language did not refer directly to desegregation or integration. It spoke about the great value of neighborhood schools, of the denial of freedom inherent in forced busing, and of the right to freedom of choice in selecting schools for one's children. Court orders were also reinterpreted in this rhetoric as dictatorial usurpations of local authority. Federal judges were burned in effigy as carpetbagging martinets appointed to violate the will of public majorities.

At the close of the 1960s, northern districts began to experiment with voluntary options such as magnet schools (Blank, Dentler, Baltzell, & Chabotar, 1984). Magnet schools then evolved rapidly after 1975 because federal grants under the Emergency School Assistance Act (later renamed the Magnet School Assistance Act) pumped about $100 million a year into their implementation as part of a congressional quest for alternatives to forced busing.

A magnet school draws together students who are racially and ethnically representative of a district's overall composition to study together based on shared interest in a program, such as science or the performing arts. Majority to minority student transfers, controlled transfer preferences, vouchers, and other variations on the older concept of open enrollment also came into renewed favor after 1970. Like Blank et al., Willie (1984) found that workable remedies most often combined mandatory assignment of students with voluntary options of various kinds so that the principle of enhanced parental choice is strengthened rather than threatened by desegregation. Very few wholly voluntary approaches have succeeded; for the most part, a combination is essential if past wrongs are to be corrected. In addition, magnet approaches alone are often vulnerable, being too slight in scope to have any districtwide effect. Philadelphia has a series of outstanding magnet schools, for example, but the number is so small as to have no impact on citywide racial segregation.

Other landmark court decisions became guidelines for other features of school desegregation plans. Such decisions as those in Kalamazoo, Michigan, and Dayton, Ohio, for instance, laid the foundation for teacher and administrative desegregation. Here the guideline became the "Singleton standard" (*Singleton v. Jackson Municipal Separate School District,* 1969) under which the share of black teachers and administrators in each building and unit in a district had to equal the share of black educators in the district as a whole. That share was established by estimating regional labor pool availability of minority personnel credentialed for employment in specified positions.

This practice was part of the evolving law of affirmative action in fair employment as regulated by the Equal Employment Opportunities Commission from 1966 to 1979. It did not correspond closely to the educational ideal of matching the racial composition of adult personnel with that of students for role modeling and support — an ideal often debated in court hearings. Singleton also did not resolve the question of what to do in the case of school system retrenchments that began in the late 1970s — when black educators were vulnerable to being laid off for lack of seniority. Staff desegregation plans often led to ironic injustices of other kinds. In Boston, for example, Dentler and Scott (1981, pp. 196–201) found that some black teachers were terribly isolated within generally hostile schools, where they were also frozen into their positions by central office administrators.

In the Reagan era, desegregation policy focused increasingly on court disengagement. The Supreme Court rulings had obligated district courts to continue to maintain jurisdiction over local remedies and to supervise them until compliance with orders had been achieved. Sometimes the process worked: for example, the district court for New Orleans terminated jurisdiction over that city's public schools after 22 years of supervision. In Charlotte-Mecklenberg, North Carolina, the court did not withdraw totally but instead put the case on the inactive docket indefinitely, after a decade of increasingly successful implementation had been completed.

Court decisions declaring districts to be racially unitary became the fashion of the day in the 1980s. With the *Milliken* (1974) and *Spangler v. Pasadena Board of Education* (1976) decisions of the Supreme Court, the period of developing school desegregation remedies came to an end. In *Spangler,* for instance, the Court reversed a district judge who had sought to update and modify a remedy. The Court concluded that if a plan had been implemented in good faith it could not be revamped solely by virtue of demographic changes in a district "merely" because the plan had come to be inadequate to prevent racial imbalance and isolation. The sphere of action in which to improve desegregation plans and their implementation was thus drastically narrowed.

The 1980s, with few exceptions, became a decade in which desegregationists fought to shore up the gains made in the 1970s and to protect against the dismantling of those gains. Unfortunately, decisions such as that of an appellate court that, in 1986, approved a plan in Norfolk, Virginia, to revert to neighborhood elementary schools in contravention of an earlier cross-busing policy signaled a return to policy positions of the 1950s.

ACCOMPLISHMENTS

As the lights of the civil rights revolution seemed to blink out one by one throughout the nation during the 1980s, it seemed a time to sum up where we had gone since Myrdal's *American Dilemma,* and where we have arrived. It was also a time for exploring and for forecasting the future.

The *Brown* decision and its aftermath — hundreds of decisions and bench orders from federal district, circuit, and supreme courts — were pivotal to the transformation of postwar American society. School desegregation was not a separate or specialized societal event. Rather, the determination that state-imposed racial segregation was an unlawful act of unequal treatment in violation of constitutional guarantees was a policy decision that intensified the roaring tides of the black and civil rights revolutions anticipated by Myrdal and his associates.

There were legal and social policy antecedents to *Brown,* to be sure, but it was a decision that was pivotal, as well as monumental, in transforming judicial, executive, and then legislative policies between 1955 and 1975. These new policies had ramifications for every sphere of education — private as well as public. Student rights, employment equity for staff, affirmative action, curriculum reform, vocational training, gender desegregation, special education, bilingual education, compensatory and remedial instruction, preschool programs, and the radical expansion of access to higher education are among the educational realms that have been transformed fundamentally and permanently by the ramifications of the *Brown* decision. *Brown* had equally profound ramifications for housing, employment, public accommodations, welfare services, health care, military service, and criminal justice systems. Its policy principles were transferred into these and other sectors, penetrating even the confines of private clubs for white males, as American society underwent stunning, extensive, and swift sociocultural changes between the years 1955 and 1980.

Some commentators on school desegregation have been unswervingly narrow in their points of view. Nathan Glazer, for example, has argued that most school desegregation policies seem to him to be designed to make hostages out of white students so that black students will have the opportunity to sit next to them and mix with them in schools (1972). David Armor has maintained for many years that school desegregation has some benefits for social learning but little else. He concedes that interracial attitudes may be improved and that students may learn something positive about living in a multiethnic society as adults, but he does not think the remedies accomplish much else. Armor also believes that segregation remedies cause great social, economic, and political disruption when they are "coercive" (1972). There are also a number of social psychologists and educators who have identified school and classroom conditions under which black students do better and note that those conditions are more likely to be found in identifiably black schools than in desegregated schools (Cohen, 1984; Hale-Benson, 1982). These researchers' findings have often been used by debaters to argue that desegregation is educationally undesirable.

The mass media, shaped as they are by market research findings about the views of their consumers, seldom explore broader points of view about school desegregation than do the commentators and researchers discussed above. For example, a decade and a half after the Boston public schools were desegregated, the *Boston Globe,* in its Boston education stories, always refers to the disruptive and politically painful aspects of the Boston desegregation crisis of 1974 and 1975. Seldom does it link the crisis with the massive improvements in the city as a whole and in the city's race relations that resulted from desegregation.

In fact, in any of the nation's school districts, desegregation works to lift the rock of custom that ordinarily covers the realm of public schooling. As the rock is lifted and the sunlight of litigation and judicial review shines beneath, the twisted creatures of administrative corruption and venality; program mediocrity; racial, ethnic, and socioeconomic deprivation and public neglect; teacher despair and burnout; parental impotence and ignorance; building dilapidation and filth; and learning failures all crawl out and scuttle about in clear public view. Obviously, there are school districts where these creatures do not dwell beneath the rock of custom, but very frequently the presence of racial segregation over a period of many years is a powerful predictor of their hidden existence.

In this respect, desegregation becomes a process through which a city or a suburb (and sometimes a whole state) reconsiders its history and revisualizes its future. When this happens, a great deal more than classroom teaching and learning are at stake: race relations, property values, character of leadership, values of universality and inclusiveness, and economics of commerce and housing are all placed on the scale of racial injustice. In the end, a school desegregation plan may do a great deal or next to nothing to transform city and suburban life, but the planning process is always an important time, for it is then that the opportunity to do much or to do nothing is offered. The plans can be hollow, as in Chicago and Philadelphia, where little more than the reinforcement of the status quo was accomplished, or they can be profoundly substantive, as they were in Buffalo, Boston, and some of the county systems of Florida.

Of course, most plans fall somewhere in between these extremes, and the period of implementation, as in St. Louis, may be freighted with painfully protracted years of delay and controversy. Nevertheless, when the record of racial segregation in public schooling goes on the docket and is tried, the bell on the hour of change clangs out. Its call may be muffled: in Mobile County, Alabama, for example, the case of *Davis v. Mobile County* (1971) is 20 years old, and the district has still not chosen to improve its reputation or reconstruct its future. Black children in Mobile County are to this day denied a decent education, let alone equal treatment, even by Alabama State Education Department standards (1987). Still, though, the chance for Mobile to begin anew remains alive. A settlement was reached in the case in 1988, but some public interest groups, including the Mobile Chamber of Commerce, feel strongly that it is time for that state to become part of "the new South."

Desegregation plans developed since 1970 have, with rare lapses, contained important educational components. Remedies have come to include reduced class sizes; updated curricular elements such as computer education; counseling and remedial services; cooperation among schools, businesses, and universities; parent participation requirements; staff training and technical assistance; and the ingredients of Edmonds' effective school recipe. Of course, limits remain on the power of courts to intervene programmatically because desegregation cases are what judges call "race cases," and there is an obligation to leave program decisions with state and local authorities. That obligation has modified progressively over the years, however; courts have done more and bolder prescribing.

At the same time, others involved in education, including school boards, have written more education substance into their planning proposals. As a result, the most recent remedies have the power to raise the achievement levels of students. This goal has been accomplished in such districts as Wilmington-New Castle County, Louisville-Jefferson County, Buffalo, and San Diego, to name a few significant educational as well as racial success stories.

No doubt, effective school desegregation, as it has come to include numerous other elements of educational reform and capital improvement, has become more expensive. If the public schools of St. Louis are to provide truly equal treatment, for example, building renovations and repairs together with annexes will cost more than an estimated $400 million. The issue of cost brings to mind the Boston experience, where Mayor Kevin White began to argue that desegregation was desirable but unaffordable because the city was spending tens of millions of dollars paying police for overtime work in protecting schools and school grounds against antidesegregationist vandals and protesters. This raises the fascinating political question of whether constitutional democracy will be cost analyzed in the future to gauge whether and when it can be afforded. Most of the new outlays associated with school desegregation, incidentally, represent a fulfillment of Thurgood Marshall's original stratagem: desegregation would force an upgrading of facilities and services, he believed, once whites were prevented from sequestering resources for their schools and denying them to blacks.

School desegregation policies from Florida to California, and from Boston to New Orleans, have also stimulated the renewal of decaying cities and metropolitan areas. Once residential real estate is not held hostage to neighborhood schools, and schools become equal in quality, property values in previously depressed localities improve. Urban renewal and industrial redevelopment are also frequently initiated with desegregation plans, often so that city leaders can claim a new era of inclusiveness, quality, and hope has come to their community. What was once feared — integration — can often be turned into an asset, and commercial, higher educational, and infrastructural improvements can be piggybacked on the changes induced by desegregation. Also, new leadership has surfaced in many desegregating communities, including black and Hispanic leaders who had been excluded or isolated before. And just as the civil rights revolution, including the Voting Rights Act, has brought African-Americans into high political office, so has school desegregation stimulated the advent of big city and county black school board members and system superintendents.

THE FUTURE OF SCHOOL DESEGREGATION

We know now, nearly half a century after Myrdal wrote *An American Dilemma,* that school desegregation, like the larger cycle of protest and constitutional inclusion of which it is a part, has tremendous social importance for African-Americans. It has the potential, simply, to improve a youth's chances, to enable him or her to move more confidently and with self-esteem through the occupational and political realms that whites dominate. Equally important, it removes from his or her thousands of hours of life in school — from first grade through high school — the affront of being separated because of race. For individuals other than African-Americans, desegregation provides an opportunity to participate in a constitutionally more just society, to cooperate and compete more authentically in school tasks because the range of talent has been expanded, and to prepare realistically for adult life in a multiethnic world. These are great contributions, and we have longitudinal evidence that children reared under desegregation are often lifelong beneficiaries of these changes.

As with other improvements in racial justice, however, school desegregation has its share of disappointments for African-Americans. These disappointments have been especially felt by the parents and students who risked their lives in bringing about desegregation in resistant cities and counties throughout the country. They have come to see that some plans were no more than hollow shams that brought no real learning opportunities. They have also come to the shocking realization that the previously all-white schools they fought to enter were sometimes without educational or cultural merit. Still others saw positive changes in school districts achieved only at an achingly slow pace. And, finally, in some localities, some withstood white resistance so intense that it has prevented desegregation progress and produced new levels of black political radicalization and alienation.

The desegregative progress, then, has been slow, uneven, and checkered with technical and substantive flaws. During the 1980s, that progress came virtually to a standstill. Standards of excellence in desegregation planning were eroded; technical resources once available from assistance centers, such as the Office for Civil Rights, the Department of Justice, the National Institute of Education, and other federal and foundation agencies, dried up; black students walked away from college teacher preparation programs by the legions, resulting in the current crisis in black teacher and educational leadership; and implementation went awry or was canceled as courts ceased to monitor progress or accepted lame arguments that called for the end of jurisdiction. In light of these trends, we must ask: can public education drift back toward racial separatism and inequality of treatment? Or, is public education in America a series of 10,000 sandpits that, in succession, will cave in every time blacks seek to escape from injustice and ignorance?

We doubt these possibilities on every count. At every turn across a period of three decades, the majesty and power of the federal courts at three levels spanned the breach between the American creed and the reality of American education. For every decision that detracts from the intent and sweep of *Brown,* there have been ten that reinforce and enrich its import. Every hollow sham of a plan has been outmatched somewhere else by exemplary planning, and today there are hundreds of local school districts in the land that have invested themselves politically in the furtherance of the objectives of *Brown.*

During the Reagan era, our nation's leaders chose to follow numerous policy avenues that resulted in serious backsliding in the educational arena. The president and his cabinet were then stunned to find that, for the American people, nothing was equal in importance to the administration's publication of a call for educational excellence. That call, while it preoccupied itself with competitive rigor and academic elitism at the expense of concerns for equity, later brought renewed appeals from all policy quarters for a melding of equity with excellence. Cynthia Brown, former deputy director of the Office of Civil Rights and the first assistant secretary for civil rights in the U.S. Department of Education writes on this question:

> While most commentators agree that the "goal of education reform today is excellence . . . not necessarily fairness and access," I would argue that there are other forces which mitigate against states ignoring equity.
>
> Neither Federal nor state efforts have eliminated inequities or made sufficient progress in providing a quality education for all children. However, I believe that Federal and state governments can work together in new partnerships and with renewed commitment to education equity and high quality education for all children. Some states, in my judgment, already have the potential to be full and equal partners in this endeavor (1985, pp. 23–31).

We would add that there are other states where equity issues continue to be assiduously avoided. Brown is right in noting evolutionary developments in state education equity policies, however, and to this we would add the federal legal foundation. That foundation may erode over time, but it is by now broad and deep. It is not inconceivable that our nation could regress to *Plessy v. Ferguson,* or even beyond, but such a scenario is improbable. That our nation is a constitutional democracy mitigates against the possibility of our return to a time when the Supreme Court itself lived under the shadow of what remained of the racial caste system after Reconstruction.

In our opinion, moreover, there remain relatively endless small opportunities for improving the quality of racial equity through the courts: old plans can be updated (many were outmoded when they were adopted), and changing conditions can bring about new motions within the framework of old cases. Even *Brown* III may not have put the original Topeka litigation to rest. But, as the role of the court reaches a plateau in civil rights adjudication of class action suits, the role of future legislatures will gain in importance. As future policies of federal funding and development are legislated, racial equity management will likely come to be a regular component of planning and implementation — as it has in the competition for magnet school funds.

We must also take note of the increasingly multiethnic constituencies of urban and urban county school districts. Black, Asian, and Hispanic households will provide statistical majorities in many metropolitan area districts before the year 2000. In these districts, the quest for multiethnic equity will attain new salience through demographic and leadership changes alone.

We, therefore, do not foresee a reversion to the pre-*Brown* era. The boldly courageous protests of the black revolution brought the nation into the postwar era as Myrdal had predicted. The conditions for regressing far from that achievement are conceivable but not likely to develop in urban America. School desegregation is far from the panacea that some idealists dreamed it was when *Brown*'s light first dawned. Progress has been spotty and frustrating; nevertheless, the struggle for constitutional justice exemplified in the fight for desegregation has brought great positive changes to American society. Those changes were diminished during the Reagan years of political reaction, but they have not been scrapped — nor will they be. Racial desegregation in schools has evolved into an even broader movement, whose goal is providing equal educational opportunities on the basis of race, ethnicity, socioeconomic status, gender, and age. What was once "biracial" is today "multiethnic" and "multiminority." Future developments in teaching and learning will most likely never again proceed in the United States without regard for the necessity of providing equal chances to succeed.

REFERENCES

Alabama State Department of Education. (1987). *Program assessment for Mobile County: System report*. Montgomery, AL: Author.

Armor, D. (1972, Summer). The evidence on busing. *Public Interest, 28*, 90–96.

Bell, D. A. (1980). *Race, racism, and American law*. Boston: Little, Brown.

Blank, R., Dentler, R. A., Baltzell, D. C., & Chabotar, K. J. (1984). *Survey of magnet schools*. Washington, DC: U.S. Department of Education, Office of Planning, Budget, and Evaluation.

Brown v. Board of Education, 347 U.S. 483 (1954); 349 U.S. 294 (1955); 671 F. Supp. 1290 (D. Kansas, 1987).

Brown, C. G. (1985, Fall). Equity in education and civil rights enforcement: The federal role and state action. *Equity and Choice, 2* (1), 22–23.

Cohen, E. G. (1984). The desegregated school: Problems of status, power, and interethnic climate. In N. Miller & M. Brewer (Eds.), *Groups in contact* (pp. 77–96). New York: Academic Press.

Coleman, J. S. et al. (1966). *Equality of educational opportunity*. Washington, DC: U.S. Government Printing Office.

Cooper v. Aaron, 358 U.S. 1 (1958).

Davis v. Board of School Commissioners of Mobile County, 402 U.S. 33 (1971).

Dentler, R. A. (1984, February). Ambiguities in state-local relations. *Education and Urban Society, 16* (2).

Dentler, R. A. (1987). The education of the baby boom generation. In R. G. Corwin (Ed.), *Sociology of education and socialization* (Vol. 7, pp. 3–28). Greenwich, CT: JAI Press.

Dentler, R. A. et al. (1983). A county consolidation plan to desegregate the public schools in Little Rock, North Little Rock, and Pulaski County, Arkansas. Little Rock: Little Rock Board of Education.

Dentler, R. A., & Flowers, C. E. (1987, July). Decentralization in the Cleveland public schools: An evaluation. *Equity and Excellence, 1*.

Dentler, R. A., & Scott, M. B. (1981). *Schools on trial: An inside account of the Boston desegregation case*. Cambridge, MA: Abt Books.

Edmonds, R. (1978, Fall). Desegregation planning and educational equity. *Theory into Practice*, 12–16.

Edmonds, R. (1979). Some schools work and more can. *Social Policy, 9*, 28–32.

Elman, P. (1987, February). [Interview with N. Silber.] The solicitor general's office, Justice Frankfurter, and civil rights litigation, 1946–60: An oral history. *Harvard Law Review, 100* (4), 817–52.

Glazer, N. (1972, March). Is busing necessary? *Commentary, 53*, 39–52.

Hale-Benson, J. E. (1982). *Black children*. Baltimore: Johns Hopkins University Press.

Hawley, W. et al. (1981, April). *Assessment of current knowledge about the effectiveness of school desegregation strategies*. Nashville: Vanderbilt University, Center for Education and Human Development Policy.

Kluger, R. (1976). *Simple justice: The history of Brown v. Board of Education*. New York: Knopf.

Milliken v. Bradley, 418 U.S. 717 (1974).

Myrdal, G. (1944). *An American dilemma: The Negro problem and American democracy.* New York: Harper and Brothers.
Newby, I. A. (1967). *Challenge to the court: Social scientists and the defense of segregation.* Baton Rouge: Louisiana State University Press.
Newman, D. K. et al. (1978). *Protest, politics and prosperity: Black Americans and white institutions, 1940–75.* New York: Pantheon Books.
Orfield, G. (1978). *Must we bus? Segregated schools and national policy.* Washington, DC: The Brookings Institution.
Plessy v. Ferguson, 163 U.S. 537 (1896).
Ravitch, D. (1983). *The troubled crusade: American education, 1945–1980.* New York: Basic Books.
Rogers, D. (1968). *110 Livingston Street: Politics and bureaucracy in the New York City school system.* New York: Random House.
Singleton v. Jackson Municipal Separate School District, 294 N. 18 (1969).
Spangler v. Pasadena Board of Education, 427 U.S. 424 (1976).
St. John, N. (1975). *School desegregation: Outcomes for children.* New York: John Wiley and Sons.
United States v. Montgomery County, 395 U.S. 235 (1969).
Willie, C. V. (1984). *School desegregation plans that work.* Westport, CT: Greenwood Press.
Willie, C. V. (1978). *The sociology of urban education.* Lexington, MA: D. C. Heath.

4

The Future of School Desegregation

Charles V. Willie

School desegregation has contributed to the enhancement of education in this nation more than any other experience in recent years. Yet, its accomplishments are a puzzlement to students, parents, teachers, politicians, researchers, and a host of other people. Many individuals spent the greater part of the 1980s and will spend the remainder of this century trying to figure out what actually has happened with desegregation and whether the outcome has been worth the hassle. Without a clear understanding of what actually has been achieved and with misleading assessments of our educational system, such as those presented by the National Commission on Excellence in Education, which declared that "the average graduate of our schools and colleges today is not as well-educated as the average graduate of 25 or 35 years ago" (National Commission, 1983, p. 11), it is difficult for us to read the educational signs of the time.

The U.S. Census Bureau, in a 1986 report *How We Live: Then and Now,* offers an assessment differing from that of the National Commission on Excellence in Education. According to the Census Bureau, Americans today are better educated than their forbears; each generation gets more education than the one before (Americans Today, 1986, p. 1). Evidence supporting this conclusion comes from figures derived from other Census Bureau studies during the 1980s. According to these figures, 90 percent to 95 percent of all school-age children are registered as matriculating students in school, two-thirds of all adults over 25 years old are high school graduates, one-third of the adult population has attended college, and one-sixth of the adult population has graduated from college (U.S. Census Bureau, 1982–83, pp. 140, 142, 143).

These educational benefits have accrued for the total population and have been experienced by blacks as well as whites and other minorities. The median number of school years completed by white adults in 1950 — before the era of school desegregation — was 9.7 years, 40 percent greater than the median of 6.9 years recorded for blacks and other minorities. Today, the difference in the median school year for these racial populations is less than 1 percent (U.S. Census Bureau, 1982–83, p. 143).

Willis Hawley believes that gains in education are associated with the school desegregation movement, which had its greatest impact, according to Karl Taeuber and Franklin Wilson, between 1968 and 1976. Taeuber and Wilson discovered a 50 percent decrease in segregation between whites and minority groups during this period (quoted in Hawley, 1981, p. 146). During this same period, Hawley reported a 50 percent decline in the dropout rate of black students (p. 148).

Regarding social interactions, the National Review Panel on School Desegregation Research discovered that "school desegregation does not lead to significant increases in school violence." To the contrary, the increased interracial contact resulting from school desegregation is "friendly" more often than not. Moreover, "blacks [in desegregated settings] are found to be less prejudiced than whites" (Hawley, 1981, p. 148).

There is evidence that the quality of education has also improved during the era of desegregation. According to 1985 National Institute of Education figures, 1,750 school districts were at that time employing effective desegregation programs. These programs, which began in inner-city elementary schools, also expanded into some secondary schools and into suburban and rural districts (Kyle, 1985, p. 2). During the height of school desegregation activity in 1976, 50 percent of the parents of public school children rated their local schools as performing at A and B levels; only 5 percent, on the other hand, said their local schools had failed (Elam, 1978, p. 261). According to a Gallup poll, this attitude continued into the 1980s: one decade beyond the nation's bicentennial year, the proportion of parents who gave their public schools A or B ratings in performance had increased to 55 percent (Gallup, 1986, p. 47). While the proportion of blacks who gave schools high ratings has been slightly lower than that of whites, only 5 percent of blacks and other minorities believed the public schools had failed (Gallup, 1986, p. 47).

In 1975, at the height of the school desegregation movement, two-thirds of blacks 18 to 24 years of age who had graduated from high school enrolled in college (College Entrance Examination Board, 1985, p. 12). While the proportion of black high school graduates lagged behind the proportion of white high school graduates by 18 percentage points that year, the proportion of black high school graduates enrolled in college was the same as that for whites. Based on these data, one can conclude that a high proportion of all racial populations continue to believe in public education, that many are inclined to give public schools high marks in performance, and that the performance of public schools has benefited blacks and other minorities as well as whites.

In the early 1980s, a poll conducted in Boston — a city that experienced some violence associated with school desegregation — indicated that 73 percent of black residents were concerned that an end to court-ordered school desegregation would be a setback for them. Moreover, 71 percent of blacks reported that if they could choose an integrated over a segregated school, they would choose integration (Willie, 1985, p. 153). In 1985, a decade after court-ordered desegregation began in Boston, the superintendent of schools said that "black, white, Asian and Hispanic students are going to school together, becoming sensitive to each other, and developing an appreciation of pluralism and learning to judge individuals on the basis of their character and not on the basis of race, religion or ethnicity" (quoted in Willie, 1985, p. 151).

Back in 1958, when the Gallup poll first asked whites if they would object to their children attending a school in which half of the children were black, 50 percent said they would not. During the peak of the school desegregation movement, the proportion of whites who said they would not object to a racially balanced learning environment for their children increased from 60 percent in 1965 to 70 percent in 1975 (Schuman, Steech, & Bobo, 1985, pp. 106–7). Among blacks 78 percent favored desegregation in 1964, but by 1974 that proportion had fallen to 62 percent. Thus, while a large majority in the black population still favored desegregation, interest had diminished. Blacks continued to believe in desegregation in schools: nationwide, 96 percent believed in 1972 that blacks and whites ought to attend the same schools, and this attitude persisted into the 1980s (Schuman et al., 1985, pp. 144–45).

With strong overall support for desegregated education among blacks nationwide, even in communities like Boston that had experienced some violence, one is hard pressed to explain the increasing skepticism among some blacks regarding school desegregation. The Boston data offer a clue confirmed by the analysis of blacks nationally. While seven out of ten blacks in Boston said they would choose desegregated schools if given an option, they were unsure as to whether busing had been a good thing.

Blacks in that city were about equally divided between those who thought court-ordered busing was a good idea and those who thought differently (Willie, 1985, p. 153). The same discrepancy can be seen in the data from a national survey comparing the attitude of blacks about school desegregation in general with their attitude about busing in particular. At the height of the desegregation movement in 1972, 96 percent of blacks thought blacks and whites should attend the same schools, but only 46 percent liked busing as a way of achieving desegregation (Schuman et al., 1985, pp. 144–45).

The level of support for desegregation within the black community depends, therefore, to a large extent, on how it is implemented. The resistance of blacks that is sometimes interpreted as resistance to desegregation as an idea or goal appears to be resistance to the way desegregated schooling has been implemented. As Mary vonEuler, formerly of the National Institute of Education, has pointed out, "Minority groups, as plaintiffs, usually provide the impetus for legal action" (vonEuler, 1981, pp. x–xv). Yet, the white majority, which is usually not the plaintiff class, has experienced the greatest amount of desegregation. A strange and anomalous outcome is that whites, the population that predominantly white school boards tend to represent as defendants in school desegregation litigation, have experienced the most school desegregation, although they initially resisted the process.

A few examples will demonstrate how whites have experienced desegregation more often than blacks or other minorities who won the court cases. The student desegregation plan for Atlanta, for example, required little movement of whites to achieve desegregation. Instead, black students were assigned to any predominantly white schools, so that they represented at least one-third of a school's student body. The Atlanta plan, therefore, permitted many schools to remain all black, while ensuring that none remained all white (Willie, 1984, p. 191). Thus, whites experienced the beneficial effects of a desegregated education in Atlanta, while an overwhelming majority of the city's blacks did not. In Dallas, the initial court-ordered plan — which was appealed by the local branch of the NAACP — desegregated six school subdistricts, stipulating that each have a racial make-up of plus or minus 5 percent of the Dallas Independent School District as a whole. However, under this plan, one almost all-black subdistrict was left isolated, meaning that half or more of the black students were left in racially segregated all-black schools (Alpert, White, & Geisel, 1981, pp. 170–72). Again in Dallas, whites — who were not the plaintiffs in the school desegregation case — received the benefits of a desegregated education, while most of the city's blacks

— who were members of the plaintiff class — continued to attend segregated schools. Milwaukee, like Atlanta, prohibited all-white schools by requiring at least a 25 percent black population in each school. At the same time, however, it left 20 of its 120 schools with all-black student bodies. Once again whites experienced a desegregated education, while some blacks did not. In St. Louis it was the same story: the city desegregated its white schools but left several schools with all-black student bodies (Willie, 1982, p. 89).

The implementation of school desegregation plans in many locales was grossly unfair to blacks. In Louisville, for instance, desegregation was achieved by busing a majority of the white students for 2 of their 12 school years and by busing a majority of black students 8 of their 12 school years. Clearly a racial discrepancy existed that favored whites, who had to use transportation the least number of years (Arnez, 1978, p. 33). In the Charlotte-Mecklenburg desegregation case, equal numbers of black and white elementary children were bused, although each black child was bused for four years while white children were bused only two years (Finger, 1976, p. 61). Milwaukee transported nine times as many blacks as whites in its school desegregation plan, placing a disproportionate burden on blacks. If the Louisville, Charlotte-Mecklenburg, and Milwaukee plans are representative of other school desegregation plans, one can understand the increasing belief among blacks that they are treated unfairly in the desegregation implementation process. John Finger, a desegregation planner for several communities, admitted that some plans may be "inequitable" (Finger, 1976, p. 61), but he did not indicate what should or could be done to overcome this injustice.

Despite the recommendation of some desegregation planners such as Derrick Bell that communities should in the future devise plans that have potential for "improving educational opportunities for blacks without the cost and disruption of busing" (Bell, 1981, p. 200), blacks have not given up on integration. Data presented in several studies demonstrate that an overwhelming majority of blacks believe that blacks and whites should attend the same schools. This data also indicate that, when options are available, black parents are inclined to choose a desegregated school over a segregated school. However, the unjust and inequitable way that desegregation has been implemented has discouraged blacks and could affect their support of desegregation in the future.

One suspects that blacks continue to support the concept of school desegregation because they are subdominant participants in the national power structure, and subdominants tend to be inclusive rather than exclusive in their orientation. The Atlanta experience is instructive. There, blacks controlled the school system in terms of numbers on the school board, and they implemented a school desegregation plan in 1970 that initially offered whites 50 percent of the administrative positions in a system in which two-thirds of the students were black. In addition, despite the dwindling proportion of white students in the system, Atlanta blacks maintained their belief in inclusiveness and retained a proportion of white teachers twice that of white students systemwide. As final proof of its inclusive orientation and belief in desegregation, the Atlanta school board elevated a white member to the position of president when the term of office of Benjamin Mays, the esteemed black educator, expired (Willie, 1984, p. 191).

It often seems that blacks continue to support the concepts of integration and inclusiveness because many can still remember when the school desegregation court cases were initiated. As long as blacks were educated separately from whites, they could be and were treated differently, which in reality meant unequally. From 1938 through 1954, under the leadership of NAACP attorneys, blacks won several victories in federal courts demonstrating the inequality of separate facilities (Willie, 1983, p. 233). Therefore, they are not about to risk a return to state-sanctioned separate facilities based on a promise that separate schools might be more effective. They know that "the reason for separating the races in the first place [was] to accord them differential treatment" and that "communities unwilling to desegregate their [black] population have been unwilling to upgrade it economically" or educationally (Willie, 1964, pp. 84–85). In an inclusive system, one racial group cannot be harmed without also harming other groups. Blacks who understand this principle are likely to continue to choose integration or, at least, desegregation.

The record shows that schools that effectively educate racial minority students, even if they can be implemented as segregated units, are too few in number and are likely to continue as a limited option. The National Institute of Education commissioned the preparation of a document that contained an up-to-date directory of school improvement programs being implemented around the country. The document was designed to synthesize and disseminate research and practical information about "successful school effectiveness programs" (Kyle, 1985, p. 1). This source book listed Effective Schools Programs in 1,750 out of a total of 15,840 school districts in 1982 — only 11 percent of school districts nationwide. This finding is not a good omen for blacks and other minorities in 89 percent of the school districts, if the effective schools approach, which is supposedly not dependent on desegregation, is used as the chief school improvement method.

If one accepts the school as the basic educational unit, the statistics are even more disappointing regarding the widespread development of effective schools. The effective schools source book found such programs in only 5,228, or 9 percent, of the nation's elementary and secondary schools (Kyle, 1985, pp. 12, 57). For a nation obligated by its Supreme Court since the *Brown v. Board of Education* decision (1954) to provide an effective education for all children, including blacks and other minorities, the effective schools model does not appear to be a comprehensive and, consequently, constitutionally effective approach.

Some aspects of implementing school desegregation that blacks have identified as inequitable have been mentioned. In addition to the disproportionate burden of busing they have suffered to achieve desegregation, blacks have been denied the opportunity to be a majority in some multiracial schools. As the following example reveals, it has been perceived as not in the public interest for blacks to be a majority in any setting that is not all black. The state of Massachusetts passed a public law in 1965, known as the Racial Imbalance Act, that declared any school with a student body more than 50 percent black racially imbalanced (Smith, 1978, pp. 39–40). A public law defines what is and what is not in the public interest legally. A principle inferred from this Massachusetts law, then, is that it *is* in the public interest for a school to be majority white (51%) but *not* in the public interest for a school to be majority black (51%). Although the intent of the Racial Imbalance Act was to foster the desegregation of blacks, it did not prevent the segregation of whites. At the same time, it offered a racist interpretation of "not in the public interest": any clustering of blacks wherein they are a majority.

The public interest is an important concept in community life. The Supreme Court in *Brown* II (1955) stated that district courts could "take into account the public interest" in fashioning school desegregation remedies. For this reason, the Massachusetts law that prohibited a black critical mass of 51 percent but did not prohibit a white critical mass of 51 percent in public schools must be classified as arbitrary, capricious, and racist.

That the Massachusetts Racial Imbalance Act represented a general attitude among whites when it was passed is indicated by the result of a 1965 Gallup poll that revealed that while most whites said they would not object to sending their children to racially balanced schools — 50 percent white and 50 percent black or other minority — nearly two-thirds said they would object to sending their children to schools that were majority black (Schuman et al., 1985, p. 106).

Not only did the Commonwealth of Massachusetts encode into public law the prejudice and fear among whites of being a minority, but several school desegregation plans throughout the nation adopted this guideline. Seattle adopted a definition of racial imbalance that permitted the racial ratio in a school to vary not more than 20 percent above the districtwide average, provided a single minority group was not greater than 50 percent (Siqueland, 1981, p. 118). Although 77 percent of school-age children in St. Louis were black, that city defined a legally desegregated school as one in which blacks were 30 percent to 50 percent of the student body (Willie, 1982, p. 89). In 1977, Milwaukee declared a school to be legally desegregated if its black student population was 25 percent to 50 percent, although the ceiling for minorities was later increased. The assumption in all of these definitions of desegregation is that "whites always ought to be the majority" (Willie, 1982, p. 89).

According to Finger, the primary goal of many school desegregation planners was to develop plans acceptable to children and parents. Finger has maintained, in fact, that the response of children and parents may be more important than "complete equity" (1976, p. 61). Of course, we must keep in mind that it was black and other minority children and their parents who usually provided the impetus for litigation in order to avoid being "misused by the educational system" (vonEuler, 1981, p. xv). Since it was clearly minorities who, through court action, were seeking equity and peaceful social change, Finger must have been referring to whites when he asserted that satisfaction and acceptance of desegregation plans by parents and children was more important than equity. Finger's attitude about desegregation planning, as well as those of other planners with beliefs similar to his, run contrary to the Supreme Court's order in *Brown* II that states "constitutional principles cannot be allowed to yield simply because of disagreement with them." Thus, white parental satisfaction with school desegregation plans should have been of less concern to desegregation planners than achieving constitutional desegregation, but it was not. Many planners gave precedence to public interest concerns or the concerns of white parents in developing school desegregation plans. This probably happened, of course, because most school desegregation planners were white.

A review of the desegregation concerns of white and black planners reveals a significant difference in what members of dominant and subdominant racial populations emphasize. Barbara Sizemore, a black educational planner, claims that the planning priorities of many desegregation experts appear to be wrong. She sees desegregation as concerned with "education, equality and equity," and in that order. She believes desegregation should fulfill the needs of black people "for recognition and respect," and that educational policy to achieve these ends should focus specifically on grouping practices, testing procedures, curriculum development, multilingual-multicultural models, disciplinary practices, in-service training, promotion standards, extracurricular activities, and counseling services (1978, pp. 66–67). To Sizemore and other blacks, these are first-generation problems that should have been, but were not, addressed in desegregation plans.

Reports prepared by Gordon Foster (1973); Finger (1976); Larry Hughes, William Gordon, and Larry Hillman (1980); and the Vanderbilt University Center for Educational and Human Development Policy (Hawley et al., 1981) indicate the prevailing interests of school desegregation planners associated with the majority group. In summary, most white educational planners are primarily concerned with "the practicalities of assigning pupils so that schools are desegregated" and residential areas remain stable without massive change in the racial composition of the population (Foster, 1973, p. 15).

Social location in society as dominant or subdominant in the power structure (member of the majority or minority group) may be associated with the planning strategies emphasized and the priorities given to different components of a desegregation plan. If increased racial diversity with enhanced educational opportunities is the twofold goal of the *Brown* decision, then a diversified planning group is essential in achieving this goal. Otherwise, only one aspect of the goal may be emphasized at the expense of the other. A review of planning strategies by educators who identify with different racial populations reveals that minority group planners tend to be more concerned with educational outcomes, while majority-group planners tend to focus more on the racial balance of student bodies (Willie, 1984, pp. 44–45). Barbara Sizemore and Nancy Arnez claim that minorities, in general, have been excluded from the desegregation planning and policy-making process and that their exclusion has resulted in "deleterious" plans for black children (Sizemore, 1978, p. 63; Arnez, 1978, pp. 28–29).

Of the many court-ordered school desegregation plans in operation, the Boston plan (*Morgan v. Hennigan,* 1974, later named *Morgan v. Kerrigan,* 1974) has probably been the most comprehensive. An explicit goal of this plan was "improving the quality of education in the city of Boston" as well as desegregating the public schools. "The lynchpin of effecting educational improvement . . . was the involvement of the city's colleges, universities, cultural institutions, and businesses." The court order matched colleges and universities with particular schools in an effort to "enable participating institutions of higher learning to share in the direction and development of curriculum and instruction with the School Department" (Smith, 1978, pp. 101–2).

The invitation to more than 20 colleges and universities in the Boston metropolitan area to participate in the education of Boston school children was a unique feature of the Boston plan. The invitation was extended first by the court-appointed masters and the court-appointed expert educational planners who assisted the judge in formulating the school desegregation plan. The masters and the experts were multiracial groups, which may explain why their plan emphasized both educational quality and desegregation (Smith, 1978, pp. 83–85). A multiracial group of educational planners is something of value, yet few courts, school boards, or plaintiffs have retained planners with these characteristics. Frequently, a single expert or master is retained to assist the court. "Usually this person is white, middle-class, middle-aged, and male . . . and is expected to recommend or oversee the development of a plan or remedy for the grievances of the plaintiffs who, in most school desegregation cases, are children and parents of black and brown racial minorities" (Willie, 1978, p. 13).

A three-person multiracial compliance assistance panel was appointed by the Court during the early 1980s in the Denver school desegregation case (*Keyes v. Community School District 1*) but was given insufficient authority to formulate a school desegregation plan. The four-person multiracial panel of masters and two-person panel of experts in Boston, on the other hand, had sufficient authority to review the various plans submitted by the parties to the school desegregation case and to recommend a plan that included the best features of all plans and their own ideas. The Boston district court's approach to obtaining assistance in designing a school desegregation plan recognized the value of diversity. Such recognition is a manifestation of the wisdom of Judge W. Arthur Garrity, who was responsible for the Boston case.

Sizemore has asked: "How can black educators assume a position of leadership in desegregation when [they] formulate none of the theory, construct none of the definitions, design none of the models and negotiate none of the decisions?" (1978, p. 63). Today, black and other minority planning, legal service, social service, advocacy, and action agencies must insist that desegregation planners, advisers, and consultants be multiracial, including planners, advisers, and consultants retained by plaintiffs, defendants, or the court. Furthermore, blacks and other minorities must insist on a multiracial body of planners both for designing and implementing school desegregation plans since self-interest is the basic motive for human action and since it is difficult for individuals in one social location in society — such as members of a majority group — to fully understand the personal and social needs of individuals in another social location — such as members of a minority group. In short, it is more likely that a multiracial group of educational planners will consider issues of quality education, as well as of desegregative student assignments. As was illustrated by the Boston experience, a diversified panel of desegregation planners increases the possibility that blacks will continue to win court cases mandating desegregation but will gain more control over the design and implementation stages than they have had in the past.

Finally, more attention must be given to the composition of the community's educational authority and chief policy-making body: the school board. This group ultimately implements school desegregation plans. Even if the litigation for school desegregation is successful and the plans are appropriate and equitable, the authority to implement such plans is that of local educational agencies. By serving as members of the board of such agencies, blacks and other minorities can ensure that the interests of others accommodate, and harmonize with, their interests. When blacks are not members of local community decision-making bodies, these groups seldom recognize the full range of interests of local citizens.

In a chapter entitled "The Continuing Significance of Race" in *A New Look at Black Families,* I quote the observations of two researchers, Lee Sloan and Robert French (Sloan & French, 1977), who prepared a case study entitled "Black Rule in the Urban South?" state that "holding the line against black power seems to be a growing problem for metropolitan white America." They state that "it is becoming increasingly evident that whites moving out may be forfeiting political control to the blacks who are left behind." Whites attempt to regain control, according to Sloan and French, by "redefining political boundaries so that the pro-portion of blacks within the new political unit is decreased drastically." They say that this method of regaining control "can assume the forms of gerrymandering or annexation." Also, they classify the at-large election as another way of retaining control as numbers of a majority population began to dwindle.

During the 1980s the Boston School Committee became more responsive to the interests of blacks and other minorities when members of these constituencies became part of this decision-making body. Today, Boston is guaranteed a diversified, local, decision-making authority in education because its school committee members are elected at-large and by single-member districts, whereas, when the school desegregation case was filed in federal court in 1972, the school committee was all white. At that time its members were elected at-large only; such a committee was not inclined to accommodate the interests of blacks and other minorities (Willie, 1985, pp. 169-70). As evidence of the responsiveness of the school committee that emerged during the 1980s one can point to the appointment in 1985 of Laval S. Wilson to the position of superintendent of the Boston School Department. Wilson was the first black person to serve as chief school officer of the Boston schools since the office of superintendent was created in 1851 (Willie, 1985, p. 175). To guarantee participation in local decision making in the future, blacks throughout the nation should push for a change in voting arrangements for local lawmakers from at-large arrangements to single-member districts, or single-member districts combined with at-large elections.

A method of dealing with "establishment" control was exemplified in Houston in the late 1970s. At that time the nation's fifth largest city, Houston continued to be managed by a network of businesspeople and developers, despite the increase in black and Hispanic populations contributing to its growth over the years. As a result of political pressure, the city adopted a new voting arrangement in which local policy makers were to be elected by districts and at-large; previously all policy makers had been elected at-large — an arrangement that diluted the voting strength of blacks and Mexican-Americans. Under the at-large arrangement, minorities — 40 percent to 45 percent of the Houston population — had only one representative on the city council. Under the new voting arrangement by single-member districts, three to four black or Hispanic policy makers were guaranteed a spot on the council (Willie, 1981, pp. 32–33).

Following desegregation litigation in several cities, blacks continued the reform movement by pressuring for change in the method of electing local lawmakers, including school board members, who have the authority to block or to approve and implement school desegregation plans. Without a diversified policy-making and implementing group, communities throughout the United States will continue to experience what Ralph McGill observed during the first decade after *Brown*: the dishonest distortion of a court decision that could have elevated inadequate school systems had it been honestly implemented (1964, p. 246).

According to McGill, history is already drawing a harsh indictment of white political leaders who distorted the "wise proportion and meaning" of the *Brown* school desegregation decision (1964, p. 246). The same may be said of blacks who dishonestly use the defective manner in which school desegregation plans have been designed and implemented in the past as the basis for turning against desegregation as a viable concept today. School desegregation deserves to continue, with appropriate modifications, so that its promise may be fulfilled for black students.

When the side benefits of the school desegregation movement are considered (benefits such as the Education of All Handicapped Children Act, governmental requirements for transitional bilingual education for children who cannot benefit from instruction in English, and the educational amendments prohibiting exclusion of persons from educational programs on the basis of sex), one must conclude that the school desegregation movement has been the greatest contribution in this century to educational reform. We therefore should press on with school desegregation and its spirit of inclusiveness for the direct and indirect benefits it promises for majority as well as minority children in years to come.

REFERENCES

Alpert, G., White, H. R., & Geisel, P. (1981). Dallas, Texas: The intervention of business leaders. In C. V. Willie & S. L. Greenblatt (Eds.), *Community politics and educational change* (pp. 155–73). New York: Longman.

Americans today healthier, wealthier than ancestors. (1986, November 1). *Atlanta Journal.*

Arnez, N. (1978). Implementation of desegregation as a discriminatory process. *Journal of Negro Education, 47*, 28–45.

Bell, D. (1981). Civil rights commitment and the challenge of changing conditions in urban school cases. In A. Yarmolinsky, L. Liebman, and C. Schelling (Eds.), *Race and schooling in the city* (pp. 194–203). Cambridge, MA: Harvard University Press.

Brown v. Board of Education, 347 U.S. 483 (1954); 349 U.S. 294 (1955).

College Entrance Examination Board. (1985). *Equality and excellence*. New York: Author.

Elam, S. M. (1978). *A decade of Gallup polls of attitudes toward education*, 1969–1978. Bloomington, IN: Phi Delta Kappa.

Finger, J. A., Jr. (1976). Why busing plans work. In F. H. Levinsohn & B. D. Wright (Eds.), *School desegregation* (pp. 58–66). Chicago: University of Chicago Press.

Foster, G. (1973). Desegregating urban schools: A review of techniques. *Harvard Educational Review, 43*, 5–35.

Gallup, M. (1986). The 18th annual Gallup poll of the public's attitudes toward the public school. *Phi Delta Kappan, 68*, 43–59.

Hawley, W. D. (1981). Increasing the effectiveness of school desegregation: Lessons from the research. In A. Yarmolinsky, L. Liebman, & C. S. Schelling (Eds.), *Race and schooling in the city* (pp. 145–62). Cambridge, MA: Harvard University Press.

Hawley, W. D. et al. (1981). *Strategies for effective desegregation: A synthesis of findings*. Nashville, TN: Center for Education and Human Development Policy, Vanderbilt University.

Hughes, L. W., Gordon, W. M., & Hillman, L. W. (1980). *Desegregating America's schools*. New York: Longman.

Keys v. Community School District 1, 413 U.S. 189 (1973).

Kyle, R. M. J. (Ed.). (1985). *Reaching for excellence: An effective schools sourcebook*. Washington, DC: U.S. Government Printing Office.

McGill, R. (1964). *The South and the southerner*. Boston: Little Brown.

Morgan v. Hennigan, 379 F. Supp. 410 (1974).

National Center for Educational Statistics. (1983). *Digest of education statistics, 1983–84*. Washington, DC: U.S. Government Printing Office.

National Commission on Excellence in Education. (1983). *A nation at risk*. Washington, DC: U.S. Government Printing Office.

Schuman, H., Steech, C., & Bobo, L. (1985). *Racial attitudes in America*. Cambridge, MA: Harvard University Press.

Siqueland, A. L. (1981). *Without a court order*. Seattle: Madrona.

Sizemore, B. (1978). Educational research and desegregation: Significance for the black community. *Journal of Negro Education, 47*, 58–68.

Sloan, L., & French, R. M. (1977). Black rule in the urban south. In C. V. Willie (Ed.), *Black/brown/white relations*. New Brunswick, NJ: Transaction Books.

Smith, R. R. (1978). Two centuries and twenty-four months: A chronicle of the struggle to desegregate the Boston public schools. In H. Kalodner & J. J. Fishman (Eds.), *Limits of justice* (pp. 25–113). Cambridge, MA: Ballinger.

U.S. Census Bureau. (1982–1983). *Statistical abstract of the United States*. Washington, DC: U.S. Government Printing Office.

vonEuler, M. (1981). Foreword. In C. V. Willie & S. Greenblatt (Eds.), *Community politics and educational change*. New York: Longman.

Willie, C. V. (1964). Deprivation and alienation: A compounded situation. In C. W. Hunnicutt (Ed.), *Urban education and cultural deprivation* (pp. 83–92). Syracuse, NY: Syracuse University School of Education.

Willie, C. V. (1978). *The sociology of urban education*. Lexington, MA: Lexington Books.

Willie, C. V. (1981). *A new look at black families* (2d ed.). Bayside, NY: General Hall.

Willie, C. V. (1982). Desegregation in big-city school systems. *The Education Forum, 67*, 83–95.

Willie, C. V. (1983). *Race, ethnicity, and socioeconomic status*. Dix Hills, NY: General Hall.

Willie, C. V. (1984). *School desegregation plans that work*. Westport, CT: Greenwood Press.

Willie, C. V. (1985). A ten-year perspective on the role of blacks in achieving desegregation and quality education in Boston. In P. L. Clay (Ed.), *The emerging black community in Boston* (pp. 145–80). Boston: Institute for Study of Black Culture, University of Massachusetts.

III

SCHOOL IMPROVEMENT

School desegregation has been used to improve the educational opportunities of black students. In addition, there has been interest in improving the schools that African-American students attend — whether desegregated or not. In the first chapter in this section on school improvement, James P. Comer and Norris M. Haynes discuss the approach they have used in New Haven, Connecticut. Their approach, considered a part of the effective schools movement, seeks to have the classroom environment reflect the black experience. This approach, which they more specifically call the "school development program," focuses on "an orderly environment, strict discipline, basic skills, and high achievement." It emphasizes relationships among parents, teachers, and students, as well as the "basics." According to Comer and Haynes, children in schools that followed this plan achieved at a higher rate than similarly situated children not in those schools.

In her chapter on school improvement, Faustine C. Jones-Wilson reviews the records of several school improvement operations and concludes that many have demonstrated remarkable turnarounds. Where students once had perennially low levels of achievement, they are now regularly achieving at high levels. Importantly, however, she concludes that it is wishful thinking to suggest that existing school improvement efforts among African-Americans will move entire systems to excellence in the near future. A primary deterrent to such success, she notes, is that school improvement has not been a national priority.

Finally, in a chapter addressing counseling and guidance issues for black and other minority children, Charles E. Flowers suggests what, in essence, is an extension of one aspect of the school improvement plan of Comer and Haynes. Flowers suggests multicultural counseling both at school and at home. He notes that low self-esteem and low motivation, in addition to the idea of the family as the culprit in determining the educational achievement of black children, present formidable impediments in the lives of urban students. Flowers argues that the assumption that students' educability derives more from the nature of the family than of the school leads to low teacher expectation, a major pedagogical problem that condemns black students to an inadequate education. Flowers joins with others in stressing that the quality of teaching is the main issue and that multicultural counseling involves everyone in the educational process. Such involvement, he says, is important because teachers and counselors must understand the cultural realities of African-American children.

5

Meeting the Needs of Black Children in Public Schools: A School Reform Challenge

James P. Comer and Norris M. Haynes

During the past 25 years several well-meaning attempts at reforming American public education have been made. Some of the reform programs were purported to redress historical inequities in education opportunities and access for blacks and other minorities. Many of the programs were based on the compensatory education model and were designed around assumptions about the causes for consistent and severe underachievement among black and disadvantaged children. Three of the most prominent of these programs were Head Start, Follow Through, and Title I of the Elementary and Secondary Education Act. Other remedial programs were also tried, and several desegregation methods such as busing and the magnet school concept were employed. However, due to their narrow focus, limited scope, and lack of sound theoretical framework, these compensatory education and reform programs have had limited and questionable effect on school adjustment and performance of black children from low-income families. Compensatory education models were found to be unresponsive to the needs of black and disadvantaged children (Bloom, David, & Hess, 1965; Gordon, 1965), and other school reform movements, identified by Bruce (1980), were not specifically designed to benefit minority and disadvantaged children and had negligible impact on their school performance.

Most recently, the effective schools movement has achieved prominence, as renewed efforts to reform schools are once more targeted primarily at inner-city schools. The effective schools model emphasizes strong school leadership, an orderly environment, strict discipline, basic skills, and high achievement (Edmonds, 1981, 1982; Weber, 1971;

Brookover et al., 1983; Rutter, Maughan, Mortinore, Ouston, & Smith, 1979; Goodlad, 1979; Clark, Lotto, & McCarthy, 1980; Venezky & Winfield, 1979; Achilles et al., 1982). This approach offers some potential benefit in raising teacher expectations and improving achievement among black children; however, it does not give any attention to the relationship between children's school adjustment and their family and cultural backgrounds. Further, it does not recognize the need for systemic organizational reform within schools. Selby (1983) and Rutter et al. (1979) note that the ethos of a school significantly influences what and how children learn.

American public education has evidently failed, to a very large degree, to address the special needs of minority and disadvantaged children. The sociocultural idiosyncrasies of black children, in particular, have not been adequately addressed. The very structure of public education and the philosophies that have guided its development and implementation have neglected to recognize and incorporate salient features of black culture and the black experience in America. In a seminal work edited by McAdoo and McAdoo (1985), researchers discuss the importance of sociocultural and psychodynamic factors as they influence the psychological, social, personal, and cognitive development of black children. The evidence shows that there is an implacable nexus between the cultural and familial experiences of black children and their social and psychological adjustment to the school environment. For example, Garibaldi (1976) and Slavin and Oickle (1981) reported that black students perform better on school-related tasks when working in groups in a cooperative goal structure rather than under individualistic and competitive conditions. This preference for cooperation over competition in the classroom directly reflects the values of sharing, caring, and cooperation stressed and fostered within the black family and community. Boykin (1979) also reported that black children perform better on school-related tasks that are culturally and experientially salient than on other tasks. Willie (1964) demonstrated that black college students in predominantly white schools performed at a higher level when the relationship between black students and white faculty members was clearly positive. We can presume that the relationship factor is even more important in primary and secondary school settings, particularly when there are racial, class, and other significant differences between students and staff.

In our own work (Comer, 1980), achievement test scores, attendance, and student behavior in two elementary schools were dramatically improved by attending to relationship issues in particular and addressing at least three problem areas related to the black experience in America.

Political, economic, and social policies and practices resulted in excessive dependency, powerlessness, and lack of control as a group. These conditions, in turn, resulted in disproportionate amounts of poverty, family and community stress, and troublesome attitudes and behavior not conducive to academic success among many black students. Simultaneously, public policies and practices created conditions, attitudes, and behaviors in schools serving low-income children that reinforced rather than overcame difficult family and community conditions.

Our approach, the school development program, was designed with the black experience in mind. It systematically empowers parents, teachers, administrators, and students through collaborative, cooperative, coordinated planning and program implementation. A central focus is creating relationships in which there is mutual respect among all the players in the educational enterprise. Teaching is based on understanding what the children have not received in preschool experiences and reinforcing these needs through relevant and meaningful activities, with an emphasis on developing basic skills. Involving parents in planning and implementation helps make the program culturally sensitive and parents and staff more accountable. The mental health or support team helps those involved use child development and relationship principles in every aspect of the school program.

A follow-up after three years on 24 students from our program and 24 students from the same community who did not attend our program and who were now attending the same middle school showed our project school students to be two years ahead in language arts and a year ahead in mathematics. Students from our project schools were more often student leaders and had fewer behavior problems. Similar results using our model have now been demonstrated in over 20 elementary schools.

Most of the education reform reports (Achilles et al., 1982) call for raised standards of course content, time, and achievement among staff and students. Very little attention was given to the issue of relationships in schools and their impact on student learning. Almost no attention was given to the special problem of relationships between what is often minority children and parents and nonminority staff. Yet serious identity issues, troublesome feelings, and attitudes about self interfere with learning among many minority students. These are the issues we feel are essential to address if we are to greatly improve the level of minority student learning.

Finally, it is possible to raise test scores through any systematic teaching and learning effort, but raising test scores is not enough if schools are to achieve their mission: to prepare students to become responsible adult members of a democratic society — competent workers, responsible family members and child rearers, and responsible members of their communities and the society. School improvement efforts must address relationship issues in order to overcome past conditions detrimental to black family functioning and child development and to make it possible for schools to prepare children for successful adult lives. The relationship factor appears to be of paramount importance, yet it has been given the least attention in school improvement efforts. Even where some attention has been given to parent-student-staff relationships, sources of tension and difficult relationships between black and low-income students and families and schools have been given grossly inadequate attention.

REFERENCES

Achilles, C. et al. (1982). *Development and use of a replication and evaluation model to track the implementation progress of effective schools elements in an inner-city setting*. Paper presented at the annual meeting of the Mid-South Educational Research Association, New Orleans.

Bloom, B., David, A., & Hess, R. (1965). *Compensatory education for cultural deprivation*. New York: Holt, Rinehart and Winston.

Boykin, A. W. (1979). Psychological behavioral verve: Some theoretical explorations and empirical manifestations. In A. W. Boykin & J. F. Yates (Eds.), *Research directions of black psychologists*. New York: Russell Sage Foundation.

Brookover, W. B., Beamer, L., Efthim, H., Hathaway, D., Lesotte, L. W., Miller, S. K., Passalacqua, T., & Tornatsky, L. (1983). *Creating effective schools*. Holmes Beach, CA: Learning Publications.

Bruce, J. (1980). *The continuous process of school improvement: learned from the past*. Reston, VA: Association of Teacher Educators.

Clark, D. L., Lotto, L. S., & McCarthy, M. M. (1980). Factors associated with success in urban elementary schools. *Phi Delta Kappan, 61* (3), 467–70.

Comer, J. P. (1980). *School power*. New York: The Free Press.

Edmonds, R. R. (1982). Prigram of school improvement: An overview. *Educational Leadership, 39*, 4–14.

Edmonds, R. R. (1981). Improving the effectiveness of New York City public schools. In *The minority student in public schools: Fostering academic excellence* (pp. 23–30). Princeton, NJ: Educational Testing Service, Office for Minority Education.

Garibaldi, A. M. (1976). *Cooperation, competition, and focus of control in Afro-American students*. Doctoral dissertation, University of Minnesota. (University Microfilms No. 77-12, 807).

Goodlad, J. I. (1979). Can our schools get better? *Phi Delta Kappan, 60*, 342–47.

Gordon, E. W. (1965). A review of programs of compensatory education. *American Journal of Orthopsychiatry, 35* (4), 640–51.

McAdoo, H. P., & McAdoo, J. L. (Eds.). (1985). *Black children: Social, educational and parental environments*. Beverly Hills: Sage.

Rutter, M., Maughan, B., Mortinore, P., Ouston, J., & Smith, A. (1979). *Fifteen thousand hours: Secondary schools and their effects on children.* Cambridge, MA: Harvard University Press.

Selby, C. C. (1983). *Need for top down and bottom up leadership.* Address delivered at the Forum on Excellence in Education, Indianapolis.

Slavin, R. E., & Oickle, E. (1981). Effects of cooperative learning teams on student achievement and race relations: Treatment by race interactions. *Sociology of Education, 54,* 174–80.

Venezky, R. L., & Winfield, L. (1979). *Schools that exceed expectations in teaching reading.* Dover, DE: University of Delaware Studies on Education.

Weber, G. (1971). *Inner-city children can be taught to read: Four successful schools.* Washington, DC: Council for Basic Education, Occasional Papers, 18.

Willie, C. V. (1964). Deprivation and alienation: A compound situation. In C. W. Hunnicutt (Ed.), *Urban education and cultural deprivation.* Syracuse, NY: Syracuse University Press.

6

School Improvement among Blacks: Implications for Excellence and Equity

Faustine C. Jones-Wilson

Historically, black Americans have been ardent supporters of and advocates for high-quality public education. Black efforts to gain systemic equality in educational policies and practices are well known: the battles for equal per-pupil expenditures; teachers' salaries; length of school terms; expenditures for buildings, facilities, equipment, and books; curricular offerings; and so on. As a result of these efforts and of political and economic changes nationally and internationally, progress has been made with respect to ending legally imposed school segregation, as well as increasing black participation in schooling for longer periods of time, that is, raising the median years of schooling completed.

In spite of this progress, however, the larger society apparently continues to perceive the black minority group as intellectually inferior. Indicators of this perception include: continued white flight from desegregated schools, the high value placed on I.Q. and other norm-referenced tests as selecting and sorting mechanisms to discriminate among individuals and groups, the numbers of blacks assigned to special education classes and vocational tracks, the numbers and proportions of blacks suspended or expelled from schools, the emphasis on attaining excellence with minimal commitment to equality and even less significance attached to equity, and so on. Most recently, the larger society has retreated from its short flirtation with urban school improvement, for example, helping "the disadvantaged." Urban school improvement is clearly not a national priority today, nor has it been a serious, purposive, continuous societal effort since public school desegregation began in the mid-1960s.

As a result of these circumstances, black educators and their like-minded allies have increasingly taken the lead in urban school improvement. One facet of this movement has been the study of schools that are effectively educating urban poor black children and making recommendations to other schools that want to replicate effective policies and programs. Foremost among these researchers are Ronald R. Edmonds, Wilbur B. Brookover, George Weber, Lawrence W. Lezotte, Daniel U. Levine, and Eugene E. Eubanks. They began by identifying public schools that were effectively teaching black children and pinpointed their common characteristics:

strong administrative leadership;
climate of high expectations;
orderly but flexible atmosphere, conducive to instruction;
philosophy that acquiring basic academic skills is the first order of business;
flexibility to allow school energy and resources to be diverted from other business in order to further fundamental objectives; and
continuous monitoring and evaluation of pupil progress with instructional strategies redesigned as needed (Edmonds, 1979a, 1979b).

This work continues, and school improvement is verifiable when the common characteristics prevail and are supported (Brookover, 1985; Glenn, 1985; Lezotte & Bancroft, 1985; Levine, Levine, & Eubanks, 1985).

In New York in 1987 the effective schools legacy was continued by J. Jerome Harris. Notably in District 13 Public Schools 11, 20, 44, 282, and 307 and Junior High School 113 are high-achieving schools; 70 percent or more of the students achieved reading scores at or above grade level for three years (Harris, 1987).

In Pittsburgh, Barbara A. Sizemore, Carlos A. Brossard, and Birney Harrigan studied three high-achieving, predominantly black public elementary schools (Sizemore, 1985). The researchers refer to these schools as "abasing anomalies" because they counter the expectation that black inner-city schools rank at the bottom of the achievement scale. Sizemore et al. found that these anomalies began with these factors:

recruitment and selection of moderately authoritarian principals who believed that black poor students could and would learn;
principals who risked differing with the system's norm of low achievement for black poor schools;

consensus among school and community actors that high achievement is the highest priority goal;
climate of high expectations for student achievement conducive to teaching and learning;
functional routines, scenarios, and processes for achieving this highest priority; and
willingness to disagree with superior officers about the choices of these routines and their implementation.

Sizemore emphasizes that the "promise of effective schools research is precisely that it shows that black poor children can learn and can be taught" (1985).

The earlier work of Bernard C. Watson (1974) supports this concept. Watson's publication *In Spite of the System: The Individual and Educational Reform* presents three case studies of school improvement at the secondary level. Maverick administrators took risks to challenge the system and, with the assistance of parents and the community, succeeded in making their schools places of learning.

In addition to individual researchers, some cities, states, and education organizations are involved in school improvement projects targeted at poor urban students. In 1980 for example, Chicago instituted a plan for mastery learning in reading to correct the widespread problem of low reading achievement. The program provided teachers with comprehensive instructional activities, corresponding pupil learning activities, formative tests for instructional feedback, and corrective instructional activities for those students who failed to master objectives. A criterion-referenced testing program served as the basis for instruction, promotion, and administrative monitoring (Katims & Jones, 1985).

Milwaukee, in 1979, instituted Project Rise, a school effectiveness program to identify the 18 lowest achieving elementary schools and work toward raising their achievement levels to city or national norms. The majority of these schools met or exceeded national norms at most grade levels by the end of the 1983–84 school year (McCormack-Larkin, 1985). The Jackson, Mississippi, schools found that in-service staff development programs were a necessary part of school improvement. Student achievement there has been enhanced through the institution of a systematic, structured, ongoing training program designed to improve teacher performance (Fortenberry, 1985). In Virginia, alternate scheduling practices that restructured the school day increased student achievement in certain elementary schools (Canady & Hotchkiss, 1985).

Since 1981 a statewide effort has been under way in Connecticut to improve effectiveness in schools. While success has varied greatly across schools, there is evidence that principals and teachers can significantly alter characteristics related to school effectiveness and improve student achievement (Gauthier, Pecheone, & Shoemaker, 1985). The Connecticut plan includes home-school relations as an essential component in its efforts to improve urban schools.

In New Jersey, Carol Ann West's research has clearly shown that administrative instructional leadership is an important factor in school outcomes. According to West, emphasis on basic skills significantly improved mathematics achievement in New Jersey elementary schools, and parental involvement contributed to reading achievement, as did teacher experience and education (1985).

The New Jersey Education Association (NJEA) in 1979 instituted a School Effectiveness Training Program designed to increase student achievement. The results from this program show lower staff absenteeism, higher participation of staff in instructional decisions, greater involvement of staff in school activities, reduced costs for vandalism, better management, and higher staff and student morale (McNeely, 1985). In 1987 the NJEA also launched an Urban Challenge Project to promote urban school improvement.

James P. Comer, director of the School Development Program at the Yale Child Study Center, is well known for his school improvement work (Comer, 1980). Following his successful efforts in the New Haven, Connecticut, area, Comer's knowledge and commitment have been spread through his work as an educational consultant to large and troubled school systems that want to solve their problems. He and his team of consultants are active in the school systems of Prince Georges County, Maryland; Norfolk, Virginia; Washington, D.C.; and other places.

The National Conference on Educating Black Children (NCEBC) — a voluntary organization with representatives from a cross-section of black groups, major national education organizations, and local grassroots community organizations — has held two national meetings designed to promote a nationwide effort to improve the education of black children. From these two conferences *A Blueprint for Action II* was developed by the participants and refined by a working committee. This blueprint consists of practical action items and implementation activities that students, teachers, administrators, parents, community members, and policy makers can employ regularly and continuously to improve schooling. NCEBC's intent is to promote a process in which all significant actors in the educational endeavor work together in positive, succinct, achievable activities and to encourage these significant actors to stop blaming each other for the educational problems that blacks continue to face (National Conference on Educating Black Children, 1987). At its Hunt Valley II conference — May 29 to 31, 1987 — the NCEBC presented six models of school improvement so that participants could know about their work, visit these schools, and replicate their successes. Elementary school models were presented from Baltimore and Atlanta, and junior high school models from Los Angeles and St. Louis were discussed. Two Chicago senior high school programs — Corliss and Hyde Park — were also presented as improving models.

In a different vein, it must be acknowledged that during the past two decades it has become increasingly apparent that larger numbers of black adults are selecting nonpublic schools for their young. In their desire to obtain the best possible education for their young, they choose private schools, including black independent schools (Arnez & Jones-Wilson, 1988). These parents say they believe private schools provide their children with better basic skills instruction, cultivate higher order thinking skills, have higher academic standards, and prepare their children for college or the work place more successfully. School improvement for them means leaving public schools. Slaughter and Schneider (1986) believe black parents' choice of private schools is "less of a rejection of public schooling, and more of an evolution of a new strategy for insuring future levels of sustained and/or upward mobility for the family." Increased black departure from public schools, however, may mean that the more supportive, motivated, caring, and accomplished parents and their children (regardless of income) are not involved in the public school system and that the system is the loser in the process. Black individuals and communities must consider the costs and benefits of education in nonpublic schools compared with education in public schools — not only for themselves, but for the nation at large. At the same time, public schools must make more headway in school improvement if they want to retain the traditional support they have long enjoyed from black families.

Many individual students can attain standards of excellence if school improvement policies and programs such as those described above are retained, consistently used, refined, and modified as evaluation results recommend. Individual schools will find that their achievement levels and test scores improve, and that many of them can attain local and national norms even if their populations are poor, or black, or both. These standards can be achieved without excluding any student from an equal opportunity to be educated.

Most urban school systems, however, have such deep-seated problems stemming from generations of social, economic, and educational inequities that it would be wishful thinking to suggest that existing school improvement efforts among blacks will move entire systems to excellence in the near future. Yet, they can make marked progress toward individual and collective competence, which is so necessary for the youth who fill school buildings.

School improvement efforts seek to make school systems fair and to provide all students with the conditions necessary for effective learning. Equity should become an essential part of a "bill of rights" for elementary and secondary school students.

Our country still has a long way to go to realize equity in the schoolrooms of our nation. All students need an equal chance to learn, which means providing equity in financing schools and programs; providing competent, caring teachers; retaining proven, compensatory programs; relating curriculum subject matter to coping with real-life situations and problems; creating and using appropriate evaluation measures; providing enrichment trips and learning opportunities to supplement classroom work; meeting individual needs; and allowing for individual differences. We who care about our youth and our democratic society must stand together to ensure that equity as both a concept and reality is not lost in the bedlam of the "excellence movement" (Jones-Wilson, 1986).

REFERENCES

Arnez, N. L., & Jones-Wilson, F. C. (1988). A descriptive survey of black parents in the greater Washington, D.C., area who chose to send their children to nonpublic schools. In D. T. Slaughter & D. J. Johnson (Eds.), *Visible now: Blacks in private schools*. Westport, CT: Greenwood Press.

Brookover, W. B. (1985, Summer). Can we make schools effective for minority students? *Journal of Negro Education, 54*, 257–68.

Canady, R. L., & Hotchkiss, P. R. (1985, Summer). Scheduling practices associated with increased achievement for low-achieving students. *Journal of Negro Education, 54*, 344–55.

Comer, J. P. (1980). *School power: Implications of an intervention project*. New York: Free Press.

Edmonds, R. R. (1979a). Some schools work and more can. *Social Policy, 9* (5), 28–32.

Edmonds, R. R. (1979b). Effective schools for the urban poor. *Educational Leadership, 37* (1), 15–18.

Fortenberry, R. N. (1985, Summer). Successful staff development for effective schools. *Journal of Negro Education, 54*, 431–37.

Gauthier, W. J., Jr., Pecheone, R. L., & Shoemaker, J. (1985, Summer). Schools can become more effective. *Journal of Negro Education, 54,* 388–408.

Glenn, B. C. (1985, Summer). Excellence and equity: Implications for effective schools. *Journal of Negro Education, 54,* 289–300.

Harris, J. J. (1987, May). Presentation at the second Hunt Valley Conference on Educating Black Children, New York.

Jones-Wilson, F. C. (1986). Equity in education: Low priority in the school reform movement. *The Urban Review, 18* (1), 31–39.

Katims, M., & Jones, B. F. (1985, Summer). Chicago mastery learning reading: Mastery learning instruction and assessment in inner-city schools. *Journal of Negro Education, 54,* 369–87.

Levine, D. U., Levine, R. R., & Eubanks, E. E. (1985, Summer). Successful implementation of instruction at inner-city schools. *Journal of Negro Education, 54,* 313–32.

Lezotte, L. W., & Bancroft, B. A. (1985, Summer). School improvement based on effective schools research: A promising approach for economically disadvantaged and minority students. *Journal of Negro Education, 54,* 301–12.

McCormack-Larkin, M. (1985, Summer). Change in urban schools. *Journal of Negro Education, 54,* 409–15.

McNeely, D. R. (1985, Summer). School effectiveness training: An education association's initiative for instructional improvement. *Journal of Negro Education, 54,* 462–72.

McNeely, D. R. (1987, June). Correspondence with the author.

National Conference on Educating Black Children. (1987). *A blueprint for action II.* Washington, DC: Author.

Sizemore, B. A. (1985, Summer). Pitfalls and promises of effective schools research. *Journal of Negro Education, 54,* 269–88.

Slaughter, D. T., & Schneider, B. L. (1986). *Newcomers: Blacks in private schools.* Final Report to the National Institute of Education (Grant No. NIE-G-82-0040, Project No. 2-0450). Evanston, IL: Northwestern University, School of Education.

Watson, B. C. (1974). *In spite of the system: The individual and educational reform.* Cambridge, MA: Ballinger.

West, C. A. (1985, Summer). Effects of school climate and school social structure on student academic achievement in selected urban elementary schools. *Journal of Negro Education, 54,* 451–61.

7

Counseling and Guidance of Black and Other Minority Children in Public Schools

Charles E. Flowers

Twenty-five years ago thoughtful educators, attempting to explain the disparity between black and white educational outcomes, determined that culturally or educationally disadvantaged children needed separate treatment, compensatory programs, and the like to make their education more equal to that of other children. Then, as now, there were those large voices in the wilderness who decried the tests, labels, separate sections, and special treatment as ill-conceived, misguided, and destructive. Then, as now, major blame and responsibility for the educational disfranchisement was laid at the feet of the disfranchised. Perhaps as we move into the 1990s, we can begin to realize more clearly the vision and direction of such eminent social scientists as Clark (1965), Dentler (1968), Hilliard (1983), Lee (1982), and Edmonds (1981), to name but a few.

> After the Egyptian and Indian, the Greek and the Roman, the Teuton and the Mongolian, the Negro is a sort of seventh son, born with a veil, and gifted with second-sight in this American world which yields him no true self-consciousness, but only lets him see himself through the revelation of the other world. It is a peculiar sensation, this *double-consciousness,* this sense of always looking at one's self through the eyes of others, of measuring one's soul by the tape of a world that looks on in an amused contempt and pity [emphasis added] (Du Bois, 1903, p. 6).

These prophetic reflections of Du Bois mirror the contemporary educational scene of black youth in the 1980s. William Raspberry (1986), describing the contemporary situation, raised the question, "What has gone wrong?" and then answered, "Virtually everything beginning, in my view, with the catastrophic level of joblessness, out-of-wedlock pregnancies, drug abuse, academic indifference (or outright hostility)." That large numbers of black and minority families live in poverty is rather consentaneous. Parents and children living in poverty must be provided with the basic essentials of food, housing, health care, and parental support for school. A quality educational experience depends upon an adequate quality of life.

The consequences of "amused contempt and pity" are visions of dismal futures for too many inner-city youngsters. They see little point in deferring gratifications, making serious academic exertions, and setting long-term goals. Inspiring black youth to prepare for decent jobs is most difficult when they see so few of their cohorts working or attending college, when so many of their friends drop out due to poor counseling, lack of money, or other reasons common to this segment (Kirsh & Jungeblut, 1986).

In an effort to identify significant issues in the counseling of black and minority students in public schools, this researcher contacted 11 professionals including counselors, counselor educators, National Urban League (NUL) researchers, and school administrators. Remarkable similarities in significant issues and their possible approaches and resolutions have been subsumed under the following rubrics.

ACCESS TO ACADEMIC ACHIEVEMENT

What Do We Know?

Virtually every respondent cited what Courtland Lee at the University of North Carolina at Chapel Hill called the "crisis of low expectations for academic achievement" (personal communications, April 1987). Riessman (1962) wrote, "'Perhaps it is not the disadvantaged who have capitulated to their environment, but the teachers who have capitulated to theirs" (p. 23). Kenneth Clark (1963b) reasoned that teachers "point to the realities of poor environment, cultural deprivation, and the lack of educational stimulation in the home as determinants of low academic achievement of the children" (p. 149). However, here in the 1990s, we are still mired as deeply as ever in ability grouping, I.Q. testing that supports the counselors' pigeonholing of students, and the concomitant low teacher expectations for underachieving black and minority students. Cicourel and Kitsuse (1963), calling counselors "educational decision-makers," railed that "the day-to-day activities of school personnel effectively control the access of students to the limited curricula available, particularly their access to the curriculum most instrumental for upward mobility, i.e., the college preparatory curriculum" (p. 135).

Rosenthal and Jacobsen (1968), Flowers (1966), Stikes (1972), Cross (1974), Gunnings and Simpkins (1972), Hilliard (1983), and others have demonstrated that the I.Q. testing program as used in education is merely a ranking and classification system. It is not diagnostic or remedial. Worse, educators too often have been able "to rationalize inaction by blaming educational failure on an assumed intellectual inferiority of disproportionate numbers of black children" (Hilliard, 1983).

Clark (1963a) wrote that low achievement as well as low performance on I.Q. tests reflected the quality of teaching, and the National Alliance of Black School Educators (NABSE) wrote in *Saving the African-American Child* (1984): "Low income, poor nutrition, noncommon language variation, etc., are not the causes of low performance of students. These things may determine what treatment students get from educators. The treatment that they get determines success or failure" (p. 27).

What Should Be Done?

Respondents decried the use of I.Q. testing and, even more vehemently, its use in classifying students. They would ban the use of I.Q. tests, as reported by NABSE (1984), and "study the validity of standardized testing instruments specifically for African American populations." Tyler (1984) cited the need for counselors and other school personnel to improve their knowledge and understanding of tests in order to end their misuse. Hilliard (1983) stated that there were too many erroneous assumptions connected with the concept and use of the I.Q. tests to correct and that "it is possible for drastic improvements in pedagogy without reference to I.Q. testing." The research of Fuller (1977), Fuerstein (1980), and Freire (1973) apparently support this thesis.

The recent increase in American College Test (ACT) scores by black and minority students was attributed to substantially increased participation in core academic courses. Completing more course work in relevant subject areas has likely resulted in higher ACT test scores (Davidson, 1986). NABSE and other respondents recommended that criterion-referenced tests replace all norm-referenced tests where tests are required.

While much of the above discussion on tests, groups, and teacher expectations for academic achievement synthesized respondents' foci on access to quality education, many suggested elements of the Effective

Schools Program as effective for improving the educational environment of schools where black and minority students predominate. Drawing heavily from Edmonds (1981, p. 13), the educability of students derives far more from the nature of their school than that of their family. The Network for Effective Schools recommended: schools must accept and practice that all children can learn; educators should drop socioeconomic biases and strive to assure that no children pass up educational opportunity; and schools should communicate high expectations, recognize achievement, and provide motivation (Edmonds, p. 15) .

PROFESSIONAL DEVELOPMENT OF COUNSELORS

What Do We Know?

According to respondents, the most frequent barrier to effective education is the counselors' lack of competence in cross-cultural counseling of black and minority children. Frank Burnett (Burnett & Suber, 1987), formerly assistant executive director of the American Association for Counseling and Development, wrote, "There are some real flaws in how counselors are trained" (p. 10). He questioned whether a counselor trained to be nondirected can become a good student advocate: "There are going to be times in helping kids when you not only have to be a good listener, but to speak up on their behalf. This means doing a little more than pounding the table occasionally, it means taking risks as educators" (p. 17).

Respondents said too few counselors are assigned to schools, resulting in very limited access to a counselor for black and minority children. All too often the visit to the counselor's office is directed by the problems approach: a focus on students' weaknesses rather than their strengths. William Warfield (personal communication, April 1987), professor of education at Western Michigan and consultant to Michigan schools, cited the lack of role models for blacks and minority youth; counselors tend to be white and female with little or no multicultural counseling or effective knowledge of the "cultural institution" referred to by Vontress (1987).

Respondents were unanimous in their concern for the plight of black males. Concerns ranged from counselors who were easily intimidated by them to the patronizing practice of approving work release from school for alternative or work/study programs. Black or minority counselors to provide role models were especially scarce.

What Should Be Done?

The need for more black and minority counselors, especially male counselors who understand the cultural realities of minorities, was reported as urgent. The legacy of racial discrimination in American society and the educational experiences of black and minority children are complexly intertwined. Increased commitment in counselor training programs must be instituted to sensitize counselors to the dynamics of the minority experience (Cross, 1974; Stikes, 1972; Toldson & Pasteur, 1976). The need for multicultural counseling, which is beginning to be recognized, will be intensified by shifts in population mix, particularly in metropolitan areas, if present trends continue. According to Lee (1987), the proportion of Hispanics in the nation's schools rose from 5.1 percent to 9.1 percent between 1970 and 1984. Asian enrollment increased from .5 percent to 2.5 percent, and black enrollment increased from 1.5 percent to 16 percent, while white enrollment declined from 78 percent to 71 percent. In the suburbs of Virginia and Maryland, the minority population boomed while the percentage of white students dropped from 78 percent to 64 percent.

"Cultural intuition" (Vontress, 1987) and "multicultural counseling" (Lee, 1987) provide direction for improved counselor training programs. As defined by Lee (1987), "multicultural counseling is the dynamic interface between counselor and client that takes both personal and cultural experiences of the counselor and client into consideration in the helping process" (p. 13). It recognizes and validates cultural pluralism and serves to invalidate the concept that blacks need the same counseling as whites. Well-trained multicultural counselors understand and accept that West Indian students have strong taboos against seeking counseling, that biculturalism induces conflict within the family, and that cultural background affects career choices (Vontress, 1987).

CAREER DEVELOPMENT — NEW CHALLENGES FOR THE 1990s

What Do We Know?

There is real concern that our minority children are not being prepared for technological jobs. Several respondents are alarmed, citing the dearth of black, native American, and Hispanic students in math and science courses. Black students and their parents too often believe that, for some unknown reason, they lack ability in math and science, which may in part explain the statistics cited by Eva Chunn (1987), senior researcher for NUL. While blacks and Hispanics represented 18.5 percent of the population, they received only 7.3 percent of the bachelor's degrees in biological science and only 5.8 percent in physical science. The percentages were even lower at the master's and doctorate levels (personal communication, June 1987).

Because day-to-day survival needs in many minority families may lessen opportunities to develop long-range plans and decision-making skills, counselors must assist teachers in encouraging students to dream and to plan. Frasier (1979), incidently, reported in a Department of Labor study that minority students often develop realistic long-range goals early in life. We should replicate this study and test this hypothesis further.

The world of work for far too many black and other minority youths and adults, especially Hispanics and native Americans, must be characterized as debilitating and destructive to the aims of education. Counselors and teachers must be alert as minority students, because of social and economic considerations, opt out of more advanced math and science courses upon entering high school, precluding opportunities in technical fields. Counselors must address personal and social concerns as they plan academic and career activities to help middle school minority students become aware of and interested in technical fields and develop the competence and self-confidence required in scientific study. According to Woods (1987), the middle-school years are critical for minority students in math, science, and computer science (Davidson, 1986).

What Should Be Done?

Any emphasis on career development must be enveloped in a program of total educational development. Table 7.1, which describes the counselor as a student development facilitator, is an example of the holistic approach to this issue. Lee (1982) further proposed that counselors conduct individual and group consultations with teachers and administrators to identify alienating or racist factors in educational attitudes, behaviors, and policies. He likewise suggested that such workshops could also instruct and encourage the inclusion of the African-American experience into curriculum and the professional development of staff. He, along with several other counselor educators, proposed additional counselors who would be assigned a 3:00 P.M. to 9:00 P.M. counseling day, during which they could conduct home visits and workshops with parents and com-munity leaders. These counselors could also coordinate alternative, work-related, and internship programs with the assistance of paraprofessionals and in association with community centers and agencies, such as Opportunities Industrialization Centers and NUL, to name a few (Lee, 1982).

COMMUNITY-BASED INVOLVEMENT OF COUNSELORS AND EDUCATORS

What Do We Know?

The NABSE report *Task Force on Black Academic and Cultural Excellence* states, "Educators must reach out and serve the needs and interests of African American parents and their children in a way that moves them into the larger society without destroying their ethnic identity or neighborhoods" (1984). Likewise, in conversations with staff in several offices of the NUL, as well as with counselors, issues related to low self-esteem and low motivation due largely to negative ethnic identity were unanimously cited as reasons for low academic achievement and concomitant behavioral problems among black, native American, and Hispanic adolescents. Problems from that "double consciousness" and "always looking at one's self through the eyes of others" to which Du Bois (1903) referred are apparently highlighted and for many predominate during middle and high school years. Their awareness of their unique characteristics, their perceptions of themselves as valued for who they really are, and their comfort with their similarities and differences among their peers are the issues of adolescents. In addition, minority youth must face racial and cultural factors. Perhaps the challenge has never been greater, considering the technological and economic changes in American society over the last 25 years. Added to the challenge are the monumental social problems, such as teenage pregnancy (well over half of all black babies born this year will be born to single women), unemployment of young black males, drug use, crime, and the high outflow of the black middle class from traditional black communities.

The gargantuan efforts to attenuate the constant negative perceptions of self that accumulates in minority children until they consider academic and personal success beyond their reach will require the involvement of the entire community. School people and especially counselors must be aware of the effects negative self-perception has on a student's academic achievement. James Coleman (Jenkins, 1987) wrote, "for children from disadvantaged groups achievement appears closely related to whether they believe the environment will respond to reasonable efforts, or whether they believe it is instead merely random or immovable" (p. 13).

TABLE 7.1
The Counselor and the Black Student — Student Development Facilitator

Counselor or Function	*Implementation*
Personal-Social Growth	
Facilitating the development of positive black self-identity	Conduct self-awareness groups emphasizing self-appreciation through cultural heritage: Use culturally specific curriculum materials and aesthetic dimensions to cultivate self-pride from a black perspective in group interactions.
Facilitating the development of positive interpersonal relations and responsible behavior	Explore the nature and importance of positive interpersonal relationships in growth groups: Incorporate traditional African-American notions of community into group interactions to develop greater interpersonal respect, particularly between young black men and women. Conduct social behavior guidance groups: Facilitate collective explorations of pragmatic strategies for enhancing behavioral repertoires for optimal school success while maintaining culturally learned response styles.
Academic Achievement	
Facilitating the development of positive attitudes toward academic achievement	Conduct motivation groups: Develop group guidance activities focusing on inherent black potential that incorporate historical and contemporary references to the educational experiences of influential African-Americans.
Facilitating the development of academic skills and competencies	Conduct guidance workshops in the following areas: (a) academic planning, (b) study skills and time management, (c) testing skills, and (d) remediation.

Career Development	
Facilitating the vocational choice and career development process	Develop relevant guidance and training experience related to the world of work: (a) conduct information forums on nonstereotyped jobs and careers; (b) sponsor career days and invite black career role models to explain their perceptions and experiences in the world of work; (c) develop internship and cooperative experience with black businesses and professionals; (d) conduct workshops on the mechanics of the world of work, that is, how to look for, apply, and interview for a job; (e) conduct workshops on the rules of work, that is, proper attire, behavior, and attitude in the work setting; and (f) conduct workshops on survival issues, that is, money and its management, tax concerns, social security, etc.

Source: Lee, C. (1982, April). School counselor and the black child. *Journal of Non-White Concerns in Personnel and Guidance, 10* (3), 96.

What Should Be Done?

Many have suggested that counselors and other school personnel lead an effort to teach and advise in storefronts, churches, or community centers during and after school hours. L. Michael Styles, counselor at Boston English High School, in such an effort, formed a comprehensive school age parenting program. After he learned, among other things, that married teen fathers were as likely as teen mothers to drop out and that boys become fathers for many of the same reasons as girls become mothers, he developed a counseling program emphasizing group cohesion and cooperation and dynamics of socialization among minority youth.

Other community-based programs, such as the National Urban Coalition's "family math" workshops, in cooperation with local schools, have provided the special impetus some black parents and students need. In the Washington, D.C., area, minority parents — including some teenage parents — take their children to science fairs and Saturday morning meetings on the importance of scientific and technological literacy, supported and funded by Women in Science, a band of committed science professionals (Holman, 1986). Counselors and other community leaders must assume primary responsibility for coordinating and promoting such efforts.

Lulu Beatty, research associate at the Washington, D.C., bureau of the NUL, called for a black alumni council to be created for the purpose of attracting the interest of black college graduates, particularly those from black colleges. She suggested that the council, besides serving as role models for inner-city students, be much more involved with the parents of black students in an effort to foster black identity activities such as plays, speeches, contests, and readings of black history and other literature. These activities were deemed especially relevant for minority families with children in desegregated/integrated schools, where these children suffer most from the double-consciousness phenomenon attendant in "acting white" or being "one-in-a-class" or an "integrated student."

From conversations with professional educators and research social scientists, as well as from a review of the literature relative to the achievement and nonachievement of black and minority children, the current assessment clearly dictates a more active involvement of the total community in support of public school education. It is imperative that counselors accept more responsibility to develop more creative approaches both within schools and within the other institutions in the community in order to meet the educational commitments required of a culturally diverse society.

REFERENCES

Burnett, F., & Suber, J. E. (1987). College admissions counseling: Burnett and Suber discuss challenges. *Black Issues in Higher Education, 4,* 8–10.

Chunn, E. (1987). Personal communication.

Cicourel, A., & Kitsuse, J. I. (1963). *The educational decision-makers.* New York: Bobbs Merrill.

Clark, K. B. (1963a). Clash of cultures in the classrooms. *Integrated Education, 1,* 7–14.

Clark, K. B. (1963b). Educational stimulation of racially disadvantaged areas. In A. H. Passur (Ed.), *Education in depressed areas* (pp. 141–62). New York: Bureau of Publications, Teachers College, Columbia University.

Clark, K. B. (1965). *Dark ghetto.* New York: Harper & Row.

Cross, A. (1974). The black experience: Its importance in treatment of black clients. *Child Welfare, 53,* 158–66.

Davidson, C. (1986). Relationship between scores and academic coursework is clear, minority students' scores show increases. *Black Issues in Higher Education, 3,* 1–10.

Dentler, R. A. (1968). *American community problems.* New York: McGraw-Hill.

Du Bois, W. E. B. (1903). *The soul of black folk.* New York: Signet. (Reprinted in 1969)

Edmonds, R. (1981, October). The characteristics of effective schools: Research and implementation. Paper presented to the National Conference on Education Issues, New York.

Flowers, C. E. (1966). *Effects of an arbitrary accelerated group placement on the tested academic achievement of educationally disadvantaged students.* Unpublished doctoral dissertation, Teachers College, Columbia University, New York.

Frasier, M. (1979). Counseling the culturally diverse gifted. In N. Colangelo & R. Zaffan (Eds.), *New voices in counseling the gifted* (pp. 304–11). Dubuque, IA: Kendall-Hunt.

Friere, P. (1973). *Education for critical consciousness.* New York: Seabury.

Fuerstein, R. (1980). *Instrumental enrichment.* Baltimore: University Park Press.

Fuller, R. (1977). *In search of I.Q. correlation.* Stonybrook, NY: Ball-Stick-Burch.

Gunnings, T. S., & Simpkins, G. A. (1972). A systemic approach to Counseling disadvantaged youth. *Journal of Non-White Concerns in Personnel and Guidance,* 4–8.

Hilliard, A. G., III. (1983). I.Q. and the courts: *Larry P. vs. Wilson Riles* and *P.A.S.E. vs. Harmon. Journal of Black Psychology, 10* (1), 1–18.

Holman, M. C. (1986). More math for minority kids. *Black Issues in Higher Education, 3,* 32.

Jenkins, D. E., Counselor. (1987). Responsibility for unparalleled student achievement. *Black Issues in Higher Education, 4,* 12.

Kirsh, I., & Jungeblut, A. (1986). *Literacy: Profiles of America's young adults.* 16-PL-02. Washington, DC: National Assessment of Educational Progress.

Lee, C. C. (1982). School counselor and the black child: Critical roles and functions. *Journal of Non-White Concerns in Personnel and Guidance*, 94–100.

Lee C. C. (1987). Multi-cultural counseling: New directions for school counselors. *Black Issues in Higher Education, 4*, 13, 14.

Lee, C. (1987). Personal communication.

National Alliance of Black School Educators, Inc., Task Force on Black Academic and Cultural Excellence. (1984). *Saving the African American child.* Washington, DC: Author.

Raspberry, W. (1986). How can we save black men? *Black Issues in Higher Education, 3*, 32.

Riessman, F. (1962). *The culturally deprived child.* New York: Harper and Row.

Rosenthal, R., & Jacobsen, L. (1968). *Pygmalion in the classroom.* New York: Holt, Rinehart & Winston.

Stikes, C. S. (1972). Culturally specific counseling: The black client. *Journal of Non-White Concerns in Personnel and Guidance, 4*, 15, 23, 105–17.

Toldson, I. L. T., & Pasteur, A. B. (1976). Beyond rhetoric: Technique for using the black aesthetic in group counseling and guidance. *Journal of Non-White Concerns in Personnel and Guidance*, 142–52.

Tyler, L. E. (1984). Testing the test: What tests don't measure. *Journal of Counseling and Development, 63*, 48–50.

Vontress, C. E. (1976). Racial and ethnic barriers in counseling. In W. Petersen, J. Lonne, & J. Draguns (Eds.), *Counseling across cultures* (pp. 87–107). Honolulu, HI: University Press.

Vontress, C. E. (1987). Cultural intuition: Implications for counseling the culturally different. *Black Issues in Higher Education, 4*, 13, 14.

Warfield, W. (1987). Personal communication.

IV

POSTSECONDARY EDUCATION

During the 1980s the proportion of blacks graduating from high school increased, but the proportion of blacks enrolled in college decreased. Black females outnumbered black males in college, but black males outnumbered black females in doctoral degree graduate programs. The proportion of black students needing financial aid to go to college has increased during the same period that federal assistance for higher education decreased, explaining the smaller proportion of college-going blacks during the 1980s, the decade harvesting the largest proportion of black high school graduates in recent decades. Antoine M. Garibaldi presents these data and their effects in the first chapter in this section.

Among the decreasing proportion of black high school graduates who manage to get federally funded grants, the proprietary career school rather than college is increasingly becoming the institution of choice. In his chapter, Robert Rothman informs us that "blacks constitute a disproportionate number of the approximately 1.5 million students in the nearly 6,000 for-profit career schools nationwide." Rothman states that reliable sources have estimated the number of blacks in such schools at one-fifth to one-fourth of all blacks enrolled in postsecondary institutions. These schools offer job-specific training in six months, which appears to give "a quick return on a student's investment." While some observers see this as a positive outcome, others believe that this education will not lead to upward mobility but, instead, will trap black, inner-city young people perpetually in low-paying jobs and a lower socioeconomic status. Indeed, observers told Rothman that some of these schools "at best, [offer] short-term opportunities, and at worse, no help at all." Rothman indicates this phenomenon deserves more attention.

James E. Blackwell reports on another educational contradiction. He writes that "the admission of black students to medical colleges is declining even though their test scores and other indices of eligibility are improving." This decline is also reflected in the number of blacks attending law school. While blacks make up 11 percent to 12 percent of the nation's population, they represent less than 4 percent of the nation's lawyers. Furthermore, blacks receive less than 4 percent of the doctorates awarded to U.S. citizens. In his chapter, Blackwell blames postsecondary schools for this development. He states that "our nation's graduate and professional schools are not recruiting, admitting, retaining, and graduating sufficient numbers of blacks." According to Blackwell, while there is a large "pool of talent available among black Americans," interest in developing it through affirmative action and other efforts by graduate and professional schools seems to have diminished.

From his examination of Title VI of the 1964 Civil Rights Act, John B. Williams confirms Blackwell's contention that our nation has little interest in cultivating the pool of talent among its minorities through higher education. Had there been the political will to do this, Williams says, Title VI provided a legal way. The law requires desegregation of public white colleges and universities and enhancement of public black institutions so that they too would attract students of all racial populations. Moreover, the law requires that states develop plans to achieve meaningful and timely results. According to Williams, little is known for certain about the outcomes of Title VI. At best, he states, no one can claim that there has been more than limited results because the federal government has done an inadequate job collecting data on Title VI's implementation.

8

Blacks in College

Antoine M. Garibaldi

Since 1940, significant gains in school attendance have been recorded for the black population. The sixteenth census of the United States in 1940 reported that the median number of school years completed by black Americans was 5.7, compared to 8.8 years for whites. Because of the pervasive segregation laws at that time, only 1.2 percent of blacks had completed four or more years of college, compared to 5.4 percent of native whites. While blacks have made significant gains in the pursuit of higher education since that time, current trends indicate that the numbers and proportional representation of blacks in college are declining rapidly, despite the fact that almost 80 percent of blacks between the ages of 18 and 24 have obtained a high school education.

Prior to 1945, almost 90 percent of all blacks in college attended historically black colleges and universities (HBCUs), institutions located primarily in the South and founded after the Civil War for the express purpose of educating blacks. The numbers of blacks in college, however, increased rapidly after 1945 with the promulgation of the GI bills of World War II and the Korean War. Even more blacks and nonwhites attended college in the mid-1960s with the promulgation of civil rights legislation that dismantled segregatory practices in public institutions through the imposition of open admissions policies. Further increases were recorded in the late 1960s and early 1970s as veterans of the Vietnam War went to college with their GI bill benefits and as the cohort of black 18- to 24-year-olds increased by a half million between 1970 and 1975 (Hill, 1983). Higher education enrollment for blacks thus peaked in

1976, when 604,000 black, full-time students were pursuing a college degree (Hill, 1983).

HISTORICALLY BLACK COLLEGES

HBCUs felt the enrollment increases of the 1960s and 1970s as intensely as other colleges. In 1966, for example, total enrollment at the nation's 105 HBCUs was 129,444; in 1977, enrollment had increased 60 percent to 212,574 (Blake, Lambert, & Martin, 1978). The academic years 1975 and 1976 saw the largest gains in first-time, first-year enrollment at the HBCUs, which admitted an average of 52,000 students each year, compared to average annual enrollments between 1966 and 1974 of 41,553 first-time students. Despite these increases, however, the proportional share of black students enrolled at HBCUs has actually declined to less than 20 percent of all black students enrolled in college (Garibaldi, 1984). This decline is attributed not only to greater competition for black students by predominantly white institutions, but also to the larger number (between 45% and 50%) of black students who attend two-year and junior colleges.

COLLEGE ENROLLMENT

Given current demographic and population trends, the numbers and proportion of black students enrolled in college today should be much higher than what they are. Between 1977 and 1984, the number of black students who graduated from high school increased by 26 percent. As noted earlier, this situation was due primarily to the expanding age cohort of 18- to 24-year-old blacks. Unfortunately, the proportion of blacks going to college decreased by 11 percent between 1975 and 1982 (American Council on Education, 1987). In 1976, blacks represented 9.6 percent of the total enrollment in U.S. colleges, compared to 8.8 percent in 1984. This decline of almost one full percentage point for the 1.1 million black students in college represents a 20 percent decrease in the number of black students in college. Thus, rather than capitalizing on the increasing size of the age cohort and the higher numbers graduating from high school, college participation rates of today's generation of black youth have regressed significantly in absolute numbers and proportional representation on college campuses.

There are many documented reasons for the declining number of black students in college. These include higher dropout rates in high school because of inadequate elementary and secondary academic preparation; an insufficient amount of federal and state grants, scholarships, and loans; higher attrition rates in the first years of college; the inflationary cost of a college education; inadequate or no college counseling in high school; and the inability of many black students to view a college education as a worthwhile investment.

GRADUATION RATES

In any analysis of black graduation rates since the mid-1970s, two points are obvious. First, the percentage of black undergraduate degrees never equals the group's proportional share of enrollment; second, black women receive between one-third and one-half more bachelor's degrees than black men. Though blacks represented 9.4 percent of all students in higher education in 1976, they received only 6.4 percent of all bachelor's degrees (59,100); in 1987, they represented slightly more than 9 percent of college enrollment but received 5.7 percent (56,554) of the bachelor's degrees awarded that year (Hill, 1983; Wilson & Carter, 1989). Whites, on the other hand, represented slightly more than 80 percent of the total undergraduate enrollment in both years and received more than 85 percent of the bachelor's degrees during those years.

Closer inspection of the National Center for Educational Statistics (NCES) data on black graduation rates (Hill, 1983; Wilson & Carter, 1989) shows that in 1976 black females received 7,900 more bachelor's degrees than black males (33,500 versus 25,600), and in 1987 they received 11,588 more (34,056 versus 22,498). This gender comparison of graduation data not only indicates a lower matriculation rate for black males but is also a result of a much larger pool of black females in college. Between 1965 and 1985, for example, the number of black women in college rose from 148,000 to 600,000. Moreover, between 1980 and 1986, black females outnumbered black males in college by an average of 194,000 for each of those six years. Black females also receive 60 percent more of the master's degrees awarded to blacks (11,000 versus 6,200 in 1981 and 8,700 versus 5,150 in 1987), and they have closed the gap on doctoral degrees (800 males and 400 females in 1976 and 311 males and 494 females in 1988). Black males, however, continue to receive more first-professional degrees than black females — 1,800 versus 1,200 in 1981 and 1,836 versus 1,585 in 1987 (Hill, 1983; Wilson & Carter, 1989).

As a final note, it is important to recognize that the HBCUs continue to award a large share of bachelor's and master's degrees. In 1976, 22,000 of the 59,100 bachelor's degrees and 4,500 of the 17,200 master's degrees received by blacks were awarded by HBCUs (Hill,

1983). That trend continued in the 1980s, and data show that HBCUs awarded an average of 37 percent of the bachelor's degrees and approximately 30 percent of master's degrees received by blacks (Wilson & Carter, 1989). Thus, HBCUs still play a major role in the college and graduate education of blacks in this country although they represent less than 5 percent of the more than 3,300 colleges and universities in America.

FIELDS OF STUDY

Between 1976 and 1981, blacks increased their proportional representation among bachelor's degree recipients in 11 of 24 disciplines. The increases occurred, in ranking order, in public affairs and services, psychology, communications, interdisciplinary studies, health professions, biological science, fine and applied arts, physical science, engineering, architecture and environmental design, and agriculture and natural resources. Declines in the number and percentage of degrees awarded to blacks occurred in the fields of education, social science, library science, computer and information sciences, and foreign studies (Hill, 1983).

Business and management was the most popular discipline among all black bachelor's degree recipients in 1981. Education and social science were next. (These were also the three most popular fields of nonwhites.) In 1981, 13,325 black students received degrees in business, 9,471 in education, and 8,091 in social science. Predominantly black colleges awarded 38.9 percent of the business degrees, 48.3 percent of the education degrees, and 29.9 percent of the social science degrees. The next highest numbers of degrees awarded to blacks were in the fields of public affairs (4,839), health sciences (3,594), and psychology (3,332). Degrees in the fields of biological science, engineering, and computer science also increased between 1976 and 1981. These disciplines produced 3,884 black undergraduates in 1981, compared to 2,022 degrees granted in 1976 (Trent, 1984). However, business and social science continue to be the two most popular majors of black and white students (Wilson & Carter, 1989).

FINANCIAL AID

Because of the poor economic condition of most black families, financial aid is essential to black students' college attendance. In 1981, for example, almost half (48%) of the black high school seniors planning to enter college came from families with incomes of less than $12,000; only 10 percent of white seniors came from such families (College Board, 1982). Cuts in federal financial aid grants during the 1980s have adversely affected all students who attend college, but the impact has been even greater on black students. As a recent study has shown, federal grants in 1979–80 accounted for 53 percent of all financial aid to students at the 43 private black colleges of the United Negro College Fund (UNCF); in 1984–85, federal grants to students at these same institutions accounted for only 37 percent of their financial aid (UNCF-NIICU, 1987). The median family income of students at UNCF schools is $11,000. Thus, without financial assistance, the majority of these students would not be able to finance their education.

Changes in eligibility requirements have also made it more difficult for students to obtain assistance. Between 1980–81 and 1981–82, the percentage of all students receiving grants declined from 43 percent to 36 percent, and similar declines have been observed for other financial assistance programs (College Board, 1985). These changing eligibility requirements and the greater demand placed on families to finance the education of black students will continue to exacerbate the college enrollment shortage.

FUTURE SUCCESS OF BLACKS IN COLLEGE

The success of blacks in college in the twenty-first century will depend upon this society's ability to solve several problems. These remedies will require more effective academic training in elementary and secondary schools, changes in public policy (increasing financial aid), more institutional support at colleges and universities (reducing attrition rates), and support from families and the black community (encouraging more youth to obtain a college education). By the year 2020, nonwhites will represent 35 percent of this country's total population. Hispanics will be the largest nonwhite group, representing nearly 15 percent of the total population, and blacks will constitute approximately 14 percent. Thus, it is imperative that this young population have every opportunity to obtain more than a secondary education. The following are some specific recommendations for achieving this goal:

Black students must obtain better academic preparation at the elementary and secondary levels. Besides learning basic skills, they must learn to think critically and analytically in order to meet the demands of a changing technological society.

High school dropout rates for black students must be curbed immediately, and there must be a concomitant increase in the absolute number and proportional representation of black high school graduates. In 1985, 79.6 percent of blacks had completed high school, compared to 84.3 percent of whites (American Council on Education, 1987). However, census data show that 25.9 percent of blacks between the ages of 14 and 34 had dropped out of high school in 1981. Schools and families must play dominant roles in reversing this trend.

The proportion of black high school graduates attending college must be increased. Between 1975 and 1980, the percentage of black high school graduates going to college declined from 32 percent to 27.8 percent (American Council on Education, 1987). This sharp decline was actually more serious in absolute numbers because 29 percent more black students had graduated from high school during this same period. Counselors and teachers at the elementary and secondary levels must constantly monitor students' academic progress and encourage them to obtain a postsecondary degree.

All colleges and universities must provide the necessary support services to assure higher persistence rates for black students. Previous studies show that almost 35 percent of black students in four-year colleges and 55 percent in two-year colleges leave before completing their education (NCES, 1979). While there are many possible explanations for this situation, the data indicate that students who do not have financial assistance are more often the ones who leave. Colleges and universities have a responsibility not only to see that students obtain the necessary financial assistance but also to provide academic and social counseling to help them matriculate and receive their degrees. This is especially important for two-year colleges, which enroll more than 40 percent of all black students but graduate less than half of that number (NCES, 1979).

HBCUs, which enroll less than one-fifth of all black college students but graduate more than 40 percent of all black undergraduates, must receive the necessary state and federal assistance for institutional development and student support services. In the past, HBCUs received the lion's share of federal support under Title III of the Higher Education Act, which was aimed at strengthening "developing" institutions. However, these institutions receive barely one-third of annual appropriations, due largely to changes in eligibility requirements and the definition of "developing" institutions (Williams, 1984; Garibaldi, 1984). Similarly, since these institutions have always depended on tuition for the vast majority of their operating expenses, changes in state and federal financial aid policies have made it difficult for them to provide an education to all students who would like to attend, the vast majority of whom come from low-income families. Public policies must be developed to remedy these inequities, given the role these institutions have played in the past and continue to play today.

Finally, as noted, financial aid policies must be thoroughly revamped so that the most deserving students can obtain more financial assistance to support their college educations.

REFERENCES

American Council on Education. (1987, May). *A status report on minorities in higher education: Background paper I.* Washington, DC: Author.

Blake, E., Lambert, L., & Martin, J. (1978). *Degrees granted and enrollment trends in historically black colleges: An eight year study.* Washington, DC: Institute for Services to Education.

College Board. (1982). *Profiles: College bound seniors, 1981.* New York: College Entrance Examination Board.

College Board. (1985). *Equality and excellence: The educational status of black Americans.* New York: College Entrance Examination Board.

Garibaldi, A. M. (Ed.). (1984). *Black colleges and universities: Challenges for the future.* New York: Praeger.

Hill, S. T. (1983, November). *Participation of black students in higher education: A statistical profile from 1970–71 to 1980–81.* Washington, DC: U.S. Department of Education, National Center for Education Statistics.

National Center for Education Statistics (NCES). (1979). *Students and schools.* Washington, DC: U.S. Department of Education.

Trent, W. T. (1984, May). Equity considerations in higher education: Race and sex differences in degree attainment and major field from 1976 through 1981. *American Journal of Education, 92* (3), 280–305.

UNCF–NIICU. (1987, April). *Access to college: The impact of federal financial aid policies at private historically black colleges.* New York: United Negro College Fund and Washington, DC: National Institute of Independent Colleges and Universities.

Williams, J. B. (1984). Public policy and black college development: An agenda for research. In A. M. Garibaldi (Ed.), *Black colleges and universities: Challenges for the future.* New York: Praeger.

Wilson, R., & Carter, D. J. (1989, December). *Eighth annual status report: Minorities in higher education.* Washington, DC: American Council on Education.

9

The Road Taken: Minorities and Proprietary Schools

Robert Rothman

At a time when lagging rates for blacks headed to college are attracting the attention of worried educators, another trend has gone largely unnoticed: the growth, over the last decade, in the number of minority students seeking postsecondary training in proprietary career schools. Although data are scarce and any relationship between the two trends remains undocumented, most observers agree that blacks constitute a disproportionate number of the approximately 1.5 million students in the nearly 6,000 for-profit career schools nationwide. According to some observers, such programs appeal to students who want to enter the job market soon after leaving high school rather than pursue the lengthy, and perhaps more intimidating, route of higher education.

The strongest indicator that minority students are fueling the rise in enrollment in these schools is the sharp increase in the number of proprietary school students receiving Pell grants, the chief form of federal aid for low-income students. Between 1980 and 1984, the number of Pell grant recipients in proprietary schools rose by 124 percent, to 578,000. By comparison, the number of grant recipients in public colleges rose by 1.6 percent during that period.

Furthermore, evidence from individual schools and states indicates that enrollment in proprietary schools is growing fastest in inner cities and in programs in which minority students predominate.

Unless otherwise noted, all references are to Rothman, R. (1987, June 10). Black students booster enrollment in proprietary schools. *Education Week.*

In Pennsylvania, one of the few states able to provide data on minority proprietary school enrollment, the proportion of black, first-year students in proprietary schools tripled between 1976 and 1984. In 1984, 22 percent of all black, first-year students enrolled in postsecondary schools were in proprietary schools, compared with 7 percent in 1976.

In New York, the proportion of black students enrolled in the state's 27 degree-granting proprietary schools rose from 17 percent in 1980 to 24 percent in 1984. During that period, overall enrollment in the schools rose from 21,688 to 30,273. Of the 400 nondegree-granting proprietary schools in the state, according to Michael King, supervisor of operations for the New York State Department of Education's Bureau of Proprietary-School Supervision, business schools in urban areas, which enroll a high proportion of black students, have been growing at a fast pace, while trade schools in rural areas, which tend to enroll a high proportion of white students, have been closing in recent years.

The Katherine Gibbs Schools, Inc., which offers business training in 11 East Coast locations, has been growing rapidly in inner cities, according to company president Eleanor Vreeland. Its recent advertisement in the *New York Times* drew attention to the issue of minority enrollment by showing a black alumnus of a Gibbs school, Quentin Headon, who is now a production manager of the Boice Dunham Group.

More comprehensive data on enrollment — particularly minority enrollment — in proprietary schools is lacking, but some may be forthcoming from the U.S. Department of Education, which is including proprietary schools in its annual survey of postsecondary institutions. "So many more students are enrolling in proprietary schools," explained Susan Hill, a statistician in the department's Center for Education Statistics. "Institutions of higher education are enrolling a smaller and smaller percentage of students going on to postsecondary institutions."

The new survey may also provide clues as to why students are attending these schools in greater numbers, despite the fact that tuitions, which average about $4,000 a year, are substantially higher than the $704 a year it would cost to attend a state-supported, two-year college. Most observers agree that the "opportunity cost" of attending a postsecondary institution is the prevailing factor and that proprietary schools appear to offer a quick return on a student's investment, since they typically offer job-specific training in six months, less than half the time it would take to earn a degree at a two-year college. Two-year colleges, moreover, include academic courses students may not find useful or enjoyable, and their structure makes it difficult to adapt to changes in the job market as quickly as the independent career schools can. Although there is no proof that these schools provide the kind of training sought by students who attend them, evidence indicates that they are successful in fulfilling the needs of the students. As Wilms notes, "job placement is the acid test" for the for-profit institutions (1987).

A sizable proportion of proprietary school enrollments are made up of low-income students and students who did not complete high school — students who are less likely than those in other institutions to succeed in school. Thus, Wilms states, "any analysis of the outcomes of training or education must take into account the characteristics of the students themselves." He concludes: "Insofar as it is possible to make all other things equal, students who choose proprietary schools are more likely to complete their programs than those who opt for comparable public programs. On the average, job placement and earnings rates appear similar" (1987).

Such evidence leads some observers to conclude that the trend toward higher minority participation in proprietary schools is a positive development. "I am encouraged by the idea that African-Americans may be pursuing alternatives allowing them to augment their lifestyles in ways that are solid and secure for them," said Patricia A. Ackerman, president-elect of the National Alliance of Black School Educators. On the other hand, some educators contend that if black enrollment in proprietary schools continues to rise while the black college-going rate stabilizes or falls, the gap in socioeconomic status between blacks and whites could widen. Black undergraduate enrollment declined from 10.1 percent in 1980 to 9.5 percent in 1984 (American Council on Education, 1986). Some observers also note that minority students could harm themselves if they continue to flock to proprietary schools. Such schools, these observers fear, offer students, at best, short-term opportunities and, at worst, no help at all. "I worry about kids who go to sleazy ones, incur debt burdens, and don't learn anything," says Gary Orfield, director of the University of Chicago's Metropolitan Opportunity Project.

REFERENCES

American Council on Education, Office of Minority Concerns. (1986). *Fifth annual report on minorities in higher education*. Washington, DC: Author.

Wilms, W. W. (1987, January-February). Proprietary schools: Strangers in their own land. *Change: The Magazine of Learning*, 10–22.

10

Graduate and Professional Education for Blacks

James E. Blackwell

In recent years, considerable attention has focused on the participation of black Americans in graduate and professional schools. A primary concern has been the declining enrollment of blacks in graduate schools and in certain professions (Blackwell, 1981, 1987; Thomas, 1981; Centra, 1980; Clewell & Ficklen, 1987; Fisher, 1981; Hall, Mays, & Allen, 1984; Hall & Allen, 1980; Lehner, 1980; Morris, 1979; and Carnegie Foundation for the Advancement of Teaching, 1987).

Perhaps as an outgrowth of consciousness raising during the civil rights movement of the 1960s and heightened sensitivity among the graduate and professional schools of predominantly white institutions, a special effort was made during the early 1970s to recruit and enroll significantly larger numbers of black Americans in graduate and professional schools. This effort was also facilitated by the implementation of an immense variety of affirmative action policies and procedures in higher education, the development of special recruitment and special admissions programs, the influence of the federal government through the allocation of capitation grants, and the authorization of various forms of minority fellowship programs (Blackwell, 1987).

Enrollment of blacks in graduate school and in such professions as medicine, dentistry, law, pharmacy, engineering, and social work reached unprecedented levels between 1970 and 1976. An examination of graduate school enrollment data by race shows that, in 1972, black students comprised 4.2 percent of total graduate school enrollment. By 1975, black representation had increased to 6.4 percent of total enrollment in graduate schools. In fall 1976, the 65,338 blacks in graduate schools comprised 6 percent of the total 1,079,307 students matriculated in our nation's graduate schools. However, between 1976 and 1984, black graduate student enrollment declined by 22.4 percent. In the four-year period between 1976 and 1980, the decline in absolute numbers was from 65,338 to 59,976 — a 15.4 percent drop. The precipitous decline continued between 1980 and 1984, when the number of blacks dropped to 50,717 in 1984; by that year, blacks comprised only 4.8 percent of total graduate school enrollment. Data from the National Center on Educational Statistics state that, between 1986 and 1988, black graduate school enrollment grew by 9 percent or up to 76,000 full- and part-time students (Blackwell, 1987; Carnegie Foundation for the Advancement of Teaching, 1987). Nevertheless, that blacks constitute only 5.1 percent of graduate enrollment disturbs American educators and policy makers committed to equity and access in American higher education.

The issue of access to professional schools and changing enrollment patterns of black students can be illustrated in such fields as medicine, dentistry, law, pharmacy, engineering, and social work. Blackwell's *Mainstreaming Outsiders: The Production of Black Professionals* (1987) is a definitive study of participation rates of black Americans in these fields and in graduate and professional education in general. Blackwell demonstrated that black student enrollment in medical colleges increased during the 1970s but decreased during the 1980s, when repeaters were removed from data on first-year enrollment. This finding was supported by a 1987 report issued by the Association of American Medical Colleges, which showed that the admission of black students to medical colleges was declining even though their test scores and other indices of eligibility were improving. The decline occurred although there was more space for first-year students in 1987 than in the early 1970s.

The absolute number of blacks in medical colleges went from 697, or 6.1 percent of first-year enrollment, in 1970, to 1,148 in 1984–85 — representing a decline to 5.9 percent of first-year enrollment. Since 1974–75, when blacks constituted 7.5 percent of first-year medical classes, the percentage of blacks has steadily declined to the 5.9 percent registered in 1984–85. Given the increase in the actual number of seats available for first-year students and the insignificant growth of medical school enrollment since 1981, declining black student enrollment must be attributed to a number of complex factors that help to explain patterns in other fields.

In dentistry the percentage of black students in first-year classes rose from 4 percent in 1970 to 5.9 percent in 1984–85. In absolute numbers, 185 blacks matriculated in first-year classes in 1970 and 299 were enrolled in 1984–85. While the proportion of black students in the predominantly black medical institutions at Howard University, Meharry College, and Morehouse College dropped during this period from approximately 80 percent to less than 20 percent, this is not the case with blacks in dentistry. Of the 299 black students in first-year dental school classes, Meharry and Howard account for 39.4 percent. As in medicine, black students in dental colleges tend to be concentrated in a relatively small number of institutions, and a significant proportion of these institutions enroll black students in essentially token numbers.

The schools of pharmacy located at historically black institutions (Xavier University of New Orleans, Florida A&M University, Howard University, and Texas Southern University) also assume a major responsibility for the pharmacy education of black students. Enrollment patterns show only a slight increase in the absolute number of black, first-year pharmacy students between 1979 and 1984. During this period, the number of black students rose from 858 to 1,033, or from 4.2 percent to 6.1 percent of all students. However, the total number of students in first-year pharmacy classes declined from 22,560 to 16,772 over the same period of time. In 1984, Xavier University enrolled 140; Howard University, 64; Florida A&M University, 103; and Texas Southern University, 111. These four institutions accounted for 418 or almost 40 percent of black student matriculation in first-year pharmacy school classes.

The number of black engineering school students increased by more than 400 percent between 1970 and 1983. Specifically, the number of first-year students climbed from 1,289 (1.8% of all students) in 1970 to 6,342 (5.8% of all students) in 1983–84. However, since 1981 the absolute number of black students has shown a steady downturn since it peaked at 7,015 in that year. This decline in the number of black engineering students has occurred at a time when overall engineering enrollment has increased and the need for engineers has grown in a high-technology economy.

Black student enrollment in law schools also grew steadily throughout the 1970s. The percentage of black, first-year law matriculants peaked in 1978 at 5.9 percent. Since that time, the representation of black students has declined to about 5.4 percent. In 1985, 2,214 blacks were first-year law students compared to 1,715 in 1971. As has been observed regarding other professional fields, increases in absolute numbers of black students have not been so dramatic as to assure significant changes in the proportion of blacks in law. Even with overall improvements in enrollments and increases in the number of blacks graduated with professional degrees, African-Americans still constitute less than 3 percent of persons in law.

In social work, parity in black student enrollment (measured by the proportion of blacks in the total population) was attained in 1970 when the 975 blacks enrolled in first-year, professional degree programs represented 15.7 percent of all students. Since that year, the percentage of black student enrollment has continued to fall so that by 1981 blacks constituted only 9 percent of first-year enrollment. Only 679 black students sought the M.S.W. degree that year.

The enrollment, retention, and graduation of black students are contingent upon six major factors (Astin, 1975, 1982; Allen, 1985, 1986, 1987; Blackwell, 1981, 1983, 1987; Chaffee, 1984; Deskins, 1983; Epps & Jackson, 1985; Linn, 1974; Messick, 1982; Morris, 1981; Nettles, Baratz, & King, 1986; Philips-Jones, 1982; Portes & Wilson, 1976; Pruitt & Issac, 1985; Sedaleck & Webster, 1978; Sexton, 1979; Tracey & Sedaleck, 1984, and Velez, 1985):

1. recruitment or outreach programs,
2. flexibility in admissions requirements,
3. availability of sound financial aid packages,
4. favorable institutional climate,
5. mentoring, and
6. good attitudes of black students.

Whenever any of these factors or conditions are not met, success in enrolling and producing black professionals will be considerably less than desired. One explanation for the declining enrollment of blacks in graduate schools, unlike the situation in such fields as medicine where the private foundations have played a major role in recruitment and financial assistance, is the lack of sound recruitment strategies. Another explanation lies in the absence of departmental commitment in many disciplines to make a special effort to recruit, enroll, and nurture black students, not only by using traditional "old boy networks," but also through the implementation of imaginative programs that require a special effort. For instance, although it is universally recognized in the literature that blacks as a group do not perform as well as whites on such objective determinants of admission as the GRE, MCAT, DAT, or OCAT, it is also true that institutions do employ both qualitative as well as quantitative admissions criteria whenever their purposes are to be pursued (Blackwell, 1987; Thomas, 1981; Morris, 1979). The predictive power of such measures beyond first-year performance or in determining the success of a student as a professional is highly disputed. Academic support programs and mentoring for students in need, as well as a critical mass of black students, are associated with success in the completion of a graduate or professional degree.

Also of special importance are such factors as the kind of financial aid programs available and the quality of the institutional climate. Learning takes place most effectively within the context of a positive learning environment, which should not be characterized by apathy, indifference, or hostility but should evince as much concern for the welfare of black students as faculty and administrators ought to have for all students. This concern is often reflected in decisions to award teaching and research assistantships. Data from the National Research Council showed that in 1984, blacks (who received 30.6% of these awards) were significantly less likely than whites (who received 48.4% of these awards) to be awarded teaching assistantships, which help defray the cost of graduate education and provide the tutelage of a mentor. Similarly, only one in every five blacks received a research assistantship. By contrast, almost four of every ten (38.2%) white graduate students were awarded this assistance (National Research Council, 1985).

Problems observed in any combination of the first five factors listed above may discourage black students who would otherwise seek a graduate or professional degree. Also, inequities in any of the six factors necessarily negatively affect the production of blacks with doctoral or professional degrees. The evidence shows that the absolute number of blacks who earned doctoral degrees increased significantly between 1973 (581 received) and 1980 (1,095 received). Since 1980, however, the number of doctoral degrees received by African-Americans has fallen yearly and is now less than 900 per year. Blacks comprised slightly more than 3 percent of doctorates awarded to U.S. citizens in 1989 (Blackwell, 1987; National Research Council, 1989).

There is a major problem not only with the paucity of numbers among black doctorates but with the maldistribution of blacks by field or discipline. While there continues to be a critical shortage of blacks in all fields including education, the compelling fact is that approximately one-half of all blacks earn doctoral degrees in education. The social and behavioral sciences follow with 21.1 percent; arts and sciences, 9.6 percent; life sciences, 9.2 percent; professions, 5.8 percent; physical sciences, 4.9 percent; and, finally, engineering with 1.4 percent (Blackwell, 1987, p. 329). Our nation's graduate and professional schools are not recruiting, admitting, retaining, and graduating sufficient numbers of blacks with doctorates in any field, but the record in the sciences and technology is especially poor. In a society that has moved rapidly into a postindustrial stage characterized by an economy based on high-technology, all available talent must be used if the nation is to remain competitive. We can no longer afford inattention to the pool of talent available among African-Americans. Their recruitment, training, and production is now in the national interest more than ever before.

REFERENCES

Allen, W. R. (1985). Black student, white campus: Structural, interpersonal, and psychological correlates of success. *Journal of Negro Education, 54* (2), 134–47.

Allen, W. R. (1986). *Gender and campus race differences in black student academic performance, racial attitudes and college satisfaction.* Atlanta: Southern Education Foundation.

Allen, W. (1987, May-June). Black colleges vs. white colleges: The fork in the road for black students. *Change: The Magazine of Learning, 19* (3), 28–39.

Association of American Medical Colleges. (1987). *Minority students in medical education: Facts and figures.* Washington, DC: Author.

Astin, A. W. (1975). *Preventing students from dropping out.* San Francisco: Jossey-Bass.

Astin, A. W. (1982). *Minorities in American higher education.* San Francisco: Jossey-Bass.

Blackwell, J. E. (1981). *Mainstreaming outsiders: The production of black professionals.* Bayside, NY: General Hall.

Blackwell, J. E. (1983). *Networking and mentoring: A study of cross-generational experiences of blacks in graduate and professional schools.* Atlanta: Southern Educational Foundation.

Blackwell, J. E. (1987). *Mainstreaming outsiders: The production of black professionals* (2d ed.). Dix Hills, NY: General Hall.

Carnegie Foundation for the Advancement of Teaching. (1987, May-June). Change trendlines: Minority access: A question of equity. *Change: The Magazine of Learning, 19* (3), 35–39.

Centra, J. A. (1980). Graduate degree aspirations of ethnic student groups. *American Educational Research Journal, 17,* 459–78.

Chaffee, E. (1984). Institutions and their processes for graduate education. In W. Manning (Ed.), *Developing a program of research on improving access of minority students to graduate education.* Princeton, NJ: Educational Testing Service.

Clewell, B., & Ficklen, M. (1987). *Improving minority retention in higher education: A search for effective institutional practices.* Princeton, NJ: Educational Testing Service.

Deskins, D. (1983). *Minority recruitment data: An analysis of baccalaureate degree production in the U.S.* Totowa, NJ: Rowan & Allanheld.

Epps, E., & Jackson, K. (1985). *Educational and occupational aspirations and early attainment of black males and females.* Atlanta: Southern Education Foundation.

Fisher, A. (1981). Black medical students: Too few for so large a task. In G. Thomas (Ed.), *Black students in higher education: Conditions in the 1970's*. Westport, CT: Greenwood Press.

Hall, M. L., & Allen, W. R. (1980). Race consciousness and achievement: Two issues in the study of black graduate/professional students. *Integrated Education, 20,* 56–61.

Hall, M., Mays, A., & Allen, W. (1984). Dreams deferred: Black student career goals and fields of study in graduate/professional schools. *Phylon, 45,* 271–83.

Lehner, J. C. (1980). *A losing battle: The decline of black participation in graduate and professional education.* Washington, DC: U.S. Department of Education.

Linn, R. L. (1974). *Test bias and the prediction of grades in law school.* LSAC-75-1. Princeton, NJ: Law School Admission Council.

Messick, S. (1982). Issues of effectiveness and equity in the coaching controversy: Implications for educational and testing practice. *Educational Psychologist, 17,* 67–91.

Morris, L. (1979). *Elusive equality: The status of black Americans in higher education.* Washington, DC: Howard University Press.

Morris, L. (1981). The role of testing institutional selectivity and black access to higher education. In G. Thomas (Ed.), *Black students in higher education: Conditions and experience in the 1970's.* Westport, CT: Greenwood Press.

National Research Council. (1985). *Survey of doctorate recipients.* Washington, DC: Author.

National Research Council. (1989). *Survey of doctorate recipients.* Washington, DC: Author.

Nettles, M. T., Baratz, J., & King, B. (1986). The effects of financial assistance upon access, attendance, and persistence in graduate school. Research Proposal, GRE No. 86-10. Princeton, NJ: Graduate Record Examination Board.

Philips-Jones, L. (1982). *Mentors and proteges.* New York: Arbor House.

Portes, A., & Wilson, K. L. (1976). Black-white differences in educational attainment. *American Sociological Review, 41,* 414–31.

Pruitt, A. S., & Issac, P. D. (1985, Fall). Discrimination in recruitment, admission and retention of minority graduate students. *Journal of Negro Education, 54* (4), 526–36.

Sedaleck, W. E., & Webster, D. W. (1978). Admission and retention of minority students in large universities. *Journal of College Students Personnel, 19,* 242–48.

Sexton, J. (1979). Admissions programs after Bakke. *Harvard Educational Review, 49,* 319–39.

Thomas, G. E. (Ed.). (1981). *Black students in higher education.* Westport, CT: Greenwood Press.

Tracey, T. J., & Sedaleck, W. E. (1984). Noncognitive variables in predicting academic success by race. *Measurement and Evaluation in Guidance, 16,* 171–78.

Velez, W. (1985). Finishing college: The effects of college type. *Sociology of Education, 58,* 191–200.

11

Systemwide Title VI Regulation of Higher Education, 1968–88: Implications for Increased Minority Participation

John B. Williams

In 1964 only 300,000 blacks were enrolled in the nation's higher education system, and most attended colleges and universities in the South that had been established solely to educate blacks. On the other hand, approximately 4.7 million whites attended college during that same year (National Center for Education Statistics, 1987). With passage of the 1964 Civil Rights Act, the federal government acknowledged this inequity in blacks' opportunity to attend college and threatened, through Title VI, to become a major source of pressure for desegregating higher education. But the potential of Title VI and the promise of government intervention to accomplish greater equity have never been realized.

Specifically, Title VI renders discriminatory agencies and institutions, including colleges and universities, ineligible to receive federal funds. Title VI allows individuals to file civil complaints with the federal government against all colleges and universities that discriminate in formal and informal ways, but it also contains the threat to withdraw funds if the federal government, through routine monitoring, finds systemwide discrimination. However, in passing the new law, Congress gave little guidance about how to formulate remedies for systematic segregation. Consequently, the character of the federal government's early civil rights intervention was unsure.

As far as Title VI is concerned, findings of systematic discrimination in public higher education were initially based upon two kinds of evidence: the existence of laws and policies prior to *Brown v. Board of Education* (1954) requiring separation of college students by race, and enrollment and employment patterns showing concentrations of students, faculty, and staff by race within state public education systems. Title VI was subsequently ruled to apply to systemwide discrimination only in the 18 states guilty of having operated legally sanctioned dual racial systems.

After correspondence, site visits, and reviews of enrollment and employment data, the director of the Office for Civil Rights (OCR) at the U.S. Department of Health, Education, and Welfare (HEW) sent letters to the governors of ten states indicating their states' failure to eliminate the lingering effects of past segregation laws and policies. He asked the ten governors to submit desegregation plans indicating measures that would be taken to eliminate the effects of discrimination. The ten states were Arkansas, Florida, Georgia, Louisiana, Maryland, Mississippi, North Carolina, Oklahoma, Pennsylvania, and Virginia. Not until 1981 were officials in the remaining eight states that had been found guilty of de jure segregation notified of Title VI noncompliance. Those states were Alabama, Delaware, Kentucky, Missouri, Ohio, South Carolina, Texas, and West Virginia.

The OCR director's 1969 letter to the governor of Virginia (Panetta) provides an example of early OCR findings of systemwide discrimination:

> The Office of Civil Rights of the Department of Health, Education and Welfare has required that all institutions of higher education receiving Federal financial assistance submit a compliance report indicating the racial enrollment at these institutions. Based on these reports particular colleges are visited to determine their compliance with Title VI of the Civil Rights Act of 1964. These visits, together with the reports received from the four-year State colleges and universities in Virginia, indicate that the State of Virginia is operating a nonunitary system of higher education.
>
> Specifically, the predominantly white State institutions providing four or more years of higher education have an enrollment which is approximately 99 percent white. The predominantly black institutions have an enrollment which is predominantly black in similar proportion. In addition to this situation which prevails in individual institutions throughout the State, the two land grant colleges, Virginia Polytechnic Institute and Virginia State College, originally devised as separate agricultural and technical colleges, one for blacks and one for whites, remain structurally separate and predominantly of one race, the latter black and the former white. Another manifestation of the State's racially dual system of higher education is evident in the city of Norfolk in which are situated two large institutions, predominantly white Old Dominion University and predominantly black Norfolk State, the enrollment of which is 98 percent Negro.

Even though letters of finding like this one were submitted beginning in 1969, requirements for remedy of past discrimination were not codified and standardized until 1977 upon order of the Federal District Court (*Adams v. Califano,* 1977). Prior to that time OCR officials dealt with each state independently, attempting to extract as many policy concessions as possible given the specific character of the segregation problem in each state. The desegregation guidelines, referred to as "criteria" in the *Federal Register* (U.S. Government, 1978, pp. 6658–64), contain the following provisions:

The proportion of black high school graduates throughout each state shall be equal to the proportion of white high school graduates entering two-year and four-year undergraduate institutions of higher education.

There shall be an annual increase in the proportion of black students in traditionally white four-year institutions of higher education.

Disparity between the proportion of black high school graduates and white high school graduates entering traditionally white institutions of higher education will be reduced by at least 50 percent by academic year 1982–83.

The proportion of black state residents who graduate from undergraduate schools and enter graduate schools shall be equal to the proportion of white state residents who enter such schools.

Increase the total proportion of white students attending traditionally black institutions.

Similar goals are required regarding faculty and staff. They are to be calculated based upon available pools of black doctoral and master's degree holders within relevant occupational fields and geographical locations.

Notably, it is difficult to ascertain from existing compliance documents the nature of the programs that were proposed and implemented by state and local officials in an effort to meet desegregation requirements. Colleges and universities in Title VI states seem to have focused effort in the direction of new recruitment projects, special scholarship programs, new instructional programs, and improved facilities at traditionally black institutions. But, with few exceptions, compliance reports do not contain sufficient and appropriate details for understanding and evaluating campus-level programs and activities that were planned and undertaken to achieve enrollment and employment increases.

Moreover, planned projects from one year are reported in subsequent years never to have been implemented. In one case, the state's higher education executive failed to convince the legislature to fund all budgetary programs for a given fiscal year. The reports also sometimes include process-defined activities, for example, indicators of the number of recruitment trips undertaken by admissions officers to predominantly black high schools, but such information gives the impression of documenting the efforts made by colleges, efforts that attract little response from potential black enrollees. There is no evidence of recruitment of the kind admissions officers know to be required for success. For the most part, the states' responses to Title VI compliance from 1968 to 1988 consisted of going through the motions — at various times with more zest than at others — of proposing and implementing relevant remedial measures. Moreover, some state policy makers — like those in Louisiana, Mississippi, North Carolina, and Ohio — for a time successfully refused to comply at all. In effect, the state role in Title VI regulation has ranged from outright defiance to polite but arrogant acquiescence.

On several occasions between 1968 and 1988, the NAACP Legal Defense Fund (LDF) asked the courts to require OCR to pressure state officials to report progress and to plan, promise, and undertake appropriate remedial actions. For example, in response to a 1982 petition from the LDF, the Washington Federal District Court concluded that, where the Arkansas, Georgia, Florida, Virginia, Oklahoma, and North Carolina community college systems were concerned,

> each of these states has defaulted in major respects on its plan commitments and on the desegregation requirements of the Criteria of Title VI. Each state has not achieved the principal objectives in its plan because of the state's failure to implement concrete and specific measures adequate to ensure that the promised desegregation goals would be achieved (*Adams v. Bell*, 1982, p. 2).

A review of state plans, state compliance reports, and OCR letters of finding (official responses to the compliance materials submitted) have consistently shown little state effort either to propose or to implement reasonable remedies for segregation. These same documents, on the whole, suggest little federal effort as well, for the documents were approved in most cases by federal officials even though they were unclear and, in many instances, notably inadequate.

Other evidence of inadequate federal effort consists of OCR's failure to respond both to complaints of discrimination against individuals and to evidence of institutionwide discrimination contained in routine annual compliance reports. In 1986 alone, OCR received 2,648 individual complaints and initiated 196 compliance reviews. OCR issued only 27 notices of opportunity for hearing between 1981 and 1985 despite finding 2,000 violations of civil rights law. Over that same period it referred only 24 additional cases to the Department of Justice (U.S. Department of Education, 1987, p. v). This pattern extends a policy of nonimplementation that began in 1970 when the original *Adams* case (*Adams v. Richardson,* 1973) was initiated. The Nixon administration's OCR also engaged in nonenforcement of individual complaints filed under Title VI (*Adams v. Weinberger,* 1975).

General agreement exists today that not much has taken place as a result of Title VI regulation of higher education over the past 20 years. The repeated judgments for further relief at the federal district court level, 1987 findings of a select congressional committee, and repeated independent policy analyses all reach the same conclusion. Moreover, federal officials do not attempt to dispel the considerable evidence that not much has taken place.

In 1984 the acting director for policy enforcement in OCR wrote to the assistant secretary for civil rights:

> Because the state systems with which it (OCR) has been dealing have not heretofore even approximated what might be considered the elimination of the vestiges of the dual systems, OCR has never defined how it would decide when that complete elimination of vestiges has been achieved in a state system (Cioffi to Singleton, November 15, 1984. Cited in U.S. Congress, Committee on Government Operations, 1987, p. 8).

Similarly, in its final review of compliance documents submitted by states whose desegregation plans expired in 1985 and 1986, OCR reported that the states did not meet the desegregation enrollment goals, with only two — Delaware and South Carolina — showing any progress. Similarly, none of the ten states involved met the employment goals they had set for faculty — though Georgia and Oklahoma met one numerical objective in the category of hiring black nondoctoral faculty. According to testimony at a hearing of the U.S. House of Representatives' Committee on Government Operations, OCR noted that four states out of the nine that had set goals for hiring doctoral-level black administrators met their goals, and six of nine setting goals for employing more nondoctoral administrators were partially successful (U.S. Committee on Government Operations, 1987, p. 10).

However, federal officials argue that most Title VI states have acted in sufficient good faith and that failure to enroll and hire more blacks in public higher education stems from factors beyond the control of government and higher education policy makers. Adopting this approach, the Department of Education (DE) ruled in 1986 that Georgia need no longer plan and implement remedies for desegregation past the period of their current plan if the measures included are completed. These measures include some physical facilities construction projects, public relations programs to encourage whites to enroll at Albany State College (a traditionally black institution), and an agricultural extension program jointly administered by Fort Valley State, a traditionally black institution, and the University of Georgia. The DE reached this decision despite convincing evidence of continuing racial inequity. For example, the percentage of high school graduates enrolling in college in Georgia declined from 17.5 percent in 1978 to 16.9 percent in 1985. White high school graduates enrolled at the rate of 16.8 percent in 1978 and 27.1 percent in 1985. Black enrollment grew from 9,907 in 1978 to 11,587 in 1985, but this increase represents only 75 percent of the state enrollment goal. Black retention rates also declined by roughly 3 percent during this same period (U.S. Department of Education, 1986).

In 1987, DE officials notified five other states — Arkansas, North Carolina (for its two-year college system), Delaware, South Carolina, and West Virginia — of compliance with Title VI. Since then, Florida, Kentucky, Pennsylvania, Texas, Arkansas, and Oklahoma have also been ruled in compliance. Alabama, Tennessee, Louisiana, Maryland, Ohio, and the state university system of North Carolina remain under the jurisdiction of the federal judiciary, which may or may not extend desegregation remedies much longer. And the Fifth Circuit Court of Appeals ruled in September 1990 that Mississippi's obligation involves simply providing open admissions/nondiscrimination policies.

The most compelling evidence of the demise of the Title VI regulatory charade in higher education emerged in 1989, when the Federal District Court in the District of Columbia ruled that plaintiffs in the original *Adams v. Richardson* court case no longer held standing to pursue relief from discrimination through the federal courts. The LDF successfully petitioned the court in 1972 to require the federal government to implement Title VI, because since 1970, under the Nixon administration, Title VI regulatory activities had withered. The *Adams* case got the federal courts involved in pressuring the OCR at the DE to implement Title VI. Favorable rulings by the court since 1973 provided almost the sole energy for sustained compliance with Title VI. Although LDF has appealed the recent decision regarding lack of standing by plaintiffs in *Adams,* the federal courts no longer monitor Title VI regulatory activities of the OCR at the DE. Without court oversight, the DE has been freed to arbitrarily release states from their civil rights responsibilities in higher education.

It is possible to argue that, despite several years of Title VI implementation, equal education opportunity for blacks at the postsecondary level has stagnated or worsened. This judgment, regardless of its accuracy, does not, however, reflect the total picture of black participation in higher education from 1969 to the present. Title VI regulation in 18 states occurred within the context of a much broader effort to secure equal opportunity for blacks in higher education. It is important to take the broader picture into account in order to suggest future strategies to overcome what seems like a very real failure.

On a national scale the following important trends, drawn from the *Higher Education General Information Surveys, 1964–1986* (National Center for Education Statistics, 1987), seem evident:

Black high school graduation rates have increased from about 56 percent in 1967 to 76 percent in 1986.

Although total black enrollment increased by 170 percent between 1964 and 1986, parity with whites has never been achieved.

Only 8 percent of black 18- to 24-year-olds enrolled in college in 1964, while 22 percent did so in 1986.

The percentage of black 18- to 24-year-old high school graduates enrolling in college increased from 23.5 percent in 1967 to 28 percent in 1986.

Despite the positive movement evidenced by these statistics, the problem is that in calendar year 1976 black 18- to 24-year-old high school graduates enrolled in college at the rate of 36 percent. Title VI regulation and all other attempts to improve black participation in higher education are held hostage to the phenomenon of recently declining rates of black high school graduates enrolling in college. The reasons for this phenomenon are unknown at this time. Another important aspect of the declining black participation phenomenon is high attrition. While the percentage of blacks completing four years of college increased by 474 percent between 1964 and 1986 (correspondingly, the percentage of black persons aged 23 to 34 holding college degrees rose from 3.9% to 10.6% over the same period), the number of bachelors' degrees awarded to blacks between 1976 and 1985 decreased by 3 percent (compiled from National Center for Education Statistics, 1987).

Despite the fact that over 50 percent of blacks in college enroll in Title VI states and roughly 46 percent of all public institutions are affected by systemwide Title VI regulation, nonimplementation of Title VI remedies at the local level does not seem to constitute much of an explanation for these trends. In fact, implementation probably expanded slightly between 1975 and 1985 as the Federal District Court in Washington, D.C., grew weary of repeated appeals for further relief by LDF and instructed OCR in more direct ways to implement the law. Still, it is during this period that black enrollment declined both in the Title VI region and nationally as well.

It may be that serious effort during the latter period of implementation occurred too late for good results to emerge. By then new barriers to participation, like reductions in federal student aid programs, had begun. The major contribution of the early years of Title VI regulation may have been the elimination of all formal laws, policies, and overt practices aimed specifically at keeping blacks excluded or concentrated in traditionally black institutions. It is during this period that most positive changes seem to have come about.

Where systemwide regulation of higher education under Title VI is concerned, clearly there have always been and remain today factors beyond the intervention that have negatively affected its outcomes. These factors include the passage of substantial federal student aid laws in 1971 and subsequent reductions in the 1980s, the rise and fall of the civil rights movement and of civil rights as a broad national political issue, seemingly unlimited growth followed by severely constrained expansion of the college and university enterprise, and changing quality of elementary and secondary education systems. All these are factors related to black participation levels in higher education over the past 20 years.

In light of this observation, even if strong evidence of Title VI implementation existed at this time, it may still have been impossible to show that this intervention itself produced results. Evaluating the impact of Title VI is complicated by several other factors, but being unable to show its impact is not synonymous with its not having had any impact. As noted earlier, the disappearance of discrimination laws and formal policies is due to colleges and universities' fears of losing federal funds, a sanction included in Title VI. Also, nonimplementation of appropriate or inappropriate remedies may amount to evidence of the actively negative impact of Title VI regulation. Successful recalcitrance by state and campus policy makers, sanctioned by the inactivity of federal officials, may in fact have led college officials to ignore their responsibility more than if Title VI regulation had not taken place.

Past experience shows the need to simultaneously implement Title VI and ensure that other factors work positively in the same direction.

Today's puzzle is not whether Title VI has had much impact. It was never substantially implemented and its influence at the campus level was at best nonsystematic and at worst disruptive. The relevant policy questions involve knowing the marginal impact of Title VI and then asking: What factors are associated with nonimplementation? What additional factors, beyond Title VI, influenced outcomes? And most important, what policy resources are needed today both to compel implementation and to positively affect the other relevant circumstances?

REFERENCES

Adams v. Bell, Civil Action No. 70-3095 (D.D.C. 1982).

Adams v. Califano, 430 F. Supp. 118, 121 (D.D.C. 1977).

Adams v. Richardson, 356 F. Supp. 92 (D.D.C. 1973).

Adams v. Weinberger, 391 F. Supp. 269 (D.D.C. 1975).

Brown v. Board of Education, 347 U.S. 483 (1954).

National Center for Education Statistics. (1987). *Higher education general information surveys, 1964–1986.* Washington, DC: U.S. Government Printing Office.

Panetta, L. (1969, December 2). Letter from Panetta, then director of the Office for Civil Rights, U.S. Department of Health, Education, and Welfare, to M. E. Godwin, then governor of the Commonwealth of Virginia.

U.S. Congress, Committee on Government Operations. (1987). *Failure and fraud on civil rights enforcement by the department of education: Twenty-second report by the committee on government operations.* Washington, DC: U.S. Government Printing Office.

U.S. Department of Education. (1987). *Office for civil rights sixth annual report.* Washington, DC: U.S. Government Printing Office.

U.S. Department of Education. (1986). *Office for civil rights factual report.* Unpublished document.

U.S. Government. (1978). *Federal Register, 43* (32), 6658–64. Washington, DC: U.S. Government Printing Office.

V

SPECIAL ISSUES

A number of special educational issues face African-Americans, in addition to those already presented in the preceding chapters. Several are addressed in this section, including the low participation of blacks in science, mathematics, and other technical fields; ethnic and cultural diversity; the shortage of black public school teachers; the impact of black studies; and the increasing rate of violence on college campuses.

According to Willie Pearson, Jr., who writes on blacks in science, mathematics, and technical education, there is ample evidence that blacks are interested in science and mathematics, especially at the undergraduate college level. Pearson has found that the proportion of blacks who express interest in a field of knowledge requiring quantitative skills is twice as large among those pursuing a bachelor's degree as among those pursuing graduate degrees. Because some institutions have been more successful than others in producing black scientists, Pearson states that "the factors that underlie the career development decisions of blacks" deserve more study.

"The trivialization of ethnic cultures" is a phrase coined by James A. Banks in his chapter, "Social Studies, Ethnic Diversity, and Social Change." According to Banks, this trivialization has resulted in insufficient study of the career development decisions of blacks and other minorities and the reasons for their varying interests in science, mathematics, business, education, sociology, social work, and other fields. A sound social studies curriculum, says Banks, should provide "knowledge about why many ethnic groups are victimized by institutional racism and class stratification." Such knowledge, he argues, may contribute to genuine equity action by the nation and would reveal that the fate and future of whites, blacks, and other minorities are intertwined. However, Banks has little hope that this will occur unless there is more effective selection and training of teachers. He calls this "the most challenging and difficult task that lies ahead" for those who believe that schooling can serve as a vehicle for human betterment.

Antoine M. Garibaldi also addresses the issue of teachers in his chapter, "Abating the Shortage of Black Teachers." He sees the declining proportion of black and other minority teachers as a very special problem facing this nation, especially since it is happening at the same time that the proportion of nonwhite students in major metropolitan school districts is increasing. Garibaldi acknowledges that the shortage of black teachers is partially because some blacks have become interested in occupations other than teaching. He also states, however, that many other blacks are staying away from teaching, not because they have been pulled to more attractive options, but because they have been pushed out of teacher training programs. He notes, for instance, that some certification requirements using standardized tests have "eliminated many prospective black teachers and discouraged other potential teacher education majors from choosing that discipline."

In his chapter, James B. Stewart states that the increased number of black students entering predominantly white colleges in the 1960s stimulated the offering of black history as a course of study. He credits the study of black history with destroying myths about blacks, such as those portraying them as passive acceptors of slavery and subjugation. Black history, according to Stewart, also documents the origins of the self-help movement among blacks and its contribution to their current progress. And, finally, black history made available to schools the record of black contributions to the world. According to Stewart, black studies, which includes black history, has established a beachhead in higher education and now needs to be integrated into the K-to-12 curriculum.

In his chapter, Wornie L. Reed describes the increase in violence against African-Americans on college campuses during the 1980s and asks, "What role does the university play in the development of racial incidents?" He answers by suggesting that universities help preserve the belief systems and value orientations of a society. Universities do this explicitly, according to Reed, through their teaching. He draws attention to the fact that, for instance, European-Americans can obtain college degrees without ever studying non-European cultures — although most of the world is nonwhite. He argues that this phenomenon devalues non-European cultures and contributes directly and indirectly to racial attacks on blacks by whites on college campuses.

In the final chapter of this volume, Charles V. Willie summarizes the results of the work of the Assessment of the Status of African-Americans study group on education and makes some policy recommendations for federal, state, and local agencies. Willie points out how the confused and contraindicated ways in which the law has been implemented have prohibited blacks from experiencing the full benefits of school desegregation and goes on to indicate how these deficiencies can be overcome. He and the other members of the study group also provide some specific changes that should be made within the present system to ensure that "excellence [in education] may be pursued without compromising equality."

12

Black Participation and Performance in Science, Mathematics, and Technical Education

Willie Pearson, Jr.

In order to sustain this country's work force in science and engineering, it is essential that all available talent be used and more attention be placed on groups, such as blacks, who are underrepresented in the American scientific community. Obviously, programs targeted at increasing black participation and performance in math- and science-related fields will be important (Frankel, 1986). This chapter reviews relevant studies on the participation and performance of black students in science, mathematics, and technical education. Materials were derived from both published and unpublished sources. In the sections to follow the focus is on black participation throughout the educational pipeline at the elementary/middle school, high school, and college/graduate school levels. These sections are followed by an assessment of current research findings and public policy strategies.

ELEMENTARY/MIDDLE SCHOOL

In a review of studies of student mathematics, science, and computer participation and performance in grades four to eight, Lockheed, Thorpe, Brooks-Gunn, Casserly, and McAloon (1985) report a number of interesting findings. Briefly, they found that few studies focused on these grade levels. They could locate only 16 studies that examined ethnic differences in mathematics performance. These studies revealed a distinct pattern of performance, with black students usually performing less well than Asians, whites, and Hispanics. Only one study reported no ethnic differences. Six studies that examined sex differences within ethnicity were identified. Lockheed et al. concluded that differences in participation and performance attributable to ethnicity may be due largely to differences in family or socioeconomic status. In another study, Johnson (1981) examined the mathematics activities (i.e., reading about mathematics, having a mathematics-related hobby, etc.) of a sample of black students in grades seven and eight and found overall low levels of participation, but no differences between sexes. In an analysis of 1981–82 National Assessment in Science data, Hueftle, Rakow, and Welch (1983) report that few studies have examined ethnic differences. They report that black and white students indicate that they use computers in school at least once a week.

Overall, studies of students in the elementary/middle school grades reveal differences between blacks and whites in mathematics and science participation and performance; however, as Lockheed et al. (1985) argue, any conclusions drawn from these studies must be tentative because most do not control for family or socioeconomic background. It is important that black students in these early years receive quality instruction in mathematics, science, and computer science. Children who are not taught science and mathematics well in their early years are unlikely to elect further courses in those subjects when they have a choice in high school (Turnbull, 1983).

HIGH SCHOOL

Davis's recent study (1989) of black student participation and performance in high school mathematics revealed some narrowing of the black/white mathematics achievement gap. However, most of the improvement was limited to rote memory and quick recall and to black students attending predominantly white high schools. She also found that taking advanced courses increased mathematics proficiency. Unfortunately, Davis found significant black/white differences in patterns of advanced course taking. In addition, she found that black students were more likely than their white counterparts to use computers for drill and practice rather than programming — especially black students attending predominantly black schools.

In a similar study of black students, Anderson (1989) focused on high school science. She, like Davis, found that black students were less likely than their white counterparts to take advanced courses, especially in physics and chemistry. This, of course, accounts for much of the black/white science achievement gap. Also, Anderson found that black students scored nearly 70 points below the national norm on achievement tests in physics, biology, and chemistry. Both Anderson and Davis reported sex differences (favoring males) among black students.

COLLEGE AND GRADUATE SCHOOL

Berryman (1983) reported that the underrepresentation of blacks in science and engineering was because they lose field and attainment ground at several points in the educational pipeline. For example, at the bachelor's level, the percentage of blacks choosing quantitative fields is 60 percent of the national average, while at the master's and doctoral levels, the percentage drops sharply to 40 percent and 33 percent, respectively.

A recent report by the National Science Foundation (1986) revealed that in 1984 black college-bound seniors were slightly more likely than their white counterparts (41% versus 39%) to indicate an intended major in math or science. However, the study showed that blacks earn a mere fraction of the degrees actually granted in science and engineering. Of the science and engineering degrees awarded in 1983, blacks earned 5.5 percent of the bachelor's, 3.8 percent of the master's, and 2.2 percent of the doctoral degrees. These figures represent substantial underrepresentation given that blacks accounted for 10 percent of overall undergraduate enrollment and 5 percent of graduate enrollment. In fact, since 1979, the proportion of blacks earning science and engineering degrees at all levels has remained relatively unchanged. The study also showed that blacks (89%) were more likely than whites (79%) to earn their bachelor's degrees in science, while whites were far more likely to earn degrees in engineering. Within science fields, however, more than four-fifths of blacks earn degrees in just three fields: psychology, life sciences, or social sciences.

Finally, the study revealed that at the master's degree level, about 54 percent of blacks (compared to 35% of whites) earned degrees in psychology or the social sciences. At the doctoral level, the largest fraction of blacks (37%) earned their degrees in psychology, while whites (30%) most often earned their degrees in the life sciences. At the final stage of the education pipeline, few blacks were found to hold postdoctoral appointments. In fact, only 215 blacks held postdoctoral appointments in 1983 and most of these were concentrated in the social (32%) and physical (32%) sciences.

It should be pointed out that studies consistently revealed gender differences among blacks, especially in terms of rates of participation in science and engineering education. These differences (usually favoring males) become more pronounced at the doctoral degree level (Leggon, 1987; National Science Foundation, 1986).

ASSESSMENT OF LITERATURE

In assessing the current literature on black participation and performance in math- and science-related education, the following issues appear to be noteworthy. First, the limited research that has been conducted examining the factors related to ethnic differences in the math and science achievement of students in the elementary/middle school grades has failed to account for socioeconomic background (Lockheed et al., 1985). Second, while there has been some speculation that the black subculture does not foster an environment supportive of the acquisition of math and science knowledge, no comprehensive systematic study has examined contextual variables (Lockheed et al., 1985). Third, despite several studies conducting analyses of large national data sets of high school students, our understanding as to why black students are not learning higher order mathematics skills remains limited. Fourth, research on the science and engineering college and graduate school experiences of black students continues to be lacking. Few institutional data exist on differential success of various colleges and graduate departments. The question is: Why have some institutions been more successful than others in producing black scientific talent? Finally, evaluative research on intervention programs is needed if we are to understand which programs are effective and which are ineffective. Correlatedly, research is needed on the postretirement plans or activities of black scientists and engineers, because these individuals represent attractive talent resources for volunteers and employees of intervention programs.

PUBLIC POLICY RECOMMENDATIONS

To improve the participation and performance of black students in math and science, policy makers must know what to target and when to initiate intervention (Berryman, 1983). With regard to target, public and private funding should be directed toward programs that improve the quality of math and science instruction in elementary/middle school grades, especially in predominantly black school systems. This is important because math and science interests are formed during this early period, and the literature consistently reveals that black students do not have the same opportunity as white students for quality instruction and facilities. The same holds for the high school level. From an educational policy position, Berryman (1983) suggests that by increasing mathematical and science high school graduation course requirements, black student preparation in these subjects would be improved. However, this presently seems an unlikely event in most states, so alternative strategies such as intervention programs must be used.

At the college level, several intervention programs have been successful in motivating black students to take math and science course electives and to choose majors in math- and science-related fields, demonstrating that the barriers to black participation in math and science are largely social and therefore subject to intervention. Consequently, intervention programs that focus on building math- and science-related skills should be evaluative, and those that work should receive public and private funding. And, of course, successful programs should be duplicated elsewhere. Such programs can compensate for the lack of in- and out-of-school math and science experiences among black students. Because a disproportionate number of blacks continue to be first-generation college students, many will need more career counseling, especially regarding opportunities for blacks in math- and science-related fields. Finally, more public and private funding must be directed toward both research projects that seek to increase our understanding of the factors underlying the career development decisions of black students (Hall & Kammer, 1985) and financial aid in the form of grants and fellowships.

REFERENCES

Anderson, B. (1989). Black participation and performance in high school science. In W. Pearson, Jr., & H. K. Bechtel (Eds.), *Blacks, science and American education*. New Brunswick, NJ: Rutgers University Press.

Berryman, S. E. (1983). *Who will do science?* New York: Rockefeller Foundation.

Davis, J. D. (1989). The mathematics education of black high school students. In W. Pearson, Jr., & H. K. Bechtel (Eds.), *Blacks, science and American education*. New Brunswick, NJ: Rutgers University Press.

Frankel, E. (1986, February 19). Demographic trends and the scientific and engineering work force. Statement before the House Committee on Science and Technology, Congress of the United States, Washington, DC.

Hall, E. R., & Kammer, P. P. (1985, October). Black math and science majors: Why so few? Paper presented at the University of Wisconsin System's Fifth Multicultural Conference, University of Wisconsin, Oshkosh.

Hueftle, S. J., Rakow, S. L., & Welch, W. W. (1983). *Image of science: A summary of results from the 1981–82 national assessment in science*. Minneapolis: University of Minnesota, Science Assessment and Research Project.

Johnson, R. C. (1981). *Psychosocial influences on the math attitudes and interests of black junior high school students*. Unpublished manuscript.

Leggon, C. (1987). Minority underrepresentation in science and engineering graduate education and careers: A critique. In L. S. Dix (Ed.), *Minorities: Their underrepresentation and differentials in science and engineering*. Washington, DC: Office of Scientific and Engineering Personnel, National Research Council, National Academy Press.

Lockheed, M. E., Thorpe, E., Brooks-Gunn, J., Casserly, P., & McAloon, A. (1985). *Understanding sex/ethnic related differences in mathematics, science and computer science for students in grades four to eight*. Princeton, NJ: Educational Testing Service.

National Science Foundation. (1986). *Women and minorities in science and engineering*. Washington, DC: U.S. Government Printing Office.

Turnbull, W. W. (1983, July). *Schooling for the age of technology: Where does America stand?* Statement before the Joint Economic Committee, Congress of the United States, Washington, DC.

13

Social Studies, Ethnic Diversity, and Social Change

James A. Banks

A series of ethnic revival movements emerged in Western countries, such as the United States, Canada, United Kingdom, and Australia, during the 1960s and 1970s. A major goal of these movements was to reform the school curriculum so that the images of ethnic groups and the roles they played in the development of their nations would be accurately and comprehensively depicted. This chapter describes the curricular visions and goals of the ethnic revival movements, the limited extent to which these goals have been realized, and the factors that have prevented significant curriculum reform. In the final parts of the chapter, a reform strategy is proposed that conceptualizes the teacher as a cultural mediator and agent of change, and a social studies curriculum that promotes social criticism and civic action to improve the human condition.

THE ETHNIC REVIVAL MOVEMENT

The black civil rights movement that emerged in the 1960s stimulated the rise of the ethnic revival movement throughout the United States as well as in other parts of the world (Banton, 1983). A major goal of these ethnic movements was to change the social, economic, and political systems so that structurally excluded and powerless ethnic groups would attain social and economic mobility and educational equality. The demand

---

for changes in the educational system was a major goal of the ethnic revival movements throughout the Western world (Banks & Lynch, 1986). Ethnic groups demanded change in the educational system because they believed the school could be an important instrument in their empowerment and liberation. Most ethnic groups have a tenacious faith in the school to help them attain social mobility and structural inclusion (Clark, 1973; Edmonds et al., 1973), despite the arguments by revisionists such as Bowles and Gintis (1976) and Jencks et al. (1972) that the school merely reproduces the social structure and depoliticizes powerless ethnic groups.

EDUCATIONAL RESPONSES TO THE ETHNIC REVIVAL MOVEMENT

In the various Western countries in which ethnic revival movements have taken place, educators responded with a wide range of programs, projects, and curricular innovations intended to silence ethnic protest, increase the achievement of ethnic groups, and close the gap between their expressed democratic ideals and practices (Banks & Lynch, 1986). Social studies, and history in particular, were among the first curricular areas to be scrutinized and criticized by ethnic reformers (Banks, 1973; Fitzgerald, 1979). A major goal of the ethnic revival movement was to shape new identities of ethnic groups and to highlight the roles that various ethnic groups had played in the development of their nations. History was seen by ethnic reformers as an important part of the curriculum that perpetuated old images and stereotypes and was therefore in need of radical revision and reconstruction (Blassingame, 1971).

Over two decades have passed since the ethnic protest and revival movements first emerged in the United States. This period has been characterized by intense ethnic polarization and debate, rapid and often superficial curriculum changes and innovations, the birth and death of promising ideas, progress and retrenchment, hope and disillusionment, and a flurry of activity related to ethnic and immigrant groups (Banks, 1984a). The current period is characterized by conservatism and a back-to-the-basics ideology ushered in partly by the movement for academic excellence, which devoted scant attention to equality and the needs of victimized ethnic groups (Johnston, 1985; National Commission on Excellence in Education, 1983).

LIFE STYLE VERSUS LIFE CHANCE APPROACHES

During the early phases of the ethnic revitalization movement in the United States, as well as in other Western nations, ethnic leaders demanded that ethnic heroes and cultures become a part of the school curriculum. Educators often responded to these demands quickly and without careful planning and sufficient in-service training for teachers. As a result, ethnic heroes such as Crispus Attucks and Martin Luther King, Jr., were inserted into the curriculum along with bits and pieces of content about ethnic cultures and traditions (Cuban, 1968). This additive approach to the study of ethnic content emanates from several assumptions that have precluded substantial curriculum reform, perpetuated stereotypes and misconceptions of ethnic cultures and life styles, and prevented teachers from dealing effectively and comprehensively with concepts such as racism, class stratification, powerlessness, and the reforms needed to empower ethnic groups.

When educators add ethnic heroes and fragmented ethnic content to the curriculum, ethnic heroes and content are assumed to be nonintegral parts of the mainstream U.S. experience. Consequently, it is assumed sufficient to add special units and festivals to teach about ethnic groups and their cultures. Particularly in elementary social studies, ethnic content is taught primarily with special lessons and pageants on holidays and birthdays. Blacks often dominate lessons during Black History Week or on Martin Luther King's birthday, but they are largely invisible in the curriculum during the rest of the year. Although blacks and other ethnic minority groups are now a more integral part of textbooks than they were prior to the 1960s, their presence is neither comprehensive nor sufficiently integrated into the total curriculum (Garcia & Goebel, 1985).

The infusion of fragmented ethnic content into the curriculum not only reinforces the idea that ethnic minority groups are not an integral part of U.S. society but also results in the trivialization of ethnic cultures. The study of Mexican-American food or of native American tepees will not help students develop a sophisticated understanding of Mexican-American culture and of the tremendous cultural diversity among native Americans. This kind of teaching about ethnic cultures often perpetuates misconceptions and stereotypes about ethnic cultures and leads well-meaning, but misinformed, teachers to believe that they have integrated their curricula with ethnic content and helped their students to understand ethnic groups better.

Superficial teaching about ethnic groups and ethnic cultures may do more harm than good. Excluding a study of ethnic cultures in the elementary social studies curriculum might be preferable to the trivialization and marginalization of ethnic cultures and life styles. The distortion of ethnic cultures that has taken place in the schools has led some critics of multicultural education to argue that teaching about ethnic groups in the schools should focus on their life chances rather than on their life styles (Bullivant, 1986b; Mullard, 1980).

A curriculum that focuses on life chances describes the ways that structurally excluded ethnic groups are victimized by social, economic, and political variables, such as institutionalized racism, class stratification, and political powerlessness. Critics of multicultural education who make this argument are concerned that a focus on cultures and life styles not only trivializes the cultures of ethnic groups but also diverts attention from the real causes of ethnic group victimization and poverty. They believe that a focus on life styles might cause majority groups to blame the victims for their victimization and help to entrench institutionalized stereotypes. Moodley (1986) writes:

> Given the complexity of cultures, they are frequently trivialized in presentations in the elementary curriculum. Werner et al. refer to the common isolated use of artifacts and other aspects of the material culture without a holistic interpretation as the "museum approach." It reinforces the "us-them" differences and highlights a "hierarchy of cultures" based on the way the outsider perceives the minority (p. 620).

Social studies teachers do not need to decide whether they will approach the teaching of ethnic content from a life style or life chance perspective. Both cultural knowledge and knowledge about why many ethnic groups are victimized by institutionalized racism and class stratification are needed in a sound social studies curriculum that accurately and sensitively reflects the experience of ethnic groups. Both perspectives are needed to help students gain a comprehensive and sophisticated understanding of the experiences of ethnic groups in the United States and in other nations. However, teaching accurately about the cultures of ethnic groups is a complex and difficult task.

To teach about ethnic cultures accurately, teachers must help students understand that ethnic cultures, especially within a modernized society such as the United States, are dynamic, complex, and changing processes (Beals, Spindler, & Spindler, 1967; Geertz, 1973). Students also need to understand that a culture consists of many aspects or variables, such as symbols, language, and behavior, and that an individual member of a culture may exemplify the characteristics of a group completely or hardly at all (Banks, 1981). Consequently, knowing what have been called African-American cultural characteristics (White, 1984) may give an individual few clues about the behavior of a particular black individual and reinforce stereotypes and misconceptions.

THE SEARCH FOR NEW PERSPECTIVES

A major goal of the ethnic revival movements of the 1960s and 1970s was not only to include more information about the culture and history of ethnic groups in the social studies curriculum but also to infuse the curriculum with new perspectives, frames of reference, and values. In textbooks and in teaching, ethnic events and heroes are often added to the curriculum, but the interpretations of and perspectives on these events and heroes remain those of mainstream historians and scholars (Garcia & Goebel, 1985). When concepts, events, and situations in the curriculum are viewed only or primarily from the perspectives of mainstream scholars and historians, students obtain a limited view of social reality and an incomplete understanding of the human experience. As James Baldwin (1985) perceptively points out in several trenchant essays, white Americans cannot fully understand their history unless they study black history from myriad perspectives because the history of blacks and whites is intricately interwoven.

In an important essay on the sociology of knowledge published in the midst of the civil rights movement, Merton (1972) discusses "insiders" and "outsiders" and their competing knowledge claims. Both insiders and outsiders claim that only they can obtain valid knowledge about group life. Insiders claim that only a member of their group can formulate accurate and valid knowledge about the group because of the special insights that result from being socialized within the group. Outsiders claim that valid knowledge results only when groups are studied by outsiders because of the dispassionate objectivity that outsiders bring to the study of group life. Merton concludes that both insiders and outsiders can make important contributions to the understanding of group life, and that insiders and outsiders should unite in their quests for knowledge.

Social and historical knowledge reflects the values, experiences, times, and social structure in which scholars are socialized and work. In an ethnically and racially stratified society such as the United States, ethnic and racial microcultures also influence the formulation of knowledge. Although social scientists and historians who are insiders in the black community and those who are outsiders are likely to agree on many observations about black life and behavior, they are likely to formulate some findings and interpretations that differ in significant ways. Many mainstream social scientists conducted studies of blacks prior to the civil rights movements of the 1960s that were strongly attacked by black social scientists in the 1970s (Ladner, 1973). Much of this controversy focused on historical interpretations of topics such as slavery and the Civil War, sociological interpretations of the black family, and descriptions and interpretations of black English and black culture. Black culture and life were frequently described as disorganized, pathological, and deviant by mainstream social scientists (Ladner, 1973). Black students were often labeled "culturally deprived" (Reissman, 1962).

Traditional research assumptions, methods, and conclusions of mainstream social scientists often differed sharply from those of the new black social scientists during this period (Banks, 1984b; Ladner, 1973). Prior to the 1960s, most mainstream social scientists viewed blacks as a "social problem" (Valentine, 1968). They developed most of their concepts and theories from studies that compared blacks to middle-class whites and concluded that black life was deviant, pathological, and culturally deprived. During the 1950s and early 1960s, most of the content about blacks in social science courses dealt with slavery and social problems such as poverty, welfare, and juvenile delinquency. The black family was often used to illustrate ways in which black life was pathological and deprived (Moynihan, 1965). Black social scientists in the 1960s and 1970s challenged the traditional conceptions of black life and formulated concepts and theories that viewed black life as different from middle-class white culture rather than deviant (Billingsley, 1968; Hill, 1971). They also viewed black culture from the inside, saw it holistically, and described it as a viable and functional culture with tremendous strengths that had enabled it to survive despite great odds (Billingsley, 1968; Blassingame, 1971; Ladner, 1973).

Although ethnicity and race often influence the knowledge claims, research, and perspectives of social scientists and historians, these influences are complex and difficult to describe precisely. Individual white, Mexican-American, or black scholars may be influenced more by their class interests, commitment to scholarly objectivity, or other values than by race or ethnicity. The revisionist and sensitive studies of blacks by white social scientists such as Baratz (1970), Genovese (1974), and Gutman (1970) during the 1970s are cases in point, as are the more conservative analyses of the black experience written by black scholars such as Sowell (1984) and Wilson (1978).

Although the influence of race, ethnicity, and class on social knowledge is complex and difficult to describe precisely, it is nonetheless significant and far-reaching. Insider perspectives on important social and historical events such as the Holocaust, the internment of Japanese-Americans, and the civil rights movements of the 1960s provide students with insights, perspectives, and feelings about these events that cannot be gained from reading accounts by individuals who have experienced these events only from a distance or from source materials (Farmer, 1985; Nakano & Nakano, 1980; Raines, 1977). Scholars who are socialized within ethnic cultures in which these events are important parts of the social and cultural history are also likely to have perspectives different from those of mainstream scholars (Blassingame, 1971; Ladner, 1973).

It is important for students in the elementary grades to have a curriculum that not only presents the experiences of ethnic and cultural groups accurately and sensitively but also enables them to see the experiences of both mainstream and minority groups from the perspective of different cultural, racial, and ethnic groups. A social studies curriculum that both includes the experiences of different ethnic groups and presents them from diverse perspectives is needed to help students understand the complexity of the U.S. experience and the ways that the nation's various groups have strongly influenced each other culturally and interacted within the social structure. Table 13.1 summarizes the dominant and desirable characteristics of multiethnic studies, described above.

IDEOLOGICAL RESISTANCE TO A PLURALISTIC CURRICULUM

After over two decades of debates and attempts to reform the school and the curriculum to reflect ethnic and cultural diversity in the United States, multiethnic reforms remain on the periphery of the mainstream curriculum in most U.S. schools. Though most examples of blatant racism and stereotypes of ethnic groups have been deleted from textbooks and teaching materials, content about racial and ethnic groups is not thoroughly integrated into mainstream textbooks and teaching materials (Garcia & Goebel, 1985). Instead, materials about racial and ethnic groups are usually relegated to special units and holidays and are appendages to the main story about the development of U.S. society.

Most content about African-Americans is studied when topics such as slavery, Reconstruction, and the civil rights movement of the 1960s are covered (Garcia & Goebel, 1985). Most frequently, a unilinear, Eurocentric approach is used to teach development of U.S. history and society. The story of the development of America is often told by

TABLE 13.1
Dominant and Desirable Characteristics of Multiethnic Studies

Dominant Characteristics	*Desirable Characteristics*
Focuses on isolated aspects of the histories and culture of ethnic groups.	Describes the history and cultures of ethnic groups holistically.
Trivializes the histories and cultures of ethnic groups.	Describes the cultures of ethnic groups as dynamic wholes and processes of change.
Presents events, issues, and concepts primarily from Anglocentric and mainstream perspectives and points of view.	Presents events, issues, and concepts from the perspectives of diverse racial and ethnic groups.
Is Eurocentric — shows the development of Americans primarily as an extension of Europe into the Americas.	Is multidimensional and geocultural — shows how peoples and cultures came to America from many different parts of the world, including Asia and Africa, and their important roles in the development of U.S. society.
Presents ethnic groups as an appendage to the regular or core curriculum.	Presents ethnic groups as an integral part of the regular or core curriculum.
Describes ethnic minority cultures as deprived or pathological.	Describes ethnic minority cultures as different from mainstream Anglo culture but as normal and functional.
Gives scant attention to concepts such as institutional racism, class stratification, powerlessness, and the victimization of ethnic and racial groups.	Makes concepts such as institutional racism, class stratification, powerlessness, and the victimization of ethnic and racial groups an important focus.
Dominates curriculum with assimilationist ideology; ignores or depicts as undesirable pluralist and radical ideologies.	Reflects a pluralistic ideology; gives some attention to radical ideas and concepts.
Focuses on lower-level knowledge, heroes, holidays, and recall of factual information.	Focuses on higher-level knowledge, such as concepts, generalizations, and theories.

Table 13.1, continued

Dominant Characteristics	*Desirable Characteristics*
Emphasizes the mastery of knowledge and cognitive outcomes.	Emphasizes decision making, citizen action, knowledge formulation, and value analysis; synthesizes knowledge with clarified values to encourage reflective decisions that guide action.
Encourages acceptance of existing ethnic, class, and racial stratification.	Focuses on social criticism and social change.

describing the sojourn of the Europeans across the Atlantic to the Americas, and then from the Atlantic to the Pacific (Cortés, 1976). The story focuses on European settlers, the way they shaped America in their image, created a nation that promised freedom for all, and made the United States a world power. Ethnic minorities such as blacks, Mexican-Americans, and native Americans are discussed primarily at points at which they interacted with the Europeans in North America.

A number of reasons have been posited to explain why the school curriculum — social studies in particular — has remained primarily Anglocentric and Eurocentric after more than two decades of attempted reform. Many teachers and principals state that they have not reformed the curriculum to reflect ethnic diversity in their schools because they do not have ethnic minorities in their school populations and, consequently, no racial or ethnic problems. These educators believe ethnic content is needed only by ethnic minority students or to help reduce ethnic conflict within schools having racial problems. This assumption is widespread and has existed at least since the early 1950s, when Hilda Taba (Taba, Brady, & Robinson, 1952) and her colleagues did their pioneering work in intergroup education.

Other reasons often given for the lack of progress since the 1960s in substantially reforming the curriculum to reflect ethnic and cultural diversity include the lack of effective teaching materials, ambivalent teacher attitudes toward ethnic diversity, and lack of administrative support. Although each of these reasons explains in part why multicultural content has not permeated the school curriculum in the last two decades, they do not reveal the basic reason. I believe that the resistance to multicultural content is basically ideological.

An ideology is a system of ideas, beliefs, traditions, principles, and myths held by a social group or society that reflects, rationalizes, and defends its particular social, political, and economic interests (Theodorson & Theodorson, 1969). Dominant ethnic and cultural groups develop ideologies to defend and rationalize their attitudes, goals, and social structures. Bullivant (1986a) writes, "In an analysis of ethnoculturally pluralistic societies the term *ideology* can be used to refer to the system of beliefs and values employed by a dominant ethnocultural group to legitimize its control over the life chances of subordinate ethnocultural groups" (p. 103). Bullivant calls this situation a form of "ethnic hegemony."

The dominant ideology related to ethnic and racial pluralism within the United States has been described using several different concepts, including the melting pot, Anglo conformity, and cultural assimilation (Gordon, 1964). This ideology states that the diverse ethnic and racial groups within the United States not only should but will eventually surrender their unique cultural and ethnic characteristics and acquire those of Anglo or mainstream Americans. Robert E. Park (Coser, 1977), the eminent U.S. sociologist who played a key role in the development of the Chicago School of Sociology, believed that race and ethnic relations were characterized by four inevitable phases: contact, conflict, accommodation, and assimilation.

Park's notion about inevitable cultural assimilation dominated U.S. social science until the ethnic revival movement emerged in the 1960s (Glazer & Moynihan, 1975). The assimilationist envisions a society and nation-state in which ethnic characteristics die of their own weight. Group affiliations within a modernized society, argues the assimilationist, are related to social class, occupation, education, and other voluntary and achieved statuses. The assimilationist believes that ethnic affiliations and attachments are antithetical to a modernized democratic society because they promote primordial affiliations, groups' rights over the rights of the individual, and particularistic concerns rather than the overarching goals of the nation-state (Patterson, 1977).

The assimilationist conception is not so much wrong as it is flawed and incomplete (Apter, 1977). By the late 1960s, ethnic minorities such as African-Americans, Mexican-Americans, and native Americans realized that no matter how culturally assimilated they became, they were often unable to attain structural assimilation and full participation in U.S. society. During most of their histories in the United States, these groups had worked diligently to become culturally assimilated and full participants in U.S. society (Glazer, 1977). In the late 1960s most nonwhite ethnic groups had become disillusioned with assimilation as an ideology and as a societal goal. They began to seriously question not only its desirability but also its latent function. Many ethnic minority leaders and scholars began to view assimilation as a tool that dominant ethnic groups used to rationalize and maintain their power and to keep victimized ethnic groups content with the status quo and yet striving to attain implausible goals (Sizemore, 1973).

During the ethnic revival movements of the 1960s and 1970s, ethnic minority scholars and leaders stridently attacked the assimilationist ideology and began to exhume and shape a pluralist ideology that they saw as more consistent with their social, economic, political, and educational aspirations (Ladner, 1973; Sizemore, 1973). This ideology maintains that the assimilationist claims about individual opportunity in the United States are a myth and that U.S. citizens are judged first as members of groups and only secondarily as individuals. The pluralists argue that individuals are rarely able to experience social and economic mobility beyond that of their ethnic or cultural group (Dickeman, 1973). Pluralists envision a curriculum that will strengthen family and ethnic attachments and help students develop a commitment to the liberation of their ethnic groups (Sizemore, 1973).

Assimilationists contend that they oppose a pluralist curriculum because it is un-American, will undercut American patriotism, will create ethnic Balkanization, and will prevent ethnic minority students from attaining the knowledge, attitudes, and skills they need to become effective participants in mainstream U.S. society and culture (Thernstrom, 1980). Pluralists maintain that mainstream Americans are strongly opposed to a pluralistic curriculum — which reinterprets the U.S. experience and presents diverse ethnic perspectives on the development of American society — because they fear it will undercut their dominant position in society and legitimize the quest of excluded ethnic groups for empowerment and significant social change (Dickeman, 1973; Sizemore, 1973).

TEACHING FOR SOCIAL CHANGE

A major goal of social studies education has traditionally been to socialize students so that they would accept, unquestionably, existing ideologies, institutions, and practices within their society and nation-state (Newmann, 1975). Political education within the United States has traditionally fostered political passivity rather than political action. Although several experimental political studies courses designed to foster political action were developed for students during the flurry of social studies curricular activity in the 1970s (Gillespie & Patrick, 1974), these projects have not substantially changed the nature of political education in the nation's schools. Students are taught to vote and to participate in the political system in ways that will not significantly reform U.S. society. Newmann (1968) writes:

> By teaching that the constitutional system of the U.S. guarantees a benevolent government serving the needs of all, the schools have fostered massive public apathy. Whereas the Protestant ethic calls for engagement (to survive economically one must *earn* a living), the political creed breeds passivity. One need not struggle for political rights, but only maintain a vague level of vigilance, obey the laws, make careful choices in elections, perform a few duties (taxes, military service), and his political welfare is assured (p. 536).

Even though the schools teach students the expressed ideals of justice and equality dominant within U.S. society, rarely do we deliberately educate students for social change and help them to acquire the knowledge, attitudes, and skills needed to help close the gap between our democratic ideals and societal realities. A major goal of the social studies curriculum should be to help students acquire the knowledge, values, and skills they need to participate in social change so that victimized and excluded ethnic and racial groups can become full participants in U.S. society. To participate effectively in social change, students must be taught social criticism. We must help them to understand the inconsistency between our ideals and social realities, what is required to close this gap, and how they can, as individuals and groups, influence the social and political systems in U.S. society (Newmann, 1975).

When conceptualizing a social studies curriculum designed to promote civic action and social change, we need to seriously ponder the arguments by the revisionists (Katz, 1975) and the neo-Marxist scholars (Bowles & Gintis, 1976). They contend that the school is incapable of teaching students to be agents of change because one of its major roles is to reproduce the social structure and to socialize students so that they will passively accept their position in our society stratified by class and ethnicity. The radical critics of the schools, especially those in the United Kingdom, have been keenly critical of multiethnic studies as a strategy to promote social change (Modgil, Verma, Mallick, & Modgil , 1986). They argue that multiethnic studies are a palliative to keep excluded and oppressed groups from rebelling against a system that promotes structural inequality and institutionalized racism (Carby, 1980). The radical scholars also claim that multiethnic studies avoid any serious analysis of class, racism, power, capitalism, and other systems that keep excluded ethnic groups powerless. Multiethnic studies, they argue, divert attention from the real problems and issues. Instead, they focus on the victim as the problem.

It is difficult to completely reject the argument that one of the school's major roles is to socialize students so that they will fit into the existing social order. However, the revisionists and other radical scholars overstate the case when they argue that the schools merely socialize students into the existing social order. The school itself is contradictory since it often expounds democratic values while at the same time contradicting them. While the school socializes students into the existing social structure, it also enables some students to acquire the knowledge, attitudes, and skills needed to participate effectively in social action and social change.

THE TEACHER AS CULTURAL MEDIATOR AND AGENT OF CHANGE

Whether it is a deliberate goal of the school or not, many students learn compassion and democratic ideals and develop a commitment to participate in social change from powerful and influential classroom teachers. These teachers are also cultural mediators who interpret the mainstream and ethnic cultures to students from diverse cultural groups and help students understand the desirability and possibility of social change. Many such teachers participated in social action in the 1960s and 1970s to promote social justice and human rights. Today, many social studies teachers are deeply concerned about apartheid in South Africa and about the possibility of a nuclear holocaust.

The school — primarily through the influence of teachers who have clarified and reflective commitments to democratic values, knowledge, and pedagogical skills and the charisma to inspire others — can play a significant role in teaching social criticism and motivating students to become involved in social change (see Figure 13.1). Some teachers have a significant influence on the values, hopes, and dreams of their students. The social studies classroom should be a forum of open inquiry where diverse points of view and perspectives are shared and analyzed reflectively. Teachers committed to human freedom and other overarching American ideals should feel free to express their views in the classroom, provided that students first have an opportunity to freely express and defend their beliefs, and that teachers defend their beliefs and moral

FIGURE 13.1 — The Teacher as Cultural Mediator and Agent of Social Change

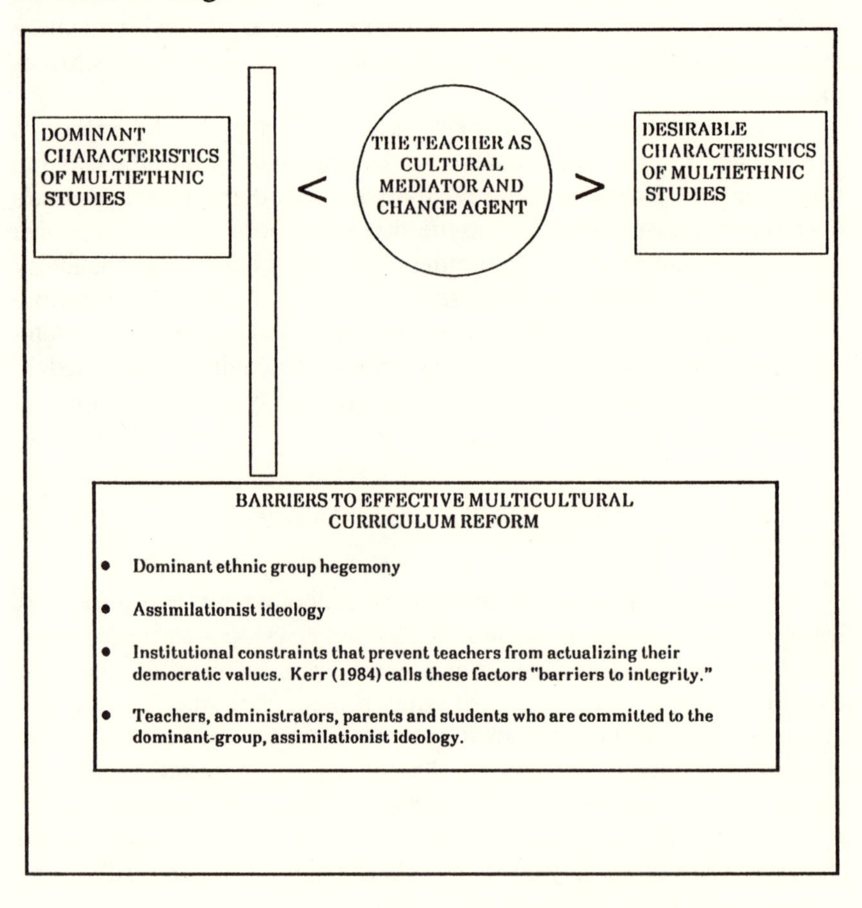

choices reflectively and in ways consistent with American democratic values, such as human dignity, justice, and equality (Oliver & Shaver, 1966).

In a democratic society, students and teachers should freely express morally and intellectually defensible values and beliefs about human freedom (Shaver & Strong, 1982). Teaching, like social science inquiry, is not a value-neutral activity. This is especially the case in the social studies, where teachers and students must deal with human problems, conflicts, and dilemmas toward which it is impossible to remain neutral. Both teachers and social scientists have often been admonished to strive for objectivity in their work. Although teachers should not use the classroom as a forum to promote partisan political beliefs, they should, like caring social scientists, become "involved observers," to borrow Kenneth B. Clark's (1965) apt phrase. Clark eloquently states his creed for social scientists, which is also appropriate for social studies teachers:

> An important part of my creed as a social scientist is that on the grounds of absolute objectivity or on a posture of scientific detachment and indifference, a true and serious social science cannot ask to be taken seriously by a society desperately in need of moral and empirical guidance in human affairs. . . . I believe that to be taken seriously, to be viable, and to be relevant social science must dare to study the real problems of men and society, must use the real community, the market place, the arena of politics and power as its laboratories, and must confront and seek to understand the dynamics of social action and social change (p. xxi).

Teachers who support human freedom, justice, and equality can motivate students to engage in social action to improve the human condition. Individual teachers — not schools per se — can and do help students develop the ideals, knowledge, and skills needed to reform society. They do this by exemplifying a commitment to democratic values in the content they select, in their interpretations of social and historical events, and in their words and deeds. While respecting the beliefs and diversity of their students and helping them to develop social science inquiry skills, social studies teachers can support democracy, equality, and the empowerment of victimized racial and ethnic groups (Cummins, 1986).

If teachers are to be the primary agents for change in schools, we must keep democratic values, teaching, and commitments foremost in mind when we select and train individuals for teaching. A major goal of our selection and training process must be to place in the classroom teachers who have strong and clarified democratic values and the knowledge and skills to implement a curriculum that will enable students to acquire the content, commitment, and competencies needed to participate in democratic social change. Training programs that are designed to help teachers to become effective cultural mediators and agents of change must help them to acquire social science knowledge, derived using a process in which the goals, assumptions, and values of knowledge are learned; clarified cultural identifications; positive intergroup and racial attitudes; and pedagogical skills [see Appendix 13] (Banks, 1986). To select and train teachers successfully is probably the most challenging and difficult task that lies ahead for those of us who would like to see the schools —

and the elementary social studies curriculum in particular — become a vehicle for social change and human betterment.

APPENDIX 13: CHARACTERISTICS OF THE EFFECTIVE TEACHER IN A MULTICULTURAL SOCIETY

Knowledge

The effective teacher has social science knowledge derived through a process by which the goals, assumptions, and values of society are learned and pedagogical knowledge of the characteristics of students from diverse ethnic, racial, and cultural groups and social classes, prejudice and prejudice reduction theory and research, and teaching strategies and techniques.

Clarified Cultural Identification

The effective teacher has a reflective and clarified understanding of his or her cultural heritage and experience and how they relate to and interact with the experiences of other ethnic and cultural groups.

Positive Intergroup and Racial Attitudes

The effective teacher has clarified and positive attitudes toward different racial, ethnic, and cultural groups and social classes.

Pedagogical Skills

The effective teacher has the skills to make effective instructional decisions, reduce prejudice and intergroup conflict, and formulate and devise a range of teaching strategies and activities to facilitate the academic achievement of students from diverse racial, ethnic, and cultural groups and social classes.

REFERENCES

Apter, D. (1977). Political life and cultural pluralism. In M. M. Tumin & W. Plotch (Eds.), *Pluralism in a democratic society* (pp. 58–91). New York: Praeger.

Baldwin, J. (1985). *The price of the ticket: Collected nonfiction, 1948–1985*. New York: St. Martin's/Marek.

Banks, J. A. (Ed.). (1973). *Teaching ethnic studies concepts and strategies*. Washington, DC: National Council for the Social Studies.

Banks, J. A. (1981). *Multiethnic education: Theory and practice*. Boston: Allyn & Bacon.

Banks, J. A. (1984a). *Teaching strategies for ethnic studies* (3rd ed.). Boston: Allyn & Bacon.

Banks, J. A. (1984b). Values, ethnicity, social science research, and educational policy. In B. Ladner (Ed.), *The humanities in precollegiate education* (83rd Yearbook of the National Society for the Study of Education, pp. 91–111). Chicago: University of Chicago Press.

Banks, J. A. (1986). Multicultural teacher education: Knowledge, skills, and processes. In *Intercultural training of teachers* (Report from a Conference in Kolmarden, Sweden, June 10–14, 1985, pp. 99–122). Stockholm: National Board of Universities and Colleges.

Banks, J. A., & Lynch, J. (Eds.). (1986). *Multicultural education in western societies*. New York: Praeger.

Banton, J. (1983). *Racial and ethnic competition*. Cambridge: Cambridge University Press.

Baratz, J. (1970). Teaching reading in an urban Negro school system. In F. Williams (Ed.), *Language and poverty: Perspectives on a theme* (pp. 11–24). Chicago: Markham.

Beals, A. R., Spindler, G., & Spindler, L. (1967). *Culture in process*. New York: Holt, Rinehart & Winston.

Billingsley, A. (1968). *Black families in white America*. Englewood Cliffs, NJ: Prentice-Hall.

Blassingame, J. W. (Ed.). (1971). *New perspective on black studies*. Urbana: University of Illinois Press.

Bowles, S., & Gintis. H. (1976). *Schooling in capitalist America*. New York: Basic Books.

Bullivant, B. M. (1986a). Multicultural education in Australia: An unresolved debate. In J. A. Banks & J. Lynch (Eds.), *Multicultural education in western societies* (pp. 98–124). New York: Praeger.

Bullivant, B. M. (1986b). Towards radical multiculturalism: Resolving tensions in curriculum and educational planning. In S. Modgil, G. Verma, K. Mallick, & C. Modgil (Eds.), *Multicultural education: The interminable debate* (pp. 33–47). London: Falmer.

Carby, H. V. (1980). *Multicultural fictions* (Occasional Paper, Race Series, SP No. 58). Birmingham, AL: Birmingham Southern College.

Clark, K. B. (1965). *Dark ghetto: Dilemmas of social power*. New York: Harper Torchbooks.

Clark, K. B. (1973). Social policy, power, and social science research. *Harvard Educational Review, 43*, 113–21.

Cortés, C. E. (1976). Need for a geo-cultural perspective in the bicentennial. *Educational Leadership, 33*, 290–92.

Coser, L. A. (1977). *Masters of sociological thought: Ideas in historical and social context* (2d ed.). New York: Harcourt.

Cuban, L. (1968, September 21). Black history, Negro history, and white folk. *Saturday Review*, pp. 64–65.

Cummins, J. (1986). Empowering minority students: A framework for intervention. *Harvard Educational Review, 56,* 18–36.

Dickeman, M. (1973). Teaching cultural pluralism. In J. A. Banks (Ed.), *Teaching ethnic studies: Concepts and strategies* (43rd Yearbook of the National Council for the Social Studies, pp. 5–25). Washington, DC: National Council for the Social Studies.

Edmonds, R., Billingsley, A., Comer, J., Dyer, J., Hall, W., Hill, R., McGhee, N., Reddick, L., Taylor, H., & Wright, S. (1973). A black response to Christopher Jenck's inequality and certain other issues. *Harvard Educational Review, 43,* 76–91.

Farmer, J. (1985). *Lay bare the heart: An autobiography of the civil rights movement.* New York: Arbor House.

Fitzgerald, R. (1979). *America revisited: History textbooks in the twentieth century.* New York: Vintage.

Garcia, J., & Goebel, J. (1985). A comparative study of the portrayal of black Americans in selected U.S. history textbooks. *Negro Educational Review, 36,* 118–27.

Geertz, C. (1973). *The interpretation of cultures.* New York: Basic Books.

Genovese, E. D. (1974). *Roll, Jordan roll: The world the slaves made.* New York: Pantheon.

Gillespie, J. A., & Patrick, J. J. (1974). *Comparing political experiences.* Washington, DC: American Political Science Association.

Glazer, N. (1977). Cultural pluralism: The social aspect. In M. M. Tumin & W. Plotch (Eds.), *Pluralism in a democratic society* (pp. 3–24). New York: Praeger.

Glazer, N., & Moynihan, D. P. (Eds.). (1975). *Ethnicity: Theory and experience.* Cambridge, MA: Harvard University Press.

Gordon, M. M. (1964). *Assimilation in American life.* New York: Oxford University Press.

Gutman, H. G. (1970). *The black family in slavery and freedom, 1750–1925.* New York: Vintage.

Hill, R. B. (1971). *The strengths of black families.* New York: Emerson Hall.

Jencks, C., Smith, M., Acland, H., Bane, M. J., Cohen, D., Gintis, H., Heyns, B., & Michelson, S. (1972). *Inequality: A reassessment of the effect of family and schooling in America.* New York: Basic Books.

Johnston, W. J. (Ed.). (1985). *Education on trial.* San Francisco: Institute for Contemporary Studies.

Katz, M. B. (1975). *Class, bureaucracy, and schools: The illusion of educational change in America* (expanded ed.). New York: Praeger.

Kerr, D. (1984). *Barriers to integrity: Modern modes of knowledge utilization.* Boulder: Westview.

Ladner, J. (Ed.). (1973). *The death of white sociology.* New York: Vintage.

Merton, R. K. (1972). Insiders and outsiders: A chapter in the sociology of knowledge. *American Journal of Sociology, 78,* 9–47.

Modgil, S., Verma, G., Mallick, K., & Modgil, C. (Eds.). (1986). *Multicultural education: The interminable debate.* London: Falmer

Moodley, K. A. (1986). Canadian multicultural education. In J. A. Banks & J. Lynch (Eds.), *Multicultural education in western societies* (pp. 51–75). New York: Praeger.

Moynihan, D. P. (1965). *The Negro family: The case for national action.* Washington, DC: U.S. Department of Labor, Office of Planning and Research.

Mullard, C. (1980). *Racism in society and schools: History, policy, and practice* (Occasional Paper No. 1). London: University of London, Institute of Education, Centre for Multicultural Education.

Nakano, T. U., & Nakano, L. (1980). *Within the barbed wire fence: A Japanese man's account of his internment.* Seattle: University of Washington Press.

National Commission on Excellence in Education. (1983). *A nation at risk.* Washington, DC: U.S. Department of Education.

Newmann, F. M. (1968). Discussion: Political socialization in the schools. *Harvard Educational Review, 38,* 536–45.

Newmann, F. M. (1975). *Education for citizen action: Challenge for secondary curriculum.* Berkeley, CA: McCutchan.

Oliver, D. W., & Shaver, J. P. (1966). *Teaching public issues in the high school.* New York: Houghton Mifflin.

Patterson, O. (1977). *Ethnic chauvinism: The reactionary impulse.* New York: Stein & Day.

Raines, H. (1977). *My soul is rested: Movement days in the deep south remembered.* New York: G. P. Putnam Sons.

Reissman, F. (1962). *The culturally deprived child.* New York: Harper & Row.

Shaver, J. P., & Strong, W. (1982). *Facing value decisions: Rationale-building for teachers* (2d ed.). New York: Teachers College Press.

Sizemore, B. A. (1973). Shattering the melting pot myth. In J. A. Banks (Ed.), *Teaching ethnic studies: Concepts and strategies* (pp. 73–101). Washington, DC: National Council for the Social Studies.

Sowell, T. (1984). *Civil rights: Rhetoric or reality?* New York: Wm. Morrow.

Taba, H., Brady, E. H., & Robinson, J. T. (1952). *Intergroup education in public schools.* Washington, DC: American Council on Education.

Theodorson, G. A., & Theodorson, A. G. (1969). *A modern dictionary of sociology.* New York: Barnes & Noble.

Thernstrom, A. M. (1980). E Pluribus Plura — Congress and bilingual education. *Public Interest, 60,* 3–22.

Valentine, C. A. (1968). *Culture and poverty: Critique and counter-proposals.* Chicago: University of Chicago Press.

White, J. L. (1984). *The psychology of blacks.* Englewood Cliffs, NJ: Prentice-Hall.

Wilson, J. W. (1978). *The declining significance of race: Blacks and changing American institutions.* Chicago: University of Chicago Press.

14

Abating the Shortage of Black Teachers

Antoine M. Garibaldi

Since 1983 all of the major educational reports have focused on the need for reform in our nation's schools. The majority of these reports have emphasized that elementary and secondary students are performing significantly below grade level due in large part to low academic standards, low expectations, and a lack of discipline. However, American education faces a much more formidable challenge as it approaches the last decade of the twentieth century, namely, the recruitment and retention of quality teachers for elementary and secondary schools. Many school systems across the country, particularly in the South and the West, are already confronted with critical teacher shortages. Even more important is the fact that as the number of nonwhite students in major metropolitan school districts approaches or exceeds 50 percent, the number of nonwhite teachers continues to decline sharply.

This chapter focuses primarily on the reduction of black teachers and delineates the critical need for these teachers as schools become more ethnically diverse. The latter half of the chapter is a summary of a recently completed research project supported by the Southern Education Foundation on the reduction of black teachers in Louisiana. Concluding thoughts are offered on what actions are necessary to prevent the extinction of black teachers.

This chapter is based on a presentation delivered in November 1986 at the Seventh Annual Conference on the Survival and Preparation of Black Teachers, Norfolk State University.

TEACHER SHORTAGES AND SCHOOL ENROLLMENTS

The adverse impact of teacher shortages is compounded by an increasingly large cohort of school-aged children entering the classroom for the first time. The U.S. Census projects that the number of children aged 5 to 13 will increase from 30.7 million to 34.4 million between 1981 and 1995. School-age populations declined slightly more than 5 percent, to 44.9 percent, between 1980 and 1984, but the number of preschoolers rose 9 percent, to an estimated 17.8 million, during that same period. Moreover, first-grade enrollments rose 185,000 during the same four-year period to 3,079,000 after experiencing a 33-year low of 2,894,000 (And Now, 1985).

Feistritzer (1985) further indicates that the "new baby boom is disproportionately non-white." While the number of white children under the age of five decreased by 2.7 percent between 1970 and 1982 (14,464,000 to 14,075,000), Feistritzer states that black children in this age group had an 11.6 percent gain (2,434,000 to 2,717,000). Further analyses for white and black children between the ages of 5 and 13 show similar trends: a 19.8 percent decline for white children and a 9.9 percent drop for black children. The 14- to 17-year age group had an overall decline of 5.6 percent; white teenagers in this cohort declined 9.1 percent, while blacks increased by 7.1 percent (Feistritzer, 1985).

Most school districts are now populated with children from many varied ethnic and socioeconomic backgrounds. There was a 5 percent increase in the number of minority children in public elementary and secondary schools between 1970 and 1981 (from 21.7% to 26.7%), and Feistritzer's analysis of school estimates projects that this number will reach one-third by 1995. With respect to socioeconomic characteristics, more poor children are also entering school today than five years ago. Approximately 13 million of the 69 million children under the age of 15 live below the poverty line, compared with 10 million of the 69 million children in 1970 (Feistritzer, 1985). In 1980 almost 27 percent of public elementary and secondary school students were from nonwhite backgrounds. Thus, Feistritzer's estimate that public school enrollments will have a minority representation of 33 percent by 1995 and Goertz and Pitcher's (1985) projection that more than 53 major metropolitan school districts will be majority nonwhite by the turn of the century is very plausible.

The Sun Belt states have experienced the greatest increase in population in recent years, and minority enrollments in schools have similarly increased. A survey of enrollments in the 50 states indicates that public elementary and secondary enrollments between 1972 and 1982 increased in seven states — all in the South and West (Utah and Wyoming had the largest increase, with enrollment gains of 21% and 19%, respectively). Elementary enrollments rose nationally by 54,000 in 1984–85, and similar gains are expected into the 1990s. Texas, for example, expects enrollments of 5.25 million by the year 2000 (an increase of almost 2 million children from 1970). California, with 4.1 million children, anticipates an additional 724,000 by the year 1991, and Florida's public school population, 1.56 million in 1984, is projected to be 2.1 million by the year 2000 (And Now, 1985). Even states that had experienced sharp declines between 1972 and 1983 — Louisiana (down 8.5%), North Dakota (down 17.6%), and Minnesota (down 21%) — increased their enrollments by an average of 3 percent between 1983–84 and 1984–85 (Feistritzer, 1985).

Marked increases in school enrollment nationwide come at a time when fewer young people are considering the teaching profession and veteran teachers are leaving the classroom because of dissatisfaction with their careers, the lure of more lucrative jobs and fields with promotional ladders, or the attainment of retirement age.

REDUCTION OF EDUCATION GRADUATES

The shortage of black teachers is not an isolated event in higher education, but rather reflects all college students' declining interest in choosing education as a career. In 1970 almost 20 percent of all first-time, full-time first-year students indicated a preference for education as a "probable career occupation." In 1982 less than 5 percent of similar students indicated a preference for education. While recent data have indicated an increasing proportion of students interested in majoring in education — 6.2 percent in 1985 and 7.3 percent in 1986 — the proportion of prospective teachers is far short of levels existing 20 years ago, and it is unlikely the supply will meet the need in the next decade (Astin, 1986).

The number of teacher education graduates has dropped significantly in absolute numbers. In 1972–73 there were 313,000 teacher education graduates; less than ten years later in 1980–81, only 141,000 teacher education students graduated, a decline of 45 percent. The greatest decline occurred between 1975 and 1977, when the number of teacher education graduates dropped from 243,000 to slightly more than 190,000 (FYI, 1983). This decline continues today and is even more acute for minority students.

COLLEGE ENROLLMENT OF BLACK STUDENTS

Until 1976, the peak year for college enrollment by black students, education was the most popular career choice among black students. In 1976 blacks received 14,095 undergraduate degrees in education, or almost one-fifth of the total awarded to the group. In 1981, however, blacks received 5,000 less education degrees (9,471) than in 1976, or almost one-seventh of their total undergraduate awards (National Center for Education Statistics, 1983). The 1976 share of degrees awarded to blacks amounted to 9.2 percent of all education bachelor's degrees awarded that year across the nation; in 1982 the proportion was 8.8 percent of the total. Clearly, percentages can be misleading, since the four-tenths of a percent difference between 1976 and 1981 does not show the magnitude of the decline of black education graduates.

On closer inspection two points become obvious in the production of black education majors. First, two-thirds (9,325) of all education degrees awarded to blacks in 1976 and 69 percent (6,518) in 1981 were awarded by southern institutions. Second, almost three-fourths of these degrees — 74 percent in 1976 and 63 percent in 1981 — were awarded by historically black institutions (Trent, 1984). These two items are obviously interrelated because 90 percent of all historically black colleges and universities are located in the southeastern and southwestern United States (Garibaldi, 1984). Though there are some predominantly black colleges in Trent's data, the bulk of the degrees were awarded by historically black institutions. Even more interesting is that black colleges accounted for more that half (55%) of all black bachelor's degrees in education in 1976 and 48 percent in 1981.

These institutions continue to play a pivotal role in producing black teacher education students, but the numbers they enroll in these programs are much smaller than ten years ago. This is clearly demonstrated in the next section, which presents results from a case study of Louisiana's declining numbers of black teachers between 1976 and 1983. Southern states such as Louisiana will therefore face the greatest challenge in employing a proportional cadre of black and other nonwhite teachers to match the ethnically diverse student populations of their schools.

REDUCTION OF BLACK TEACHERS IN LOUISIANA

In 1982–83 the state with the highest proportional share of minority teachers (35.3%) was Louisiana; at that time Louisiana had a minority student population of 43.3 percent. However, as the previously discussed National Center for Education Statistics (NCES) data indicate, graduation rates of black education majors have been declining nationally. Thus, a study was conducted to assess the extent of the decreasing numbers of black teachers in Louisiana between 1976 and 1983. The study, entitled *The Decline of Teacher Production in Louisiana (1976–1983) and Attitudes Toward the Profession* (Garibaldi, 1986), originally set out to prove that there had indeed been a decline in the number of black teacher education graduates. However, the acquisition of more extensive data made it possible to determine that there had also been a decline in the number of white teachers in this state. The results of the study are based on the following information:

analyses of education degrees awarded between 1976 and 1983 for Louisiana's 21 schools, colleges, and education departments, using institutional data submitted for the federal government's Higher Education General Information Survey (HEGIS);

estimates of the number of black education graduates certified to teach shortly after receiving their degrees;

surveys and interviews with 101 black and white education majors and 214 black and white noneducation majors, assessing their attitudes toward the teaching profession and those factors they considered important in enticing them into a teaching career; and

analyses of passing rates on the National Teachers Examination (NTE) for black and white test takers in Louisiana between 1978 and 1982.

Because of space limitations, the majority of the results for each of these sections will be discussed only briefly.

Production of Education Graduates in Louisiana

Results from the HEGIS analyses demonstrated that there had indeed been a marked decline in the number of education graduates in Louisiana. In 1982–83, there were almost 1,500 fewer education graduates among Louisiana's schools, colleges, and departments of education than there were in 1976. In 1982–83, only 1,864 bachelor's degrees in education were conferred, compared to 3,386 in 1976–77.

Declines at the five historically black colleges have been significant. In 1976–77, these five institutions graduated 745 education majors, or 22 percent of all education degrees awarded in the state. But in 1982–83, Louisiana's black colleges only awarded 242 education bachelor's degrees, or 13 percent of all education degrees in the state. Nevertheless, the five black colleges accounted for the lion's share of all education degrees awarded to black education majors in the state: 67 percent in 1982–83 compared to a previous high of 79 percent in 1976–77.

Although the above data are very disturbing, the reader must recognize that teacher surpluses in many school districts during the late 1970s, as well as newly imposed certification requirements in the state in 1978 (e.g., the NTE), eliminated many prospective black teachers and discouraged other potential teacher education majors from choosing the discipline. The best documentation for that assertion comes from the declining proportion of education graduates to the total number of bachelor's degrees awarded in the state's postsecondary institutions. For example, the average percent decline of education graduates to total undergraduate degrees awarded by the state's 21 schools, colleges, and education departments, when comparing 1976–77 data to 1982–83 data, was 8 percent. But the average percent decline for the five black colleges during those years was more than 17 percent. More specifically, 37 percent of all bachelor's degrees awarded by two of the state's public black colleges and 20 percent of the two private black colleges in 1976–77 went to education majors; in 1982–83, only 12 percent of the total undergraduate degrees awarded by the two public black colleges and less than 5 percent awarded by the two private institutions were in the field of education.

Education and Noneducation Majors Surveys

Survey questionnaires were developed and modeled after similar instruments devised by Mangieri and Kemper (1984) to assess how education and noneducation majors rated the present state of classroom teaching and preservice teacher education. For noneducation majors, the questionnaire focused more on key factors that might interest them in choosing teaching as a career. Both questionnaires allowed students to provide their answers on a Likert-type scale of agreement to disagreement: strongly agree, agree, no opinion, disagree, strongly disagree. An example of a statement for an education major is: "I want to become a teacher so I can serve others." However, all statements for noneducation majors began with the same stem: "I would become a teacher if . . . starting salaries were higher." There were 18 items for the 101 education majors and 17 statements for the 214 noneducation majors. The total sample included 154 black and 161 white students.

The results clearly showed that both groups of students agreed that salaries and fringe benefits for teachers should be increased. While both groups recognized the importance of serving others as an incentive to become teachers, noneducation majors believed that more career advancement opportunities and job security were much more important. Furthermore, these majors agreed with education majors that teachers deserve greater respect from the communities in which they teach.

A small sample of education majors (95) and noneducation majors (30) at a few of the institutions were also interviewed to amplify the data obtained on the survey questionnaires. Approximately 80 percent of both groups felt that academic and admission criteria were not too high and that the education curricula were challenging and difficult. Neither group believed that academic requirements should be lowered to attract more students into the profession. Noneducation majors indicated that if more college financial aid was offered, they might indeed consider majoring in a preprofessional teacher education program. On the other hand, education majors were strongly committed to their academic field and future profession and stated that they would have pursued education even if financial aid was not available. Ninety-five percent of education majors said that service to others was their most important reason for studying to become a teacher.

Finally, the surveys and interviews confirmed that both black and white education majors were concerned about passing the NTE. However, while black students had significantly more anxiety about passing certification exams, white students tended to be much more concerned about the poor working conditions of the teaching profession. By way of general comparison, many students said that the obstacle to their interest in teaching was the working conditions (69%), while only 20 percent were concerned about the required certification exams.

Teacher Certification and the National Teachers Examination

The most significant result of this study was the small numbers of black Louisiana education majors who were certifiable after completing their preprofessional education programs. The primary reason for their noncertifiable status must be attributed to their inability to achieve the NTE qualifying scores prescribed by the state. The legislative requirement to pass the NTE for certification was established by the state in 1978.

Though more than 40 states now require teacher education majors to pass some form of competency exam to obtain a teaching certificate, the high failure rates of black and other minority education majors on these types of certification exams has been documented in recent years by a number of researchers.[1] This issue is important because, with already smaller numbers of black education graduates, there is no guarantee that those who graduate will be eligible to teach in most states unless they are able to pass these examinations.

Trying to estimate the number of blacks (and whites) who actually became certified to teach in Louisiana shortly after graduation was difficult in this study, since the department responsible for teacher certification did not keep data by race. However, it was possible to make some interpolations for blacks since the five historically black institutions in the state are 98 percent black. Thus, comparisons were made between the number of black education graduates from these five historically black institutions (three public and two private) and the number of black individuals certified to teach by the state. While these are estimates, they are fairly approximate indicators of how many blacks were certified during the years data were available (1979–83).

Despite the production of representative numbers of black education graduates by the state's black and predominantly white institutions (see Table 14.1), estimates suggest that meager numbers of blacks were being certified to teach in Louisiana. Only 3 percent, or 80, of the teaching

TABLE 14.1
Total Education Degrees Awarded by All Louisiana Institutions and Historically Black Colleges and Universities (HBCUs), 1976–83

Academic Year	*Total Ed. Degrees*[a]	*HBCU Ed. Degrees*[b]	*HBCU % of Total Ed. Degrees Awarded*
1976–77	3,386	745	22
1977–78	2,847[c]	732	26
1978–79	2,907	750	26
1979–80	2,352	567	24
1980–81	2,061	402	20
1981–82	1,869	302	16
1982–83	1,864	242	13

[a]N = 21
[b]N = 5
[c]N = 19

Source: HEGIS data cited in Garibaldi, A. M. (1986). *The decline of teacher production in Louisiana (1976–1983) and attitudes toward the profession.* Atlanta: Southern Education Foundation.

majors from the five black colleges and universities were certified in 1978–79 and 1979–80, even though there were 750 black college education graduates in 1978–79 and 567 in 1979–80. (Both graduation years are cited here because an individual usually applies for certification immediately after graduation or during the subsequent year.) In 1982–83, only 6 percent, or 116, teaching certificates were awarded to black graduates from these same five institutions, although there were 544 graduates between the 1981–82 and 1982–83 academic years.

The only reasonable and documented evidence for this large discrepancy between the number of black college education graduates and the number of individuals from these schools who obtained state certification is their less-than-20-percent passing rate on the NTE during those years (see Table 14.2). Between 1978 and 1982, only 211 (18%) of 1,400 Louisiana blacks who took the NTE met the qualifying scores of the state. However, 4,000 of 5,200 whites who took the test during this same period achieved the qualifying score, a pass rate of 78 percent. These data clearly explain why large numbers of education graduates from predominantly white institutions, the vast majority of whom were white, and fewer graduates from historically black institutions were being certified to teach shortly after receiving their degrees.

While recent data show that the state's black college students are doing much better on the NTE — 70 of 111 (63%) during 1984–85 and 29 of 36 (81%) tested in fall 1985 met the qualifying score — the number of black students entering and finishing these programs is quite small.

TABLE 14.2
Distribution of Louisiana NTE Test Takers by Race, 1978–82

Year	*Blacks*	*Blacks as Percentage of Total*	*Whites*	*Whites as Percentage of Total*
1978–79[a]	536	24.0	1,720	76.0
1979–80	390	22.6	1,357	77.4
1980–81	298	19.3	1,175	80.7
1981–82	170	21.1	970	84.9
Total	1,394	21.1	5,222	78.9

[a]Academic years cited reflect three test administrations in December, May, and August: 1978–79 includes December 1978, May 1979, and August 1980.

Source: Derived from Louisiana Board of Regents Planning and Research Committee. (1983). Performance of Louisiana students on the NTE by race — December 1978–August 1982.

Significant efforts by the black colleges in revising curricula, providing test-taking seminars, and admitting students with higher college entrance scores have all helped produce education graduates eligible to teach. But expanding the pool of black teachers — the greatest challenge ahead — will first require the enrollment of more black students in college and, second, the recruitment of more black students to the field of education.

CONCLUSION AND RECOMMENDATIONS

The future shortage of quality teachers is just one of the many problems American education must resolve before entering the next century, for educational reforms cannot be successfully implemented without highly qualified teachers in elementary and secondary schools. To abate this shortage of teachers, the general public, national and state legislators, educators, business leaders, and professionals must advocate the importance of teaching and education in society. Thus, America's greatest challenge will be to develop effective teacher recruiting strategies. Below are a few of the author's strategic recommendations, some of which are now being implemented.

Salaries for teachers must be increased in all regions of the country and maintained at a level comparable to the national average.

Financial incentives (e.g., scholarships and forgivable loans) should be offered to academically talented high school graduates interested in teaching.

Liberal arts, science, and undecided majors should be recruited to apply their academic skills as teachers.

Junior and senior high schools should establish future teachers clubs and offer seminars or courses in the art of teaching.

Local citizens, civic and community organizations, businesses, the media, and other sources of influence must assume leadership in improving the image of education and the teaching profession.

Specific institutional remedies should be established to improve the performance of blacks on certification exams such as the NTE.

These efforts, combined with a larger pool of black students in college, will undoubtedly help to assure that the shortage of black teachers is abated before the turn of the century.

NOTE

1. See particularly Goertz, M., and Pitcher, B. (1985). *The impact of NTE use by states on teacher selection.* Princeton, NJ: Educational Testing Service; and Garcia,

P. A. (1986). *A study on teacher competency testing and test validity with implications for minorities and the results and implications of the use of the Pre-Professional Skills Test (PPST) as a screening device for entrance into teacher education programs in Texas.* Edinburgh, TX: Pan American University.

REFERENCES

And now, a teacher shortage. (1985, July 22). *Time,* p. 63.

Astin, A. C. (1986). *The American freshman: National norms for fall 1986.* Los Angeles: University of California, Higher Education Research Institute.

Feistritzer, C. E. (1985). *The condition of teaching: A state by state analysis, 1983.* Princeton, NJ: Carnegie Foundation for the Advancement of Teaching.

FYI: Enrollment projections suggest teacher shortage in late 1980's. (1983, January & February). *Journal of Teacher Education, 34* (1).

Garibaldi, A. M. (1984). *Black colleges and universities: Challenges for the future.* New York: Praeger.

Garibaldi, A. M. (1986). *The decline of teacher production in Louisiana (1976–1983) and attitudes toward the profession.* Atlanta: Southern Education Foundation.

Goertz, M. E., & Pitcher, B. (1985). *The impact of NTE use by states on teacher selection.* Princeton, NJ: Educational Testing Service.

Mangieri, J. N., & Kemper, R. E. (1984). *Factors related to high school students' interest in teaching as a profession.* Fort Worth, TX: Texas Christian University.

National Center for Education Statistics. (1983, November). *Participation of black students in higher education: A statistical profile from 1970–71 to 1980–81.* Washington, DC: U.S. Department of Education.

Trent, W. T. (1984, May). Equity considerations in higher education: Race and sex differences in degree attainment and major field from 1976 through 1981. *American Journal of Education.*

15

The Field and Function of Black Studies

James B. Stewart

> The university must become not simply a center of knowledge but a center of applied knowledge and guide of action. And this is all the more necessary now since we easily see that planned action especially in economic life is going to be the watchword of civilization. . . . [S]tarting with present conditions and using the facts and the knowledge of the present situation of American Negroes, the Negro university expands toward the possession and the conquest of all knowledge. It seeks from a beginning of the history of the Negro in America and in Africa to interpret all history; from a beginning of social development among slaves and freedmen in America and Negro tribes and kingdoms in Africa, to interpret and understand the social development of all mankind in all ages. It seeks to reach modern science of matter and life from the surroundings and habits and aptitudes of American Negroes and thus lead up to understanding of life and matter in the universe.
>
> — W. E. B. Du Bois

This vision of the developmental objective of historically black institutions of higher education articulated by W. E. B. Du Bois in 1933 (1973, pp. 5–6) provides a historical context for the modern black studies

Adaptation of the title of the Fisk Memorial Address delivered by W. E. B. Du Bois in 1933 entitled *The field and function of the Negro college*.

movement and its development over the last two decades. Black studies builds on Du Bois's mandate via its emphasis on:

looking backward to understand the present;
institutionalizing itself in centers of learning while maintaining strong ties to and active involvement in black communities;
becoming a self-perpetuating enterprise; and
looking forward in efforts to contribute to the development of viable public policies that can insure black progress into and during the twenty-first century.

This chapter reviews the progress made toward realizing each of these objectives.

THE MARCH OF HISTORY

For black studies scholars looking backward has meant an emphasis on history and historical analysis. Karenga (1982) argues that black history is "indispensable to the introduction and development of all the other subject areas. Black history places them in perspective, establishes their origins and developments, and thus, aids in critical discussion and understanding of them" (p. 43).

In response to the combination of intellectual alienation created by the absence or distortion of the black experience in pre-existing curricula and cultural alienation generated by the unfamiliar and antagonistic milieu, the first wave of black students entering predominantly white colleges and universities in the mid-1960s offered black history as simply a starting point. It was inevitable that a broader call for a comprehensive interdisciplinary curriculum that used history as a foundation would be made. Historical support for this approach can also be found in the writings of Du Bois (1905):

> [W]e can only understand the present by continually referring to and studying the past; when any one of the intricate phenomena of our daily life puzzles us; when there arises religious problems, political problems, race problems, we must always remember that while their solution lies in the present, their cause and their explanation lie in the past (p. 104).

Five of the most significant results of the historical search of black studies have been:

destruction of the myth of the passive acceptance of subjugation by blacks; peoples of African descent have always attempted to shape their own destinies (Marable, 1981; People's College Press, 1977);

documentation of the critical role of collective self-help in laying the foundations for black progress (Davis, 1975; Morris, 1984);

restoration of the record of ancient and modern contributions of blacks in developing high technology and establishing early civilizations in North and South America (Diop, 1974; Jackson, 1980; Van Sertima, 1976, 1982, 1983);

exploration of the contemporary implications of psychic duality (Cross, 1978a, 1978b; Semaj, 1981), building on Du Bois's classic formulation of the concept of Afrocentricity (Asante, 1987) as a guiding principle; and

explication of the critical role played by black women in shaping the black experience (Harley & Terborg-Penn, 1978; White, 1980).

Not all of these developments have emerged from within the enterprise of black studies itself. Many scholarly contributions to black studies have been produced under the auspices of traditional disciplines but have also provided data that undergird black studies as a disciplinary development.

A BEACHHEAD IN HIGHER EDUCATION

Du Bois's emphasis on building a permanent base in institutions of higher education has been put into operation by black studies professionals principally through the formation of a national professional organization, the National Council for Black Studies (NCBS), which represents both black studies scholar/activists and black studies administrative units. NCBS initiatives include developing and disseminating position statements regarding the desirable organizational characteristics of black studies units; establishing an accreditation mechanism and promoting curriculum standardization to insure coherency and quality standardizations in history, the social and behavioral sciences, and the arts and humanities; and assessing the state of black studies through annual surveys.

The environment in which these initiatives have been pursued is dominated by continuing challenges to the legitimacy of black studies by its critics and the weak attachment of many scholars to the black studies movement and to black studies units even when the research of such scholars examines the black experience. But the extent to which black studies has established a beachhead in higher education can be seen from selected responses to the first annual NCBS survey (Stewart, 1985b):

88.5 percent reported that the number of full-time faculty members with appointments solely in black studies is stable or increasing;
91.4 percent reported that the number of full-time faculty members with joint appointments in black studies and another academic unit is either stable or improving;
70.2 percent indicated that the number of full-time faculty members who have appointments outside black studies but who are teaching courses included in the black studies curriculum is either stable or improving;
79.5 percent indicated that the overall budgetary situation was either stable or improving;
46.4 percent indicated that new faculty members had been hired during the 1984–85 academic year; and
45.3 percent reported that new courses were offered during the 1984–85 academic year.

SELF-PERPETUATION: CHALLENGES AND POSSIBILITIES

For black studies the process of becoming a self-perpetuating enterprise has many dimensions. These include:

research into the history and development of the black studies movement to guide current planning;
ongoing assessment of the intellectual products of black studies;
development of specialized black studies journals and other outlets for research;
creation of black studies graduate programs;
integration of black studies knowledge into the K-to-12 curriculum; and
development of alliances with other organizations.

Research examining the history and development of black studies has been useful in correcting the misconceptions used by detractors to slander the discipline. For example, the misconception persists that in the late 1960s and early 1970s as many as 700 black studies units were established, only to be followed by a precipitous decline in the 1980s. Research by Daniel (1978) has clearly documented, however, that the number of units with an identifiable administrative structure never numbered more than approximately 300. The first NCBS annual survey (Stewart, 1985b) reveals that there are currently approximately 220 identifiable black studies units in institutions of higher education and that the vast majority of black studies units are responding creatively to new challenges in higher education, including the general education reform movement. At the same time, however, it is critical to recognize that black studies units remain in a state of flux; the results of the first NCBS annual survey reveal that 20.7 percent of respondents indicated that a change in the organizational format of the unit had occurred in the 1984–85 academic year, and 29.9 percent reported a change in unit leadership during the 1984–85 academic year. Currently, NCBS has approximately 100 institutional members and has established a Council of Institutional Members to improve interunit cooperation and to better protect units under attack.

The implications of organizational flux and challenges to legitimacy have influenced intellectual developments in several ways. First, there has been a continuing search for a sustainable self-definition that coherently captures the essence and defines the scope of inquiry and related activities. At the highest level of abstraction, Turner (1984b) argues cogently that the term *Africana studies* best achieves this goal. However, for this term to become standard, it will be necessary to clearly articulate the distinction vis-à-vis traditional African studies (Young & Martin, 1984). At present a variety of terms are used to describe the enterprise, including *black studies, Afro-American studies,* and *African-American studies*. In general, these terms refer principally to the study of African-Americans in the United States, although studies of classical African civilization, postclassical Africa, and the African diaspora are also integral components of the data base.

Aside from the issue of an overarching designation for the field of inquiry, the basic dilemma that continues to perplex black studies theorists was identified almost a decade ago by Allen (1974), who lumped into three general categories the various conceptions of the field that have been advanced:

an academic conception whereby the mission of black studies is to research black history and illuminate the contributions of blacks;
an ideological political conception whereby black studies is seen as an instrument of cultural nationalism; and
an instrumental political conception whereby black studies is considered a vehicle for social change with a functional relationship to the black community.

Allen's second category masks the importance of ideologies other than cultural nationalism important in the continuing development of black studies. These include Marxism (People's College Press, 1977; Alkalimat & Associates, 1984) and the black women's studies movement (Hull,

Scott, & Smith, 1982). As the third conception of black studies has become increasingly submerged in search of credibility within academe, the Outreach Center at Ohio State University (Allen's first category) is one of the few examples of systematic institutional pursuit of stronger community ties (Upton, 1984).

The intellectual momentum of black studies that cuts across all of the distinct approaches identified above has been manifested in the establishment of a number of specialized black studies journals, such as *The Journal of Black Studies, The Western Journal of Black Studies, UMOJA,* and the *New England Journal of Black Studies*. A new national black studies journal, *Africanology,* appeared in 1988.

The volume of black studies research output has created the desire to rank units based primarily on published research and has resulted in greater participation of blacks on editorial review boards (McWorter, 1981). There have also been attempts to analyze factors contributing to variation in published research in periodicals (Brossard, 1984; Stewart, 1983). In addition, a special issue of the *Journal of Negro Education* has been devoted to examining the evolution and contemporary status of black studies (Young, 1984). *The Black Scholar* has also been a regular outlet for black studies materials. One of the most recent contributions to the continuing examination of the developmental profile of black studies has been provided in the volume edited by Turner (1984a). The publications that most clearly demonstrate the maturation of black studies as an area of inquiry are, however, the general introductory texts (Karenga, 1982; People's College Press, 1977; Alkalimat & Associates, 1984; Stewart, 1979).

Increased visibility of black studies has led to the funding of major projects examining black studies curriculum development (Institute of the Black World, 1981, 1982). More recently, Huggins (1985), under the auspices of the Ford Foundation, produced an assessment of black studies that has been roundly attacked by many in the field of black studies (Asante, 1986). Huggins's report envisions, in the long run, the resubmersion of black studies into a traditional discipline. This approach plays into the hands of the enemies of black studies, primarily those administrators who have sought ways to reduce the autonomy of black studies units. The emerging pattern of attacks involves one or more of the following strategies:

downgrading units from departmental to program status;
submerging black studies into larger administrative units, for example, ethnic studies;

allowing only joint faculty appointments with traditional academic units; and

appointing a new generation of administrators not originally part of the black studies movement who naively support administration policies.

The central issues in faculty and chair appointments are: To what academic unit will a faculty member/administrator develop principal allegiance? Will the approach to the study of the black experience pursued by a scholar reflect the emergent black studies paradigm or simply recast traditional disciplinary perspectives? Appointing persons endorsing Huggins's approach obviously works against one of the most critical dimensions of black studies: promoting self-perpetuation through the development of cognate graduate units. The most hopeful development in this area is the establishment of a doctoral program in African-American studies at Temple University. If black studies is to become a truly self-perpetuating discipline, a cadre of scholars must be trained under the auspices of black studies; these scholars should be able to unite in ways that insure principal loyalty to black studies.

Even a free-standing academic unit with appropriately trained faculty is not a sufficient condition for the perpetuation of black studies. A necessary condition is a campus-based and noncampus-based constituency that serves as a watchdog against attacks. The current wave of attacks on black studies has been undertaken under the auspices of a broader retrenchment. Black studies departments and programs have been particularly vulnerable during this period because of the perception (and reality) of a declining commitment to black studies by African-Americans in the late 1970s and early 1980s as individual careerist initiatives flourished. The declining student support was observed by some administrators who leaped at the opportunity to move against black studies.

The erosion of black student support for black studies in part indicated the failure of the first wave of black studies advocates to achieve one of their principal goals. In the minds of the early black studies visionaries and in the original developmental profile of NCBS, the strategy of developing graduate programs to promote self-perpetuation was to be pursued simultaneously with efforts to introduce black studies knowledge into the K-to-12 public school curriculum. This was to lead to a continuing and growing base of student support in higher education. One of the factors working against success in this area has been the somewhat remarkable absence of black studies in colleges and schools of education. As a result, the preparation of teachers during the last decade did not include an introduction to black studies knowledge. As a consequence, the students of these teachers became the next generation of victims in what Woodson (1933) described as the "miseducation of the Negro."

In addition, black studies has not been able to effectively use either the popular media or community organizations to overcome its general exclusion from the public school curriculum. Thus, the image and nonimage of African-Americans reinforced their treatment in the primary and secondary curricula. However, the Reagan era appears to have pushed the latest wave of African-American students into a new realization of the continuing validity of Du Bois's often-quoted declaration that the problem of the twentieth century is the problem of the color line. The new racism on college campuses is creating a new interest in and a black student support base for black studies.

This organic development is occurring simultaneously with the NCBS's pursuit of crucial alliances with critical organizations including the National Alliance of Black School Educators, the Assault on Illiteracy Program, the Black United Fund, the NAACP Legal Defense Fund, Occupational Industrialization Centers of America, the Association for the Study of Afro-American Life and History, and the African Heritage Studies Association. These initiatives will hopefully broaden the impact of black studies during this decade.

ALL OUR PAST PROCLAIMS OUR FUTURE

Aside from the challenges posed by the continuing attacks from its detractors, black studies faces an even greater challenge in putting Du Bois's vision into practice. In particular, Du Bois spoke of the study of "modern science of matter and life" (1973). Black studies, as traditionally conceived, has encompassed the subject areas associated with the arts and humanities, the social and behavioral sciences, and, to a lesser extent, education. No systematic attempt has been made to integrate the subject matter of the natural and physical sciences and technology with black studies.

It is also important to note that, even within traditional subject matter, black studies analysts have tended to overemphasize the descriptive approach characteristic of traditional disciplines rather than focus on concrete application, policy development and analysis, or developing linkages to appropriate "helping professions," for example, social work, administration of justice, and so on. This pattern is only partially the result of inattention to these issues. Some black studies advocates have raised these issues sporadically (Anderson, 1974; Stewart, 1976). At the time the NCBS core curriculum was developed, there was some desire to include policy studies as a curriculum track. Unfortunately, that initiative failed, but this oversight may be corrected in the forthcoming revision to the core curriculum guide.

Another modern challenge to which black studies has begun to respond is the educational impact of microcomputers (Harvey, 1983; Hendrix, Bracy, Davis, & Herron, 1984). There are now first-generation black studies educational software packages (Harris, 1985; Stewart, 1985a). In addition, a major conference held at St. Cloud State University, hosted by Robert Johnson under the auspices of the Minority Studies Academic Program entitled "The Use of Computers in Minority Studies and Related Disciplines," has laid the groundwork for a subgroup of specialists to collaborate on additional projects in this area.

The various developments cited above can, if coordinated and nurtured, provide the foundations for the realization of Du Bois's vision. What Du Bois had in mind as the ultimate intellectual outcome of the systematic study of the black experience was a theory of history and social change in which scientific and technological developments are explained endogenously. Such a macrotheory could not only potentially reconcile the competing schools of thought within black studies but also provide a fully developed paradigm for black studies that would finally cut the rotting umbilical cord to traditional disciplines. Such a scientific revolution would also give new direction to contemporary educational and economic development initiatives designed to meet the challenges of high technology and economic transformation. In this way, the nightmares of the past and present may give way to a brighter future, where the problem of the twenty-first century will not be the problem of the color line.

REFERENCES

Alkalimat, A., & Associates. (1984). *Introduction to Afro-American studies: A peoples college primer* (5th ed.). Urbana, IL: University of Illinois at Urbana.

Allen, R. L. (1974, September). Politics of the attack on black studies. *Black Scholar, 6* (1), 2–7.

Anderson, S. E. (1974, March). Science, technology and black liberation. *Black Scholar, 5* (6), 2–8.

Asante, M. (1986). A note on Nathan Huggins' report of the Ford Foundation on African-American studies. *Journal of Black Studies, 17*, 255–62.

Asante, M. (1987). *The Afrocentric idea* (rev. ed.). Philadelphia: Temple University Press.

Brossard, C. (1984). Classifying black studies programs. *The Journal of Negro Education, 53*, 278–95.

Cross, W. E. (1978a). Black families and black identity: A literature review. *The Western Journal of Black Studies, 2*, 111–24.

Cross, W. E. (1978b). The Thomas and Cross models on psychological nigrescence: A literature review. *Journal of Black Psychology, 4*, 13–31.

Daniel, T. K. (1978). A survey of black studies in midwestern colleges and universities. *The Western Journal of Black Studies, 2*, 296–303.

Davis, K. (1975). *Fundraising in the black community*. Metuchen, NJ: The Scarecrow Press.

Diop, C. A. (1974). *African origins of civilization, myth or reality*. (M. Cook, Ed. & Trans.). Westport, CT: Lawrence Hill.

Du Bois, W. E. B. (1905). The beginnings of slavery. *Voice of the Negro, 2*.

Du Bois, W. E. B. (1973). The field and function of the Negro college. (Alumni Reunion Address, Fisk University, 1933). Reprinted in H. Aptheker (Ed.), *W. E. B. Du Bois, the education of black people, ten critiques 1900–1960*. Amherst: University of Massachusetts Press.

Harley, S., & Terborg-Penn, R., (Eds.) (1978). *The Afro-American woman, struggles and images*. Port West, NY: National University.

Harris, N. (1985). *Blackfacts*. West Lafayette, IN: North Star Gateway. A computer-based black history educational exercise.

Harvey, W. B. (1983). Computer instruction and black student performance. *Issues in Higher Education, 9*.

Hendrix, M. K., Bracy, J. H., Davis, J. A., & Herron, W. M. (1984). Computers and black studies: Toward the cognitive revolution. *The Journal of Negro Education, 53*, 341–50.

Huggins, N. (1985). *Report to the Ford Foundation on Afro-American studies*. New York: Ford Foundation.

Hull, G., Scott, P. B., & Smith, B. (1982). *All the women are white. All the blacks are men. But some of us are brave: Black women's studies*. Old Westbury, NY: Feminist Press.

Institute of the Black World. (1981). *Black studies curriculum development course evaluations*. Conference I. Atlanta: Institute of the Black World.

Institute of the Black World, (1982). *Black studies curriculum development course evaluations*. Conference II. Atlanta: Institute of the Black World.

Jackson, J. (1980). *Introduction to African civilizations*. Secaucus, NJ: Citadel Press.

Karenga, M. (1982). *Introduction to Afro-American studies*. Los Angeles: Kawaida.

McWorter, G. A. (1981). *The professionalization of achievement in black studies* (Preliminary Report). Chicago: The Chicago Center for Afro-American Studies.

Marable, M. (1981). The modern miseducation of the Negro: Critiques of black history curricula. In *Institute of the black world, black studies curriculum development course evaluations*. Conference I (pp. C1–C28). Atlanta: Institute of the Black World.

Morris, A. D. (1984). *The origins of the civil rights movement: Black communities organizing for change*. New York: Free Press.

People's College Press. (1977). *Introduction to Afro-American studies* (4th ed., vols. 1 & 2). Chicago: Author.

Semaj, L. T. (1981). The black self, identity and models for a psychology of black liberation. *The Western Journal of Black Studies, 5*, 158–71.

Stewart, J. B. (1976). Black studies and black people in the future. *Black Books Bulletin, 4,* 21–25.

Stewart, J. B. (1979). Introducing black studies: A critical examination of some textual materials. *UMOJA, 111,* 5–18.

Stewart, J. B. (1983). Factors affecting variation in published black studies articles across institutions. *The New England Journal of Black Studies, 4,* 72–83.

Stewart, J. B. (1985a). *Liberation 2000? The black experience in America.* [Computer program]. State College, PA: Dynastew Educational Software.

Stewart, J. B. (1985b). *The state of black studies.* Final Report, National Conference of Black Studies Annual Survey.

Turner, J. E. (Ed.). (1984a). *The next decade: Theoretical and research issues in Africana studies.* Ithaca, NY: Africana Studies and Research Center.

Turner, J. E. (1984b). Africana studies and epistemology: A discourse in the sociology of knowledge. In J. E. Turner (Ed.), *The next decade: Theoretical and research issues in Africana studies* (pp. v-xxv). Ithaca, NY: Africana Studies and Research Center.

Upton, J. N. (1984). Applied black studies: Adult education in the black community — a case study. *The Journal of Negro Education, 53,* 322–33.

Van Sertima, I. (1976). *They came before Columbus: The African presence in ancient America.* New York: Random House.

Van Sertima, I. (Ed.). (1982). Egypt revisited. *Journal of African Civilizations, 4.*

Van Sertima, I. (Ed.). (1983). *Blacks in science ancient and modern.* New Brunswick, NJ: Transaction Books.

White, D. G. (1980). *Ain't I a woman: Female slaves in the plantation south.* New York: W. W. Norton.

Woodson, C. G. (1933). *The mis-education of the Negro.* Washington, DC: Associated.

Young, C. (1984). *An assessment of black studies programs in American higher education.* Special issue of *The Journal of Negro Education, 53.*

Young, C., & Martin, G. (1984). The paradox of separate and unequal: African studies and Afro-American studies. *The Journal of Negro Education, 53,* 257–67.

16

The Role of the University in Racial Violence on Campus

Wornie L. Reed

Racial violence against blacks on college campuses across the country has become a source of considerable and legitimate concern. This chapter reviews the nature and extent of these incidents, discusses the national social context of their occurrence, and examines the role universities play in the development of these incidents.

The number of racial incidents reported on college campuses in recent years has been on the rise. The International Institute against Prejudice and Violence, located in Baltimore, documented racial incidents at 175 colleges for 1986–87. Since this figure is based solely on the events that received newspaper coverage, it does not adequately reflect the total number of incidents.

William Damon gives this report in the May 3, 1989, issue of the *Chronicle of Higher Education*:

> Racism and bigotry are back on campus with a vengeance. Black students have been chased and beaten at the University of Massachusetts at Amherst, taunted with defamatory posters at Pennsylvania State and Stanford Universities, subjected to racist jokes on a University of Michigan radio station, and presented with a "mock slave auction" at a fraternity house at the University of Wisconsin at Madison. Ku Klux Klan signs and other white-supremacist graffiti have been splattered on dozens of college buildings across the country, from Harvard University to the University of California (p. B1).

VIOLENCE AGAINST AFRICAN-AMERICANS[1]

During the past ten years several research centers have collected information on racially motivated violence.[2] A study of the data reveals an upsurge of racism and racist violence — with the most deadly attacks against the African-American community. There has been an increase in the number of incidents of white mobs wielding baseball bats, threatening and even attacking blacks if they are caught stopping in segregated residential areas. There has been a steady increase in the fire bombing of homes purchased by black families in predominately white neighborhoods. A study of violence in residential neighborhoods conducted by the Southern Poverty Law Center indicates that between 1985 and 1986 there were at least 45 cases of vigilante activity directed at black families moving into predominately white communities (Dennis, 1987).

The incident in Howard Beach, New York, that led to the death of 23-year-old Michael Griffith reflects a long-standing problem of racist violence in white communities in Brooklyn. Another example is an incident in 1982 when a gang of young white men beat three black transit workers who stopped in Brooklyn for pizza on their way home from work; one of the workers was killed on the spot. Black youths working in or traveling through white communities have been attacked and regularly beaten in New York City. By summer 1987, racially motivated assaults had increased to at least one a week in New York City. The Chicago Police Department reported a 58 percent increase in racial attacks for the first six months of 1986 over the same period in 1985. The New York City Police Department reported an increase in racially motivated violence over the last eight years. These attacks go mostly unreported in the news media.

The Community Relations Service of the Justice Department and the Center for Democratic Renewal provide data that demonstrate a sharp upturn in violent racial attacks nationally. The increase of 42 percent between 1985 and 1986 was largely fueled by the boldness of white terrorist groups in the United States. Nationally, the Community Relations Service reports an increase in all cases of racial confrontations from 953 in 1977 to 1,996 in 1982. In cases of racial violence involving the Ku Klux Klan, the Department of Justice reported a 460 percent increase from 1978 to 1979 and a startling 550 percent increase from 1978 to 1980.

VIOLENCE ON COLLEGE CAMPUSES

Violence and hostilities toward blacks have occurred at a wide variety of universities. Two years ago, at the Citadel Military Academy, five white cadets dressed in Klan robes invaded a black student's room. A few months later a cross was burned in front of a black cultural center at

Purdue University, and two weeks later the phrase "death to Niggers" was found carved into an office door. Buildings at Smith College were defaced with racist slogans, and graffiti and fliers were spread around at Florida State University. Following a speech by Jesse Jackson in February 1987 at Northern Illinois University, flyers with racist threats and swastikas were spread over the campus, and a student magazine printed racist poetry. One of the "poems" went as follows:

> O.K.,
> Look nigger,
> We are white.
> White is supreme.
> Jesus was white.
> God is white.
> All of our Presidents have been white.
> Thank you God.

Several black students at Columbia University filed a lawsuit after being attacked by a gang of white fraternity members on campus. A mob of white students chased and beat a small group of black students at the University of Massachusetts at Amherst following a World Series baseball game in 1986. Around the same time, black women at Mount Holyoke College complained that they were being harassed by white men from the same Amherst campus. A survey of campuses across the country suggests that racial hostility between students is extensive.

Influenced by adult organizations of the racist right, students at Sacramento State organized the White Student Union in 1979 as an offshoot of the Aryan Youth Movement. Since then the White Student Union is reported to have grown from an initial 3 chapters to some 20 chapters across the country. A group of students claiming association with the White Student Union assaulted black students at the University of Texas at Austin. They threatened to drop a black student leader, whom they were hanging by his heels, from a dormitory window if a planned antiapartheid demonstration on campus was not called off.

In 1986 a white campus bus driver at Cornell University threatened to run over three black male students as they crossed the street in front of the bus he was driving. At Princeton University a black football player's room was broken into, and the epitaph "nigger" was sprayed across the walls. At California State-Fullerton black faculty members returning to their offices after the Christmas vacation in January 1987 were greeted with spray-painted terms such as "mud race" and "nigger." In May of that year, the director of the University Center at Fullerton approved a poster to advertise a talent show that depicted a minstrel character. And during a party at the same institution, a white fraternity displayed a 15-foot plywood cutout of a black man with a bone in his hair, huge red lips, and a Tarzan outfit. In a campus poll in winter 1987, students at the University of Virginia said that racism is the school's biggest problem.

While racist behavior is hardly a new phenomenon in colleges and universities, the evidence clearly demonstrates that racial incidents took place with increased frequency during the 1980s. From student magazines or student newspaper articles defaming and ridiculing black people to outright physical aggression, racial conflict is present in a cross-section of American schools. There is a national mood on campuses that tolerates, and even encourages, campaigns to demean, harass, and intimidate black students and other minorities.

THE SOCIAL CONTEXT

As bad as they are, these racial incidents are only symptoms of the slowdown in racial progress during the 1980s. This slowdown was aided and abetted, if not engineered, by the Reagan administration, which waged a virtual war against racial progress with code words, code activities, and some overt actions. They used such code words as "welfare hustlers" and "welfare queens," and suggested distinctions between the "deserving" and "undeserving" poor. Perhaps their most significant coded activity was the presidential campaign kickoff in 1980 in Philadelphia, Mississippi, a city distinguished only by the lynching of three civil rights workers — James Chaney, Andrew Goodman, and Michael Schwerner — there in 1964. This was as clear as any signal the infamous Governor Theodore G. Bilbo could have given. Once in office, the Reagan administration began a relentless attack on civil rights laws and regulations. Even Richard Nixon was too far left for them: they tried to repeal Nixon's affirmative action Executive Order.

Affirmative Action

I am convinced that one reason for the outbreak of racial violence on college campuses is that faculty as well as students — who have no vested interest in civil rights gains, progress, or peace — are reacting to the misuses and abuses of affirmative action. Many individuals were in favor of civil rights gains made by blacks in the 1960s; others went along because it brought peace, and they preferred peace to strife. Today, however, we have a new generation, one that holds neither of these perspectives on civil rights. In addition, we have the maligned affirmative action laws: many majority group faculty members, as well as students, consider affirmative action programs to be racial preference programs that unfairly discriminate against white individuals — a view that amounts to a misinterpretation of racism.

In 1981, before the Reagan administration's reorganization and redirection of the U.S. Commission on Civil Rights, the commission affirmed its "unwavering support for affirmative action plans and the full range of affirmative action measures necessary to make equal opportunity a reality for historically excluded groups." They supported this position by concluding that "a steady flow of data shows unmistakably that most of the historic victims of discrimination are still being victimized" (U.S. Commission on Civil Rights, 1988). And yet, arguments against affirmative action have been raised under the banner of reverse discrimination. Obviously, there have been incidents of arbitrary action against white males, but the charge of reverse discrimination, in essence, equates efforts to limit the process of discrimination with that process itself. Such an equation is profoundly and fundamentally incorrect. Affirmative measures should end when the discriminatory process ends. On the other hand, it is highly unlikely that the discriminatory process will ever end without affirmative intervention.

On university search committees we often hear the term *affirmative action candidate*. In other words, the search committee has identified a minority person to interview in order to have an appropriate affirmative action search. I cannot think of a more perverse misuse of the process. No person should be interviewed unless he or she has the qualifications for the position. And when such persons do qualify they should be considered seriously. Not taking such issues more seriously demeans the process and effectively demeans the minority person involved. When white professors and university staff members reject or misuse affirmative action in their recruitment practices, they indirectly invite white students to reject the process and the minority students that process was designed to serve.

Competition for Dwindling Resources

Some observers also see the increase in violence against blacks as a result of the perception of whites that they are in competition for dwindling resources and that black students are not only competing against white students for entry into universities but also for jobs after graduation. Thus, black students are seen as an increasing threat to the future welfare of middle-class white students.

IS THE UNIVERSITY CULPABLE?

What role does the university play in the development of racial incidents? In other words, is the university culpable?

Universities have cultural goals, often so strongly suggested as to be transparent. One of these implicit goals is the preservation of the belief system and the value orientations of society. Universities contribute to this preservation by transferring the cultural heritage from generation to generation through teaching. It is in teaching that what is to be valued in the society is transmitted. It is not a long leap from *what* is to be valued to *who* is to be valued. In one sense it is strange that European-Americans can obtain college degrees without ever studying non-European cultures, when most of the world is nonwhite and when the population of the United States is significantly nonwhite and with the nonwhite proportion growing. But, in another sense, in the context of culture preservation, it is not strange at all.

In this country we have had, in the past couple of decades, substantial discussions and analyses of the potentially harmful effects to minority youth of never seeing themselves, or persons like themselves, in their readings and course work. As a result, more and more grade school texts are including pictures and references to nonwhite persons. On the other hand, we have had relatively little discussion and analysis of the effects this situation has on white students. White students must learn *who* is of value as well as *what* is of value in society by what they study in school. If their course work does not include the study of nonwhite persons, then it seems highly plausible that many of these students would act differently from the way they would if their course work routinely included material on non-European cultures. By definition, then, non-Europeans tend to be seen as people who are not to be valued.

The university plays a major role in determining what happens on campus. If no changes are made in defining the "worthwhile" culture to be transmitted, we may have no change in the current racially charged atmosphere. If changes are made so that the culture that is transmitted reflects a multicultural society — a world society — then we may be on the way toward changing the racial hostility on campus in particular and throughout the country in general.

NOTES

1. Data in this section taken from Turner, J. E. (1987). *Racism and Racial Antagonism in Contemporary American Society*. Unpublished manuscript.

2. These centers include the Southern Poverty Law Center, the Center for Democratic Renewal, and the Klan Watch.

REFERENCES

Damon, W. (1989, May 3). Learning how to deal with the new American dilemma: We must teach our students about morality and racism. *Chronicle of Higher Education.*

Dennis, R. (1987, April). Racism on the rise. *Black Enterprise,* 17.

U.S. Commission on Civil Rights. (1988). Affirmative action in the 1980s: Dismantling the process of discrimination. In P. Rothenberg (Ed.), *Racism and sexism: An integrated study*. New York: St. Martin's Press.

17

Summary and Recommendations

Charles V. Willie

REVIEW AND ANALYSIS

In Chapter 1, "The Civil Rights Movement and Educational Change," historian Meyer Weinberg states that the significance of the modern version of this movement is that blacks have taken control of its leadership. Improved education for blacks was a major goal of the movement, and Weinberg agrees with Martin Luther King, Jr.'s assessment that the public policy for educational change "was written in the streets" through demonstrations, marches, and acts of civil disobedience. The legal strategy of the civil rights movement, again according to Weinberg, was to challenge the inherent inequity of a dual system of education — one system for whites and another for blacks, separate and unequal.

After this system was declared illegal in the courts, concern for equity and equality slackened, leaving, in Weinberg's view, an unfinished agenda, especially in large cities where schools are so underfunded that they provide an inadequate education for all students, black and white. Urban education issues, Weinberg believes, must be addressed, and at a higher level of priority.

The limited assistance that blacks have received to improve their educational status during the second half of the twentieth century has been, as mentioned earlier, a stop-and-go process. In effect, blacks forced the nation to pay attention to them when they decided to cease cooperating in their own oppression. My chapter, "The Social and Historical Context: A Case Study," about the Rockefeller Foundation, contributes to the discussion of this thesis.

On December 1, 1955, Rosa Parks was arrested in Montgomery, Alabama, for refusing to give up her seat on a city bus to a white person, as required by the law. Some characterized this brave act and the support that Parks received as the beginning of the "black revolt." Blacks, in their reaction to this event, sent a message to whites that the age of passive subservience had ended.

Challenges to inequality in other sectors of society escalated and led to the 1963 March on Washington, where King, a college-educated black minister, delivered the historic speech about his dream of freedom and justice in America. The nation responded. That year, for example, the Rockefeller Foundation designed and implemented a new program that was called the Equal Opportunity Program.

The actions of the Rockefeller Foundation are particularly appropriate to observe because of that foundation's historic interest in the education of blacks. Initial grants in the new program were designed to open the doors of "good schools" to minority candidates. To implement the program, several awards were made to prestigious, predominantly white colleges. The foundation was struggling to make an appropriate response to the black revolt. However, its efforts in the early 1960s were conditioned by habits of yesteryear. Support was given largely to predominantly white institutions because the foundation wanted to attract black students into the mainstream. Predominantly black colleges and universities were not recognized by the establishment as the mainstream.

Blacks found certain students, faculty members, and administrators in these mainstream schools to be insensitive, insulting, and untrustworthy. Some blacks felt that the Rockefeller Foundation's recruitment program for these predominantly white schools was an invitation to a briar patch rather than to a rose garden. Estrangement increased between black students and white students on several white college campuses. The hoped-for racial reconciliation did not materialize.

The foundation modified its Equal Opportunity Program during the mid-1960s and included some predominantly black colleges as grant recipients. But the grants made to such schools were not comparable to the larger sums that had been offered to predominantly white colleges. Nevertheless, this modest midcourse correction indicated that the white establishment was becoming sensitive to feelings in the black community that whites tended to discount the value and legitimacy of their institutions in the new drive toward racial integration.

The Rockefeller Foundation began to internalize these new findings. It consulted more and more with predominantly black institutions of higher education. It turned toward these institutions as a partner rather than as a patron. Slowly but surely the Rockefeller Foundation changed its focus from the paternalistic rescue of selected black individuals to institutional change in society on terms acceptable to blacks. This was a commendable shift.

However, the foundation discovered that it was unprepared for this new thrust. The absence of blacks on its staff was both a source of embarrassment and a liability for an organization determined to change its old ways of doing business, determined to relate to minorities in new and different ways. The experience of a homogeneously white staff was too narrow to correctly interpret the needs of blacks. As the 1960s decade closed, the foundation diversified its staff and broadened its mission so that the Equal Opportunity Program could bring minorities into the mainstream and sponsor activities designed to effect institutional change in society.

The trials and tribulations of the Rockefeller Foundation during the 1960s were not unlike those of other predominantly white, establishment-oriented institutions. New occasions were teaching new duties. But, as we have already seen, these new findings did not immunize establishment leaders, especially those in education, against the possibility of backsliding. All of this is to say that there is no linear pattern of progress in the attainment of educational equity. With two steps forward there is sometimes one step backward. Nevertheless, the educational innovations and changes of the 1960s were real and valuable. The United States was set on a course unlike any it had pursued before. And while it might digress from time to time, the mood of minorities would prevent a return to the old paternalistic ways of offering help to people of color.

If responses to the arrest of Parks in Montgomery and the March on Washington were significant events that helped change the way whites relate to blacks in the United States, the assassination of King in Memphis in 1968 was a decisive event. King was an articulate, well-educated, and cosmopolitan minister who advocated a nonviolent approach to social change. His murder was seen as the ultimate form of rejection. After the death of King, many whites in America, including some in charge of major institutions, realized that the racial prejudice they harbored was a form of social pathology that harmed whites as well as blacks.

Blacks realized that in King they had presented their best. If he was unacceptable, none could aspire to be acceptable. After the death of King, blacks saw with increasing clarity that they were rejected in this society not because of their behavior but because of their race. The Rockefeller Foundation understood this as well as any white-dominated organization, and in 1969, the year after King died, it deliberately adopted a goal of diversifying its staff. The Rockefeller Foundation and other institutions in the United States recognized that they must root out racial discrimination within their own organizations so that they could offer genuine help to others.

By confessing their faults, the people of power were acknowledging that, in the past, they had been self-centered rather than concerned about others. Their altruistic activity, including educational philanthropy, was orchestrated primarily to fulfill the needs of the helpers and only secondarily the needs of those being helped. Before King was killed, many whites in America believed that their way of life should be the model for all and that minorities should conform to white norms.

It is interesting that Robert A. Dentler, in his chapter on the history of the school reform movement led by blacks, begins his analysis with Gunnar Myrdal and the *American Dilemma,* published in 1944, since Myrdal misunderstood the significance of education among blacks in their freedom movement and misread the early signs that pointed toward school desegregation. Indeed, Myrdal reported that "Negroes are divided on the issue of segregated schools" (1944). What Myrdal and other social scientists missed, according to Dentler, was the link between the push by African-Americans for desegregation in employment practices and housing covenants, on the one hand, and schooling, on the other. While the Supreme Court's *Brown* decision established the principle of a right to a desegregated education in 1954, Dentler observes that "the legal foundation of racial segregation and discrimination" had been "shattered" in earlier challenges in housing and employment in the 1940s.

Dentler adopts the conclusion of the NAACP legal team: while the *Brown* decision against segregated education "accomplished something of profound importance," the implementation of this principle was faulty and required a decade and a half before "a full range of tools" were developed to accomplish school desegregation. Dentler tells us that as late as 1974 (20 years after *Brown*), a report prepared for the federal government "found four in every ten [black students] enrolled in racially identifiable and isolated schools."

Dentler also reports that not only has the implementation of the principle of desegregation in education been slow and halting, but there is increasing effort to blunt the effects of this principle. He offers as evidence a plan in Norfolk, Virginia, approved by a U.S. court of appeals in 1986, "to revert to neighborhood elementary schools in contravention of an earlier cross-busing policy" and the finding by a U.S. district court in 1987 that the Topeka Board of Education, an original party in the *Brown* case, now operates a unitary school system, although "racial balance does not exist in the district's schools" (*Brown v. Board of Education,* 1987). Dentler concludes that official actions such as these tend to nail shut "the coffin of court-ordered school desegregation" and represent "serious backsliding in the educational arena."

In my chapter, "The Future of School Desegregation," I assert that school desegregation has contributed to the enhancement of education in this nation probably more than any other experience in recent years. Among the benefits of school desegregation have been the decline in the school dropout rate for black students and the increase in the high school graduation rate for all students. Desegregation, not segregation, was the expectation of the 1970s. Public opinion polls revealed that seven out of every ten black parents preferred an integrated school for their children and that seven out of every ten white parents would not object to a desegregated education for their children.

As noted earlier, backsliding is an ever-present possibility. At the end of the 1980s, blacks again had been denied; their expectations and preferences had not been fulfilled. Court-ordered desegregation seldom desegregated black schools. Actually, the whites who usually were the defendants in desegregation court cases experienced more school desegregation than the blacks who usually were the prevailing plaintiffs. In Atlanta, Milwaukee, St. Louis, and other communities, court-sanctioned school desegregation plans prohibited any all-white schools but permitted several all-black schools. Since school desegregation was a beneficial experience and contributed to many school improvements such as magnet schools, bilingual education, and other innovations, the people in power hoarded these plums for their own kind.

Initially, school desegregation in this nation was widely conceptualized as a student experience. Little attention was given to integrating local education authorities such as school boards. Since self-interest is the basic motive for human action, these white-dominated decision-making bodies fulfilled the interests of whites and granted all of their children a desegregated education while denying such education to a substantial proportion of black students. I have visited school districts throughout the nation and heard superintendents under court order to desegregate ask, "How many one-race schools will the court let us get away with?" Despite such attitudes, I maintain that school desegregation has been the greatest contribution in this century to educational reform and that it deserves to continue, with appropriate modifications, so that its promises are fulfilled for black and other minority students, indeed for all students.

During the concluding years of the 1970s, blacks realized increasingly that some court-ordered school desegregation plans could be legal but still unfair. As the 1980s began, blacks had two contrasting reactions: some embraced desegregation, others rejected it, outraged by persisting inequities in many court-ordered plans. On balance, more blacks favored desegregation than opposed it. The major complaint was that the burden of desegregation fell inequitably on blacks. Thus, blacks who were against inequitable desegregation were not against an equitable integration.

A major concern of these blacks was the need for systemic rather than cosmetic change. Merely mixing and matching children by race was considered educationally inadequate. James P. Comer and Norris M. Haynes explain in their chapter, "Meeting the Needs of Black Children in Public Schools," that the academy must consider the special needs of blacks and other population groups. Unwittingly, schools to date have dealt largely with the normative behavior and needs of affluent whites. By fashioning an educational program that addresses the problems of dependency, powerlessness, and the absence of group control often characterizing the black experience in the United States, Comer and Haynes believe that educational outcomes can be significantly changed. In New Haven, Connecticut, a program designed with the black experience in mind "empowers parents, teachers, administrators and students through collaborative, cooperative, coordinated planning in a few schools." The program created "relationships in which there is mutual respect among all . . . in the educational enterprise."

In essence, the program described by Comer and Haynes focuses on relationships as well as basics. The relationship factor, they believe, is of paramount importance. Using traditional test score measures of outcome, the New Haven program worked beautifully. Schoolchildren that followed the Comer model out-achieved other schoolchildren. Moreover, the program helped students become responsible adult members of a democratic society. Comer believes that the New Haven experience can and should be replicated elsewhere.

Faustine C. Jones-Wilson indicates why the Comer model has not been widely replicated. She states in her chapter, "School Improvement among Blacks: Implications for Excellence and Equity," that urban school improvement has not been a national priority, especially during the 1980s. An essential ingredient for school improvement among blacks and other minorities, according to Jones-Wilson, is the hiring of professionals who believe that poor children and minority children can learn. New York, Pittsburgh, Milwaukee, and other cities and communities have some schools with histories of lower achievement now exhibiting high achievement. Jones-Wilson claims that there are plenty of "practical action items" available from the National Conference on Educating Black Children and other sources for educators who want to do the right thing for blacks and other minorities. To achieve these successful outcomes, school systems must "seek to be fair," which is to say that equity in education should not be lost in what Jones-Wilson calls "the bedlam of the excellence movement."

Charles E. Flowers, like others who have contributed to this discussion, pinpoints "low teacher expectation" as a major pedagogical problem condemning many black and minority students to an inadequate education. Flowers and other scholars make a case, and make it emphatically, that the quality of teaching is the main issue. In Flowers's opinion, the school can have a positive effect independent of family circumstances if educators are willing to take risks. While Comer and Haynes would probably support this argument, they add an important codicil: schools will do what they ought to do when parents of students are involved. In other words, good schooling is a community affair.

Flowers reminds us that the middle school years are critical for minority students, particularly in developing their capacity to handle mathematics and science. This is a time when racist attitudes can be particularly alienating. To cement relationships among students, parents, and teachers, Flowers and others advocate home visits and school-initiated workshops with parents and community leaders. Such activities, he believes, are particularly appropriate for counselors. These and other suggestions are offered by Flowers in his chapter, "Counseling and Guidance of Black and Other Minority Children in Public Schools."

The 1980s have been a decade of contradictory happenings in education for blacks. While the proportion of blacks graduating from high school increased, the proportion of blacks enrolled in college decreased. Black females outnumbered black males in college, but black males outnumbered black females in doctoral programs. Business and management has replaced education as the popular degree among young, college-educated blacks; yet, a higher proportion of white-collar blacks are professionals rather than managers. The proportion of black students who need financial aid to go to college increased during the same period that federal assistance for higher education decreased. This last coupling explains the smaller proportion of college-going blacks during the 1980s, a decade that harvested the largest proportion of black high school graduates ever. These interesting data were assembled by Antoine M. Garibaldi in his chapter, "Blacks in College."

Among the decreasing proportion of black high school graduates who manage to win federally funded grants, the proprietary career school rather than the college is the institution of choice. In "The Road Taken: Minorities and Proprietary Schools," Robert Rothman tells us that "blacks constitute a disproportionate number of the approximately 1.5 million students in the nearly 6,000 for-profit career schools nationwide." Rothman states that reliable sources have estimated the number of blacks in such schools at one-fifth to one-fourth of all blacks enrolled in postsecondary institutions. These schools offer job-specific training in six months, "a quick return on a student's investment." While some observers see this as a positive outcome, others believe that the education received will not lead to upward mobility but will instead trap black inner-city young people in a lower socioeconomic status. Indeed, observers told Rothman that some of these schools offer, at best, short-term opportunities and, at worst, no help at all.

James E. Blackwell reports that the contradictory trends among blacks in education at the college level are also seen at the postgraduate level. He offers as evidence the findings of a 1987 Robert Wood Johnson Foundation report indicating that "the admission of black students to medical colleges is declining even though their test scores and other indices of eligibility are improving." Blacks, who are 11 percent to 12 percent of the nation's population, provide less than 4 percent of the nation's lawyers. Also, they receive less than 4 percent of the doctorates awarded to U.S. citizens. In his chapter, "Graduate and Professional Education for Blacks," Blackwell concludes that "our nation's graduate and professional schools are not recruiting, admitting, retaining, and graduating sufficient numbers of blacks." He states that there is a "pool of talent available among black Americans" but that the interest of graduate and professional schools in developing it through affirmative action and other efforts seems to have diminished. Because of the increasing proportion of minorities in the U.S. population (predicted to be at one-third two decades into the twenty-first century), we ignore them, their education, and the cultivation of their talents at our peril.

John B. Williams's chapter, "Systemwide Title VI Regulation of Higher Education, 1968–88," confirms Blackwell's contention that our nation has little interest in cultivating through higher education the pool of talent among its minorities. Had there been the political will to do this, Williams said, Title VI provided a legal way. The law required desegregation of public white colleges and universities and enhancement of public black institutions so that they too would attract students of all racial populations. Moreover, the law required states to develop plans to achieve meaningful and timely results. According to Williams, little is known for certain about the outcomes of Title VI. He states none can claim better than limited results, at best. To date, the federal government has done an inadequate job of data-collection on the implementation of public policy aimed at civil rights goals, particularly with reference to higher education.

Rather than enhancing higher educational opportunities for blacks by using Title VI, Williams states that the federal government seems to have conspired with other institutions to limit such opportunities by reducing federal student aid since 1980. This, in turn, reduced the states' capacity to enroll black students in public as well as private colleges and universities. By ignoring or continuing to limit the opportunities of minority students who wish to receive a higher education, state governments are following the lead of the federal government.

Williams reports that "no state system over the last twenty years has been found in compliance with Title VI." And he found "no enthusiasm by the federal government to regulate public higher education in the direction of achieving civil rights goals." Williams states that, consequently, one would be hard pressed to identify a single traditional public higher education institution with a creditable civil rights record of achievement. Although possessing a government of laws, the United States appears reluctant to enforce these laws on behalf of black students wishing to attend white institutions. It is hard to explain the failure of the federal government to enforce a legal requirement of equity. Williams wonders whether such short-sighted, illegal, and in general contra-indicated action manifests a fear that access for blacks to colleges and universities "will compromise the vitality of the American higher education community."

Whenever inequity is unchallenged by the nation's highest authorities and opinion molders, discrimination festers and turns ugly. This is precisely what has happened on college and university campuses throughout the United States. Wornie L. Reed, in his chapter, "The Role of the University in Racial Violence on Campus," attributes the violent and insensitive behavior shown by some white students to their black and other minority schoolmates to the slowdown of racial progress in the 1980s, which he feels was "aided and abetted, if not engineered, by the Reagan administration." Due to the Reagan administration's "war against racial progress," many whites on college and university campuses have misunderstood the reason why affirmative action programs are needed and interpret them as acts of discrimination against whites. Without affirmative action, Reed informs us, "it is highly unlikely the discriminatory process will ever end." Reed states that the idea that whites are entitled to privileges others do not receive is transmitted in the teaching and learning experiences of higher education. Young college students who feel that their privileged position is threatened tend to respond violently.

Willie Pearson, Jr., and James A. Banks see the issue raised by Williams — the compromising of the vitality of American higher education — as more of a problem for blacks than for whites. In their opinion, the educational enterprise has compromised, marginalized, and even victimized blacks. The educational enterprise has marginalized blacks by consigning them to selected fields of study and by failing to invite, encourage, and sustain them as worthy participants in science and mathematics. The educational enterprise has compromised blacks by not incorporating ethnic material in the curriculum and by denying the validity of the culture of blacks and other minorities. The educational enterprise has victimized blacks by inadequately cultivating their research skills, underfunding their research proposals, and ignoring the findings of their research reports.

According to Pearson ("Black Participation and Performance in Science, Mathematics and Technical Education"), there is ample evidence of blacks having an interest in science and mathematics. The proportion of blacks expressing interest in a field of knowledge that requires quantitative skills is twice as large among those pursuing a bachelor's degree as among those pursuing graduate degrees. We do know that some institutions have been more successful than others in producing black scientists, but the education community has shown no interest in studying such schools to discover why. Also, there seems to be no interest in determining why black commitment to fields requiring quantitative skills erodes. Pearson claims the factors underlying the career development decisions of blacks deserve more study.

"The trivialization of ethnic cultures" is a phrase coined by Banks in his chapter, "Social Studies, Ethnic Diversity and Social Change." This trivialization has resulted in our failure to study the career development decisions of blacks and other minorities and the reasons for their varying interests in science, mathematics, business, education, sociology, social work, and other fields. A sound social studies curriculum, according to Banks, should explain why many ethnic groups are victimized by institutional racism and class stratification. Such knowledge can contribute to genuine action by the nation to make institutions more equitable. It would reveal that the fate and future of whites, blacks, and other minorities are intertwined. However, Banks has little hope that this will occur unless there is more effective selection and training of teachers. He calls this "the most challenging and difficult task that lies ahead."

Antoine M. Garibaldi, in his chapter, "Abating the Shortage of Black Teachers," mentions the declining proportion of black and other minority teachers as a very special problem facing this nation. It is a special cause for concern because the proportion of nonwhite students in major metropolitan school districts is increasing. In some communities the proportion has already exceeded 50 percent. Garibaldi acknowledges that some blacks are attracted to occupations more attractive than teaching, but that other blacks are not going into teaching only because they have been pushed out of teacher-training programs. He states that some certification requirements use standardized tests that have "eliminated many prospective black teachers and discouraged other potential teacher education majors from choosing that discipline." Clearly, the National Teacher Examination (NTE) favors whites over blacks. Between 1978 and 1982, Garibaldi reports, only 18 percent of Louisiana blacks who took the NTE achieved the passing score of the state; among whites, 78 percent passed. Garibaldi, like other scholars mentioned in this discussion, believes America's greatest challenge will be to develop effective teacher-recruiting strategies, which should help blacks obtain certification.

In his chapter, "The Field and Function of Black Studies," James B. Stewart affirms the observation of W. E. B. Du Bois that we understand the present better by studying the past. The increased number of black students entering predominantly white colleges in the 1960s stimulated the offering of black history as a course of study, and Stewart credits black history with destroying myths about blacks, such as those portraying them as passively accepting slavery and subjugation. Black history, according to Stewart, also documents the origins of the self-help movement among blacks and its contribution to their current progress. And, finally, black history makes available, through schools, the record of black contributions to the world. Although the program occupies a tenuous position in the curriculum, black studies, which includes black history, "has established a beachhead in higher education," according to Stewart, and now needs to be integrated into the K-to-12 curriculum. Moreover, this domain of inquiry should be extended from the humanities and the social and the behavioral sciences to the natural and physical sciences. Ultimately, black studies, if pursued comprehensively as recommended by Stewart, should contribute to theories of history and social change. Stewart's comprehensive conception of black studies would prove beneficial to all learners.

SUMMARY AND INTERPRETATION

Following the celebration of the bicentennial, the upward trend in the proportion of blacks enrolled in colleges and universities turned downward. The upward turn of the 1960s and early 1970s could be interpreted as fulfilling the constitutional requirement of equal protection of the laws for all, while the downward turn in the 1980s suggests a lack of national commitment to the higher education of African-Americans. Blacks had hope during the late 1950s and the 1960s, but despair thereafter, as local education agencies desegregated more whites than blacks and gave whites greater access to magnet schools and other improvements.

This review suggests that, even during periods of progress in attaining racial justice, the forces against such justice are ever present. Recognizing the coexistence of yin and yang, good and evil, within any community, including the nation-state, should protect against undue optimism in times of success and undue pessimism in times of failure. The seeds of racial retrogression in educational opportunities were latent during the season of racial progress; likewise, the experience of commitment to racial justice is not absent but in remission as we witness a national mood that accepts and sanctions inequity.

We learn from this analysis that racial progress in education is neither inevitable nor continuous. A period of arrested racial justice in education need not become permanent. The progress toward equality depends on the action or inaction of people in power and people out of power.

This nation consists of several population groups — racial and ethnic, among others — that interact and influence each other through the mediums of power that each commands. Groups classified as dominant have greater power potential than others; groups classified as subdominant have less power potential. Power is the capacity to influence or force others to behave in a prescribed way.

Size, organization, and resources are power attributes. In the United States, whites are the majority; they have operational control over most organizations and institutions and access to many of the resources valued in this nation. Whites, therefore, may be classified as the dominant people of power among racial populations. It should be stated, however, that a population group dominant in one sector of society may not be dominant in all sectors. Also, a dominant group may not always be dominant. Likewise, a group subdominant in one sector of society could be dominant in another. Among population groups in the United

States, blacks in most sectors are subdominant, but they may not be subdominant always or in all sectors of society.

Subdominant groups have less capacity to influence or force others to behave in a prescribed way. No group, including subdominant ones, is without power. Subdominants as well as dominants have veto power. They can disrupt orderly ways of doing things. Because disruption is usually invoked to express discontent, it is a method more frequently used by subdominants. Subdominants, however, are reluctant to use their veto power because they, as well as dominants, could come to harm as a result.

When dominants act in ways that harm subdominants and refuse to change their harmful policies and practices, subdominants have alternatives: they may submit or resist. Neither action guarantees relief from oppression. An intransigent dominant group is not likely to change conventional ways of doing things unless challenged to do so by subdominants. Subdominants who are reluctant to challenge unjust customs are likely to continue to experience oppression for a long time.

As we review the happenings in education in this nation since the 1940s, we see that substantial improvements that benefited blacks and other minorities resulted only after they challenged the establishment, the dominant people of power, to behave differently. The legal challenges of segregated education by blacks under the leadership of the NAACP and other civil rights groups resulted in the 1954 and 1955 *Brown* I and II decisions by the Supreme Court. These decisions declared segregated education inherently unequal, and therefore illegal. Since our nation did not make a timely response to requirements of the Court, blacks increased their pressure on the establishment to do the right thing through a series of veto actions. This pressure was provided by King, the Southern Christian Leadership Conference, the Congress of Racial Equality, the Student Nonviolent Coordinating Committee, and other individuals and groups. The pressure was stepped up through disruptive demonstrations and marches, a new category of response called "nonviolent direct action." Such challenges resulted in the 1964 Civil Rights Act and the 1965 Voting Rights Act.

The Civil Rights Act contained titles that prohibited racial discrimination in publicly supported schools and other sectors of society. The goals of the Voting Rights Act were to enhance representative government and to achieve more diversity in official policy-making bodies. Eventually, this act would affect the racial and ethnic composition of elected school boards. White-dominated governmental structures at local, state, and federal levels demurred in fully implementing the changes required by these laws. But, after the death of King and the unrelenting veto actions set loose by this tragic event, the nation began to respond appropriately to challenges by blacks for change, particularly in education. Thus, the mid-1970s marked the apex of racial desegregation in elementary and secondary schools and institutions of higher learning. In the light of retrogressive activity during the 1980s, one could conclude that the sacrificial death of King in 1968 influenced the conscience of the dominant people of power in this country for nearly a decade.

Obviously, new challenges by blacks are needed to sustain and maintain the equity in education that was begun. One can understand how the energies of one generation of blacks to mount new challenges have been spent and exhausted. It is not yet clear what kinds of challenges will be taken on by future generations of blacks, but one fact is certain: challenge will be necessary in a nation that is unresponsive to the desire of subdominant people to be free and to participate as responsible decision makers in the community. Through challenge, subdominants cease cooperating in their own oppression and become courageous resisters of injustice. In the United States, as in other human societies, injustice for one person is ultimately injustice for everyone. Thus, subordinates who resist injustice act on behalf of the whole society.

We also have learned from this review and analysis that challenge, while necessary and essential, need not be disruptive if dominant people of power make an appropriate response. An appropriate and effective response for dominants is to pursue justice with compassion, for justice cannot coexist with injustice; fairness that is not universal and impartial is not in the end fairness at all. Compassionate people offer more than they are required to give and take less than they are entitled to receive. When dominant people of power follow this course of action, there may still be a need for subdominants to challenge, but no need for them to disrupt, since a compassionate response will be timely.

Whites, in general, have not responded with generosity or magnanimity to three decades of challenge by blacks that this nation live up to its creed of justice and equality for all in education. They did not do what they ought to have done, and they did many things that they ought not to have done. Because there was no justice, the nation reaped a whirlwind of social discord in the 1950s and in the 1960s. During the first half of the 1970s, whites began to make a compassionate response to the courageous challenges of blacks. At long last the challenges and responses were synchronized and in harmony. Consequently, disorder diminished and disruption through direct action disappeared; change was orderly and continuous. The gap between the races decreased in various measures of educational progress.

As stability and peace returned to our cities and disruptive challenges faded into history, the dominant forces began to backslide and ceased to respond with compassion. They forgot how stability and peace had been won and became less generous and magnanimous, more self-centered and arrogant. Practices of oppression returned during the 1980s. Whites blamed black victims for failures in their home life and in their schooling. Our nation suffers from loss of recent memory. It has forgotten how it coped with strife one generation ago, how courage and compassion helped to overcome our division and unite our people in trust. These synchronized processes were something of great value. They are necessary and essential today.

This book challenges the nation to rediscover courage and compassion in education and other sectors of our society. This is the major lesson we have learned: failure to courageously challenge injustice is folly; failure to make a compassionate response is folly. Thus, dominant and subdominant people have a joint responsibility to reform the educational enterprise. Subdominants have the responsibility of initiating proposals to redress reform. Dominants have the responsibility of refining such proposals and integrating them into the laws and practices of the society.

The Supreme Court in the *Brown* II decision of 1955 errorneously assigned the primary responsibility for fashioning desegregation plans for segregated public school systems to school authorities. The Court did not require school authorities, the dominant people of power, to consult with or otherwise enlist the help of the plaintiff class, the subdominant people, in developing remedial plans. Again ignoring the principle of joint responsibility, the Court also incorrectly assigned the initiation of redress and reform that is uniquely a property of subdominants to the dominant people of power. It was inappropriate to ask the same people who established, maintained, and operated segregated schools to devise a plan to disestablish them. They were not the appropriate group to initiate reform.

We assert that initiation of redress or reform proposals should be a prerogative of subdominants. Reforms designed to fulfill the needs and interests of the least among us are likely to fulfill the needs and interests of the society as a whole. But, reforms designed for the brightest and best learners may be of little, if any, help for the handicapped, for the oppressed, for the slow learner. Traditionally, the dominant people of power have focused on outcome as the criteria of successful education. Subdominant people of power tend to focus on input and process as the essentials of effective education. Since input, process, and outcome all contribute to education, the focus of both dominants and subdominants is necessary to achieve reform.

CONCLUSIONS AND RECOMMENDATIONS

Gunnar Myrdal found that segregation in public schools was a means of perpetuating economic discrimination against blacks. Using the Fourteenth Amendment as the constitutional base, the NAACP won several court cases demonstrating that blacks did not receive equal protection of the law because their segregated and inadequately financed schools did not provide an education equal in quality to that received by whites. The Supreme Court found in *Brown v. Board of Education* that segregated education is inherently unequal. The court ruling seemed to sustain Myrdal's finding. Based on evidence reviewed and analyzed, the nation is obligated to eliminate all forms of segregated education. This is the lawful way to redress the grievances brought by blacks in that landmark court case.

In the process of implementing school desegregation law, confusion and contradiction appeared. White-dominated school boards that opposed integrated education designed desegregation plans that produced more desegregation of whites than of blacks. Whites also urged courts to declare school systems unitary even though more whites than blacks experienced desegregation and some blacks remained in segregated schools. Some blacks, according to the review and analysis, point to the achievements of effective schools following the Comer model as evidence that racial separation is not always detrimental to the education of blacks. However, they acknowledge that a white-dominated governmental system that initiated segregation in the past for the purpose of discriminating against subdominant people is unlikely to appropriate sufficient funds to make racially segregated black schools effective.

We conclude that the full benefits of school desegregation have been experienced less often by blacks because of the confused and contra-indicated way in which the law has been implemented. For example:

The Court did not provide criteria for determining the educational effectiveness of desegregation.

The Court did not provide any definition of a unitary public school system.

The Court did not indicate how promptly a segregated school system should be desegregated.

The methods of achieving desegregation evolved over a decade and a half in a haphazard and piecemeal fashion.

The Court did not identify sources of technical assistance for developing school desegregation plans.

The Court did not always cite the state as a coconspirator in desegregation cases, although the state is the ultimate educational authority.

The Court seldom found that segregated schooling was harmful to whites as well as to blacks and other minorities.

The following prescriptions were contraindicated in the Court order granting relief:

Local educational agencies operating segregated schools were delegated the responsibility of planning and implementing a unitary system of desegregated schools.

Local educational agencies were instructed to proceed in good faith and with deliberate speed but were not required to desegregate schools promptly.

Local educational agencies were permitted to delay the implementation of desegregation plans if, in the public interest (as opposed to the interest of the plaintiff class), more time was needed.

Local educational agencies were required to implement a plan that provided immediate relief to segregated schools but were not required to demonstrate how continuing relief under changing demographic conditions would be maintained.

Local educational agencies were not required to diversify the membership of school boards so that the participation of majority and minority parents in educational public policy is guaranteed.

To overcome these deficiencies, we recommend the following:

State governments should be held accountable by the Court as the public authority responsible for guaranteeing equal access to public schools and will therefore be required to help finance desegregation and monitor its implementation.

Definitions of unitary school systems that do not accommodate segregated schools and that recognize desegregation as valid and achievable regardless of whether blacks and other racial populations or whites are the majority in a local school system should be promulgated.

The Court should adhere to the dictum that justice delayed is justice denied and require all segregated school systems to desegregate promptly and to implement plans that will grant continuous desegregative relief under conditions of changing demography.

State or federal law should require that local school authorities be elected by single-member districts rather than at-large to guarantee diversity in the decision-making structure or, if local school authorities are appointed, that persons of dissimilar racial and ethnic backgrounds be chosen.

A majority of blacks prefer a desegregated education for their children, and a majority of whites will send their children to racially balanced schools. Most reform plans have provided desegregation for whites more often than for blacks. We conclude that school desegregation has been the engine for social reform in this nation and that it has been relatively successful in all parts of the nation, but it has been less beneficial for blacks because they have been excluded by school authorities from the process of reform and because they have disproportionately shouldered the burden of transportation to accomplish systemic desegregation.

To overcome such unfairness, we recommend that:

The rights of blacks who won the school desegregation Court cases should be protected and not compromised, and their grievances should be lawfully redressed regardless of the attitudes of whites about the requirements of the Constitution to grant equal protection of the law.

Desegregation of all school systems should proceed promptly, and all population groups should have proportional access to all schools in accordance with their representation in the local school district, even in school systems in which whites are a minority (this principle should apply to all programs, including magnet schools, gifted and talented programs, and special education programs).

Better methods of desegregation planning involving multiracial teams of planners that do not hold student assignments hostage to segregated neighborhood zones, which contributed to the original crisis of segregated schools, are needed.

Finally, we recommend that:

The common school should fulfill its mission to majority and minority students by relating to each student group in a population-specific way.

School authorities should be taught that all students can learn, that no one is unworthy of receiving a quality education, and that such education is more likely in settings of sympathetic understanding that consider the whole student, including his or her particular learning style and cultural uniqueness.

Blockages in entry to a variety of higher education opportunities should be eliminated for blacks by eliminating admissions requirements, such as standardized tests, that are unrelated to school performance and job success.

The federal government must provide more assistance to black students. (In historically black institutions, more than 80% of the students have large loans; grants, not loans, should be available to these students.)

Since historically black colleges and universities have always accepted the majority of the so-called disadvantaged and underprepared cohort of black students, they should receive more institutional aid, enabling them to expand their academic programs so that needy black students can have the chance to obtain a college degree and prepare for professions in law, medicine, or graduate education.

More recruitment of black teachers is needed to guarantee that our youth will be taught by teachers who have knowledge of and respect for ethnic history and diversity.

More black students must be directed toward careers in science and mathematics by providing them with more exposure to these fields at secondary school levels and by sustaining their interests in these fields through graduate study.

Specific strategies should be employed to promote more research on racial and ethnic issues in education.

Research and evaluation studies of school reform should be conducted by racially diversified research staffs so that the academic progress of students is studied comparatively. Such researchers are likely to investigate the experiences as unique to each population group, not as deviant and outside the mainstream.

Foundations, religious organizations, and other voluntary associations should provide resources and other assistance to blacks for community organization and community development that will enable subdominants to effectively challenge dominants to make effective responses in educational reform.

These recommendations, if adopted and diligently pursued by the nation, should enhance the educational reform process so that excellence may be pursued without compromising equity. Moreover, the fulfillment of these recommendations will indicate that fairness is the central criterion against which the efficacy of all educational reform should be assessed.

REFERENCES

Brown v. Board of Education, 347 U.S. 483 (1954).

Myrdal, G. (1944). *An American dilemma: The Negro problem and American democracy.* New York: Harper and Brothers.

Appendix: Status of African-Americans Project Study Group Members and Contributors

PROJECT LEADERS

Wornie L. Reed (director); William Monroe Trotter Institute, University of Massachusetts at Boston

James E. Blackwell (co-chair); Department of Sociology, University of Massachusetts at Boston

Lucius J. Barker (co-chair); Department of Political Science, Washington University

STUDY GROUP ON EDUCATION

Charles V. Willie (chair); School of Education, Harvard University

Antoine M. Garibaldi (vice-chair); College of Arts and Science, Xavier University

Robert A. Dentler, Department of Sociology, University of Massachusetts at Boston

Robert C. Johnson, Minority Studies Academic Program, St. Cloud State University

Meyer Weinberg, Department of Education, University of Massachusetts at Amherst

STUDY GROUP ON EMPLOYMENT, INCOME, AND OCCUPATIONS

William Darity, Jr. (chair); Department of Economics, University of North Carolina

Barbara Jones (vice-chair); College of Business, Prairie View A&M University

Study Group on Employment, Income, and Occupations (continued)

Jeremiah P. Cotton, Department of Economics, University of Massachusetts at Boston

Herbert Hill, Industrial Relations Research Institute, University of Wisconsin

STUDY GROUP ON POLITICAL PARTICIPATION AND THE ADMINISTRATION OF JUSTICE

Michael B. Preston (chair); Department of Political Science, University of Southern California

Diane M. Pinderhughes (vice-chair); Department of Political Science, University of Illinois/Champaign

Tobe Johnson, Department of Political Science, Morehouse College

Nolan Jones, Committee on Criminal Justice and Public Protection, National Governors Association

Susan Welch, Department of Political Science, University of Nebraska

John Zipp, Department of Sociology, University of Wisconsin at Milwaukee

STUDY GROUP ON SOCIAL AND CULTURAL CHANGE

Alphonso Pinkney (chair); Department of Sociology, Hunter College

James Turner (vice-chair); Africana Studies and Research Center, Cornell University

John Henrik Clarke, Professor Emeritus, Department of Black and Puerto Rican Studies, Hunter College

Sidney Wilhelm, Department of Sociology, State University of New York at Buffalo

STUDY GROUP ON HEALTH STATUS AND MEDICAL CARE

William Darity, Sr. (chair); School of Public Health, University of Massachusetts at Amherst

Stanford Roman (vice-chair); Morehouse School of Medicine

Claudia Baquet, National Cancer Institute

Noma L. Roberson, Department of Cancer Control and Epidemiology, Rockwell Park Institute

STUDY GROUP ON THE FAMILY

Robert B. Hill (chair); Institute for Urban Research, Morgan State University

Andrew Billingsley (vice-chair); Department of Family and Community Development, University of Maryland

Eleanor Engram, Engram-Miller Associates

Micheline R. Malson, Department of Public Policy Studies, Duke University

Roger H. Rubin, Department of Family and Community Development, University of Maryland

Carol B. Stack, Social and Cultural Studies, Graduate School of Education, University of California at Berkeley

James B. Stewart, Department of Labor Studies and Industrial Relations, Pennsylvania State University

James E. Teele, Department of Sociology, Boston University

CONTRIBUTORS

Carolyne W. Arnold, College of Public and Community Services, University of Massachusetts at Boston

James A. Banks, School of Education, University of Washington

Margaret Beale Spencer, College of Education, Emory University

Bob Blauner, Department of Sociology, University of California at Berkeley

Larry Carter, Department of Sociology, University of Oregon

Obie Clayton, School of Criminal Justice, University of Nebraska

James P. Comer, Department of Psychiatry, Yale Medical School

Charles E. Flowers, Department of Education, Fisk University

Bennett Harrison, Urban Studies and Planning, Massachusetts Institute of Technology

Norris M. Haynes, Child Study Center

Joseph Himes, Excellence Fund Professor Emeritus of Sociology, University of North Carolina at Greensboro

Hubert E. Jones, School of Social Work, Boston University

James M. Jones, Department of Psychology, University of Delaware

Faustine C. Jones-Wilson, *Journal of Negro Education,* Howard University

Barry A. Krisberg, National Council on Crime and Delinquency

Hubert G. Locke, Society of Justice Program, University of Washington

Contributors (continued)

E. Yvonne Moss, William Monroe Trotter Institute, University of Massachusetts at Boston
Willie Pearson, Jr., Department of Sociology, Wake Forest University
Michael L. Radelet, Department of Sociology, University of Florida
Robert Rothman, *Education Week*
Diana T. Slaughter, School of Education, Northwestern University
A. Wade Smith, Department of Sociology, Arizona State University
Leonard Stevens, Compact for Educational Opportunity
Wilbur Watson, Geriatrics Department, Morehouse School of Medicine
Warren Whatley, Department of Economics, University of Michigan
John B. Williams, Graduate School of Education, Harvard University
Rhonda Williams, Afro-American Studies, University of Maryland
Reginald Wilson, American Council on Education

Index

About the Editors and Contributors

James A. Banks is professor of education at the University of Washington, Seattle. He is a former chairman of curriculum and instruction at the University of Washington and a past president of the National Council for the Social Studies. His expertise is in the areas of social studies education and multicultural education. His books include *Teaching Strategies for Ethnic Studies,* 5th ed. (1990), *Multicultural Education: Issues and Perspectives* (1989), and *Teaching Strategies for the Social Studies,* 4th ed. (1990).

James E. Blackwell has recently retired as professor of sociology at the University of Massachusetts at Boston. His current research foci includes minorities in higher education and social movements in the black community. Blackwell has published extensively, including the following books: *The Black Community: Diversity and Unity,* 3rd ed. (1990), *Mainstreaming Outsiders: The Production of Black Professionals,* 2nd ed. (1987), and *Networking and Mentoring: A Cross-Generational Study of Experiences of Blacks in Graduate and Professional Schools* (1983).

James P. Comer is Maurice Falk Professor of Child Psychiatry at the Yale Child Study Center, director of the School Development Program at the Child Study Center, and associate dean at the Yale School of Medicine. Comer contributes a regular column to *Parents Magazine* and is the author of a number of books including: *Maggie's American Dream* (1988), *School Power: Implications of an Intervention Project* (1980), *Black Child Care* (1975), and *Beyond Black and White* (1972).

Robert A. Dentler is professor of sociology at the University of Massachusetts at Boston and editor of *Sociological Practice Review.* Prior to going to the University of Massachusetts Dentler was senior sociologist at Abt Associates, Cambridge, Massachusetts. He is the author of many books including: *University on Trial: The Case of the University of North Carolina* (1983), *Schools on Trial: An Inside Account of the Boston Desegregation Case* (1981), and *Urban Social Problems: Perspectives and Solutions* (1977).

Charles E. Flowers is an assistant principal at the Fairfield Elementary School in the Virginia Beach School District. He has served as an educational consultant to the U.S. Office of Education, the Southern Association of Colleges and Schools, and the Integrated Systems Approach to Improving Management Program. He has also served as adjunct associate professor of education at the University of the District of Columbia. Flowers has published extensively in his areas of interest — educational administration and guidance and counseling.

Antoine M. Garibaldi is dean of the College of Arts and Sciences and professor of education at Xavier University of Louisiana. Before going to Xavier in 1982, he was a research associate at the National Institute of Education, the U.S. Department of Education. His areas of interest and expertise include blacks in higher education, minority teacher recruitment and retention, and urban education. His publications include the following books: *Teacher Recruitment and Retention* (1989), *Educating Black Male Youth: A Moral and Civic Imperative* (1988), and *Black Colleges and Universities: Challenges for the Future* (1984).

Norris M. Haynes is assistant professor and director of research for the School Development Program at Yale University's Child Study Center. Prior to going to Yale, Haynes was assistant professor in psychoeducational studies at Howard University. His interests are in psychoeducation development, minority achievement, school restructuring, and social policy. Haynes has published many journal articles in his area of expertise and has contributed chapters to the following books: *Going to School* (1990), *Black Education: A Quest for Equity and Excellence* (1989), and *Readings on Equal Education* (1990).

Faustine C. Jones-Wilson is professor of education in the Foundations of Education Department at Howard University. She is also the editor of *The Journal of Negro Education* published at Howard. Along with numerous journal articles, Jones-Wilson contributed a chapter entitled "The State of African-American Education" to the book *Going to School: The African-American Experience* (1990).

Willie Pearson, Jr., is professor of sociology at Wake Forest University and was formerly Congressional Science Fellow/Analyst at the Office of Technology Assessment, the U.S. Congress. His books include: *Blacks, Education, and American Science* (1989) and *Black Scientists, White Society and Colorless Science: A Study of Universalism in American Science* (1985).

Wornie L. Reed is director of the William Monroe Trotter Institute and chair of the Department of Black Studies at the University of Massachusetts at Boston. Before going to the University of Massachusetts in 1985, Reed was the director of the Institute for Urban Research at Morgan State University. His areas of interest include the hiring and promotion of black faculty and diversity in the curriculum. Reed was the director of the Study on the Assessment of the Status of African-Americans, which resulted in this book as well as the forthcoming book *African-Americans: Essential Perspectives.*

Robert Rothman is associate editor of *Education Week,* a national newspaper with a circulation of 60,000 that focuses on elementary and secondary education. Rothman has written extensively on minority access to higher education, and he has contributed articles on education issues to *The Scientist, Governing,* and other publications.

James B. Stewart has been vice provost and associate professor of labor studies and industrial relations at Pennsylvania State University since 1990. Prior to that time he was director of the Black Studies Program at Penn State. Stewart is coauthor of *Black Families: Interdisciplinary Perspectives* (1990) and *Regulation, Values, and the Public Interest* (1980).

Meyer Weinberg is professor emeritus in the Afro-American Studies Department at the University of Massachusetts at Amherst and also serves as the director of the Horace Mann Bond Center for Equal Education. Weinberg is the founding editor of *Integrateducation,* and his most recent books include *Racism in the United States* (1990), *The Education of Poor and Minority Children* (1986), and *Search for Quality Integrated Education* (1983).

John B. Williams is associate professor of administration, planning, and social policy at Harvard University's Graduate School of Education and faculty chairperson for the Urban Superintendents Program, also at Harvard. His areas of interest include public policy implementation, program evaluation, and civil rights. He is editor of *Desegregating America's Colleges and Universities: Title VI Regulation of Higher Education* (1988) and coauthor of the forthcoming book *Highest Honors: American Public Schools in the 1990s.*

Charles V. Willie is professor of education and urban studies at Harvard University's Graduate School of Education. Before going to Harvard in 1974 Willie was affiliated with Syracuse University for 25 years. His special interests are school desegregation and the recruitment and retention of minorities in higher education. He has published more than 20 books including *African-Americans and the Doctoral Experience* (1991), *Social Goals and Educational Reform* (1988), and *Five Black Scholars* (1986).